DOCTOR WHO
THE ELEVENTH DOCTOR

THE SAPLING VOL
GROWTH

"Amazing! It hit all the right notes, and got the Doctor perfect! 9/10"
COMIC BOOK CAST

"A truly fantastic *Doctor Who* adventure that rewards loyal readers and long-time fans of the show."
POP CULTURE BANDIT

"Fun, energetic events liven things up with some thrilling twists!"
SNAPPOW

"A riveting story with magnificent set pieces and dazzling imagery!"
BLOGTOR WHO

"Excellent script with great artwork. I've become a fan of Alice Obiefune – what a character she has become!"
TM STASH

"The tone of the Eleventh Doctor is strong in this one."
WARPED FACTOR

"Captures the feel of the series while still taking advantage of the unlimited boundaries comics can provide."
CAPELESS CRUSADER

"A great job creating a companion who can keep up with the Doctor. 10 out of 10!"
PROJECT FANDOM

"Nails the tone and spirit right out of the gate!"
COMIC BOOK RESOURCES

"Rob Williams' script is a real treat, and the art proves equally skillful. A wonderful start for The Eleventh Doctor's third year!"
KABOOOOOM

"Full of dramatic reveals."
SCI FI ONLINE

"9.5 out of 10!"
NERDS UNCHAINED

"Very unsettling visuals, brilliantly done."
NERDLY

TITAN COMICS

COLLECTION EDITOR
Jessica Burton

SENIOR COMICS EDITOR
Andrew James

ASSISTANT EDITORS
Amoona Saohin,
Lauren McPhee

COLLECTION DESIGNER
Andrew Leung

PRODUCTION SUPERVISOR
Maria Pearson

PRODUCTION CONTROLLER
Peter James

SENIOR PRODUCTION CONTROLLER
Jackie Flook

ART DIRECTOR
Oz Browne

SENIOR SALES MANAGER
Steve Tothill

PRESS OFFICER
Will O'Mullane

COMICS BRAND MANAGER
Chris Thompson

ADS & MARKETING ASSISTANT
Tom Miller

DIRECT SALES & MARKETING MANAGER
Ricky Claydon

COMMERCIAL MANAGER
Michelle Fairlamb

HEAD OF RIGHTS
Jenny Boyce

PUBLISHING MANAGER
Darryl Tothill

PUBLISHING DIRECTOR
Chris Teather

OPERATIONS DIRECTOR
Leigh Baulch

EXECUTIVE DIRECTOR
Vivian Cheung

PUBLISHER
Nick Landau

For rights information contact Jenny Boyce
jenny.boyce@titanemail.com

Special thanks to Steven Moffat, Brian Minchin, Mandy Thwaites, Matt Nicholls, James Dudley, Edward Russell, Derek Ritchie, Scott Handcock, Kirsty Mullan, Kate Bush, Julia Nocciolino and Ed Casey for their invaluable assistance.

BBC WORLDWIDE

DIRECTOR OF EDITORIAL GOVERNANCE
Nicholas Brett

HEAD OF UK PUBLISHING
Chris Kerwin

DIRECTOR OF CONSUMER PRODUCTS AND PUBLISHING
Andrew Moultrie

PUBLISHER
Mandy Thwaites

PUBLISHING CO-ORDINATOR
Eva Abramik

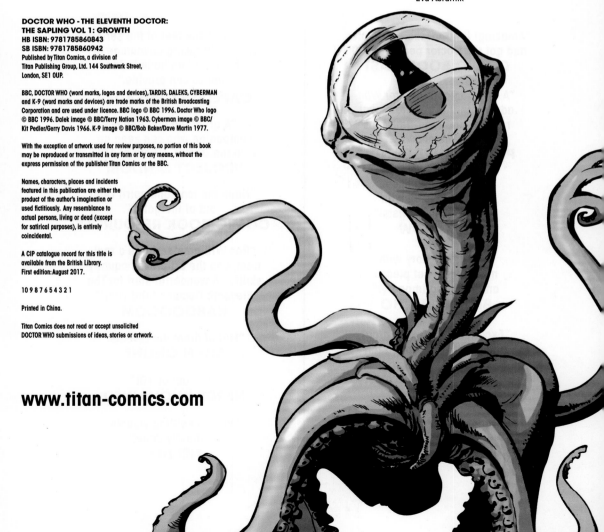

DOCTOR WHO - THE ELEVENTH DOCTOR:
THE SAPLING VOL 1: GROWTH
HB ISBN: 9781785860843
SB ISBN: 9781785860942
Published by Titan Comics, a division of
Titan Publishing Group, Ltd. 144 Southwark Street,
London, SE1 0UP.

A CIP catalogue record for this title is available from the British Library.
First edition: August 2017.

10 9 8 7 6 5 4 3 2 1

Printed in China.

Titan Comics does not read or accept unsolicited
DOCTOR WHO submissions of ideas, stories or artwork.

www.titan-comics.com

BBC

DOCTOR WHO

THE ELEVENTH DOCTOR

THE SAPLING VOL 1
GROWTH

WRITERS: ROB WILLIAMS & ALEX PAKNADEL

ARTISTS: I.N.J. CULBARD, SIMON FRASER, LEANDRO CASCO, WELLINGTON DIAZ

COLORISTS: TRIONA FARRELL, GARY CALDWELL

LETTERS: RICHARD STARKINGS AND COMICRAFT'S JIMMY BETANCOURT

BBC
DOCTOR WHO
THE ELEVENTH DOCTOR

ALICE OBIEFUNE

Alice Obiefune is a former Library Assistant. She has saved the Doctor from himself and others on multiple occasions. She and the Doctor now trust each other implicitly.

THE DOCTOR

Last of the Time Lords of Gallifrey, an alien that walks like a man. Never cruel or cowardly, the Eleventh Doctor is a gangly boy professor with an old soul. He has made many mistakes in his time – but owns all of them.

THE TARDIS

Bigger on the inside, this unassuming blue box is your ticket to unforgettable adventure! The Doctor likes to think he's in control – but often the TARDIS takes him exactly where and when he needs to be!

PREVIOUSLY...

Accused of genocide. Chased across time and space by an undefeatable, indefatigable bounty hunter. Thrown into the terror of the Time War. The Doctor and Alice faced their darkest days and came through (mostly) unscathed – though many lessons have been learned.

After spectacularly proving the Doctor's innocence, and banishing a race of malignant gods in the process, they've more than earned some downtime. But the universe, as always, has other plans...

When you've finished reading the collection, please email your thoughts to doctorwhocomic@titanemail.com

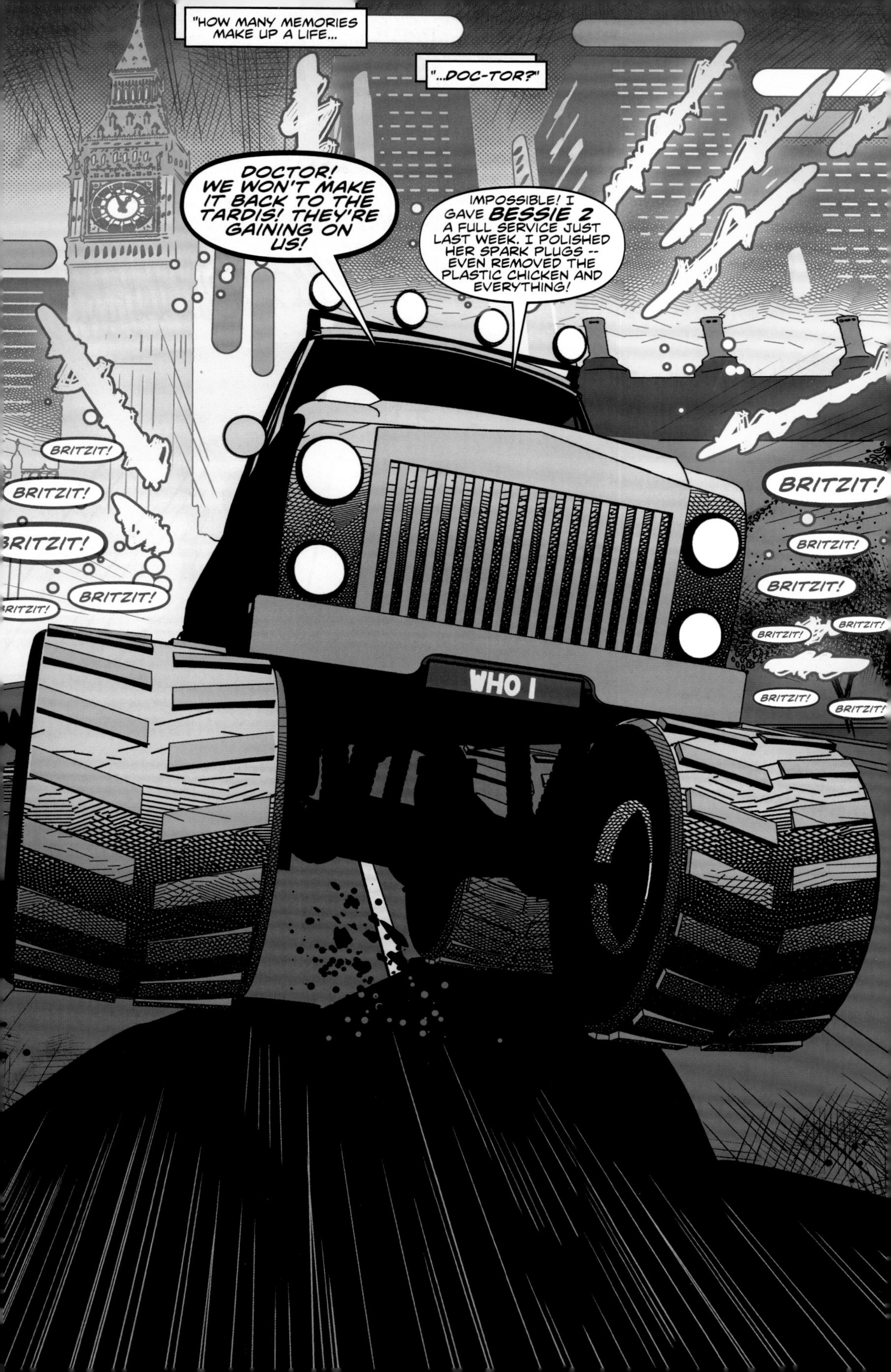
"HOW MANY MEMORIES MAKE UP A LIFE...
"...DOC-TOR?"
DOCTOR! WE WON'T MAKE IT BACK TO THE TARDIS! THEY'RE GAINING ON US!
IMPOSSIBLE! I GAVE BESSIE 2 A FULL SERVICE JUST LAST WEEK. I POLISHED HER SPARK PLUGS -- EVEN REMOVED THE PLASTIC CHICKEN AND EVERYTHING!
BRITZIT!
BRITZIT!
BRITZIT!
BRITZIT!
BRITZIT!
BRITZIT!
BRITZIT!
BRITZIT!
BRITZIT!
BRITZIT!
BRITZIT!
BRITZIT!
WHO I

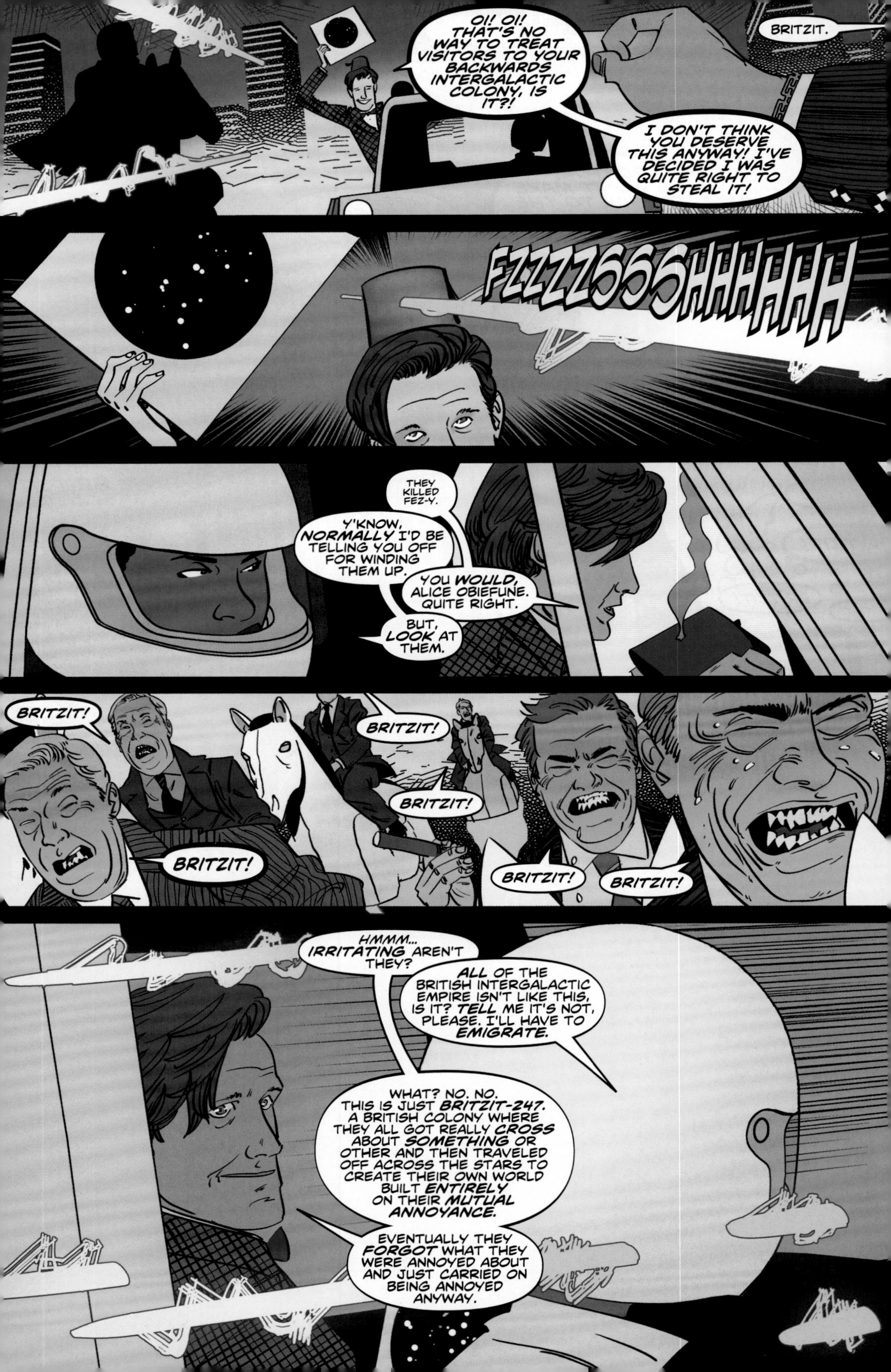

OI! OI! THAT'S NO WAY TO TREAT VISITORS TO YOUR BACKWARDS INTERGALACTIC COLONY, IS IT?!
BRITZIT.
I DON'T THINK YOU DESERVE THIS ANYWAY! I'VE DECIDED I WAS QUITE RIGHT TO STEAL IT!
FZZZZGGGHHHHHH
THEY KILLED FEZ-Y.
Y'KNOW, NORMALLY I'D BE TELLING YOU OFF FOR WINDING THEM UP.
YOU WOULD, ALICE OBIEFUNE. QUITE RIGHT.
BUT, LOOK AT THEM.
BRITZIT!
BRITZIT!
BRITZIT!
BRITZIT!
BRITZIT!
BRITZIT!
HMMM... IRRITATING AREN'T THEY?
ALL OF THE BRITISH INTERGALACTIC EMPIRE ISN'T LIKE THIS, IS IT? TELL ME IT'S NOT, PLEASE. I'LL HAVE TO EMIGRATE.
WHAT? NO. NO. THIS IS JUST BRITZIT-247. A BRITISH COLONY WHERE THEY ALL GOT REALLY CROSS ABOUT SOMETHING OR OTHER AND THEN TRAVELED OFF ACROSS THE STARS TO CREATE THEIR OWN WORLD BUILT ENTIRELY ON THEIR MUTUAL ANNOYANCE.
EVENTUALLY THEY FORGOT WHAT THEY WERE ANNOYED ABOUT AND JUST CARRIED ON BEING ANNOYED ANYWAY.

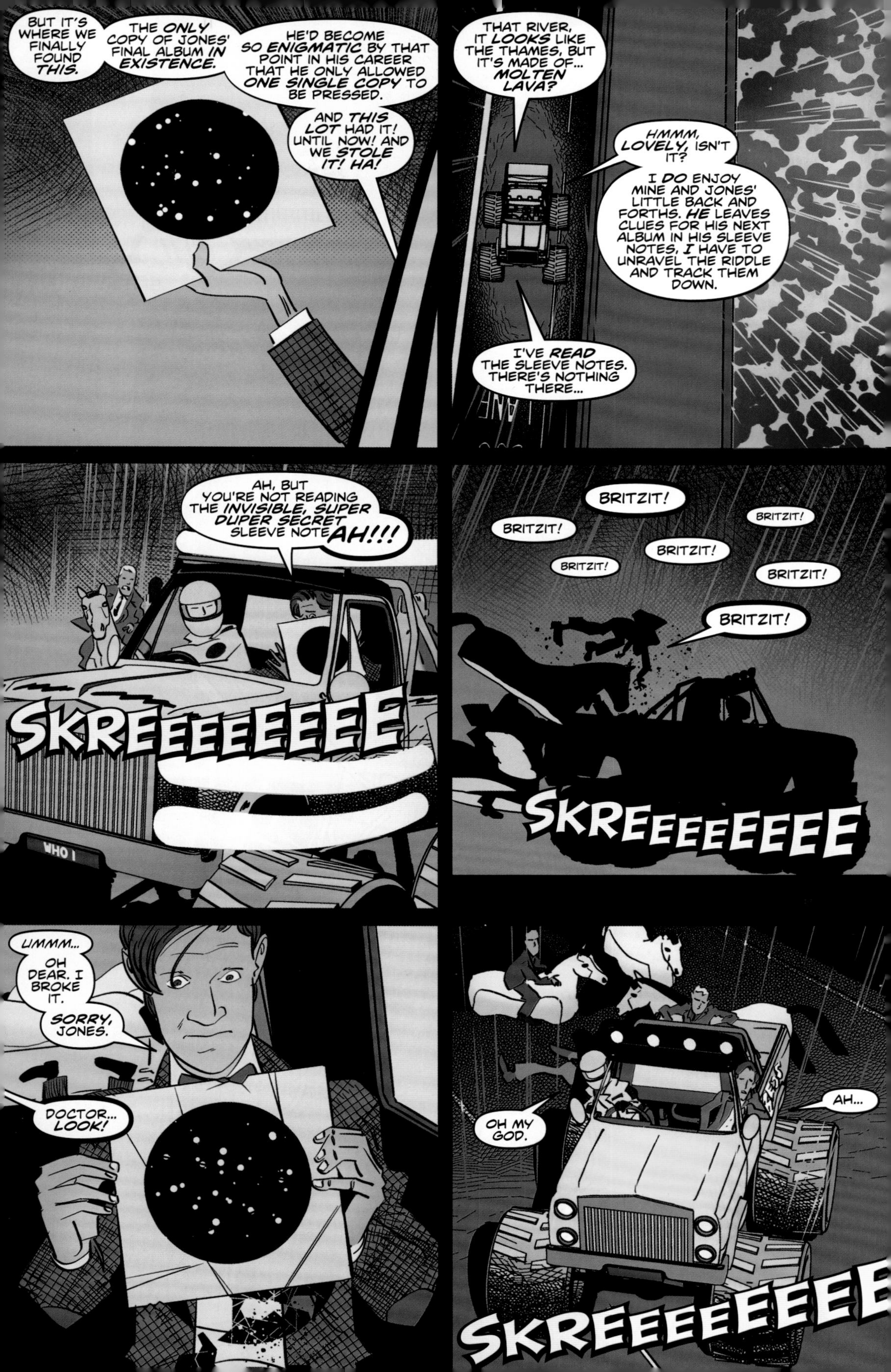
BUT IT'S WHERE WE FINALLY FOUND THIS.
THE ONLY COPY OF JONES' FINAL ALBUM IN EXISTENCE.
HE'D BECOME SO ENIGMATIC BY THAT POINT IN HIS CAREER THAT HE ONLY ALLOWED ONE SINGLE COPY TO BE PRESSED.
AND THIS LOT HAD IT! UNTIL NOW! AND WE STOLE IT! HA!
THAT RIVER, IT LOOKS LIKE THE THAMES, BUT IT'S MADE OF... MOLTEN LAVA?
HMMM, LOVELY, ISN'T IT?
I DO ENJOY MINE AND JONES' LITTLE BACK AND FORTHS. HE LEAVES CLUES FOR HIS NEXT ALBUM IN HIS SLEEVE NOTES, I HAVE TO UNRAVEL THE RIDDLE AND TRACK THEM DOWN.
I'VE READ THE SLEEVE NOTES. THERE'S NOTHING THERE...
AH, BUT YOU'RE NOT READING THE INVISIBLE, SUPER DUPER SECRET SLEEVE NOTEAH!!!
SKREEEEEEEEE
WHO 1
BRITZIT!
BRITZIT!
BRITZIT!
BRITZIT!
BRITZIT!
BRITZIT!
BRITZIT!
SKREEEEEEEEE
UMMM... OH DEAR. I BROKE IT.
SORRY, JONES.
DOCTOR... LOOK!
OH MY GOD.
AH...
SKREEEEEEEEE

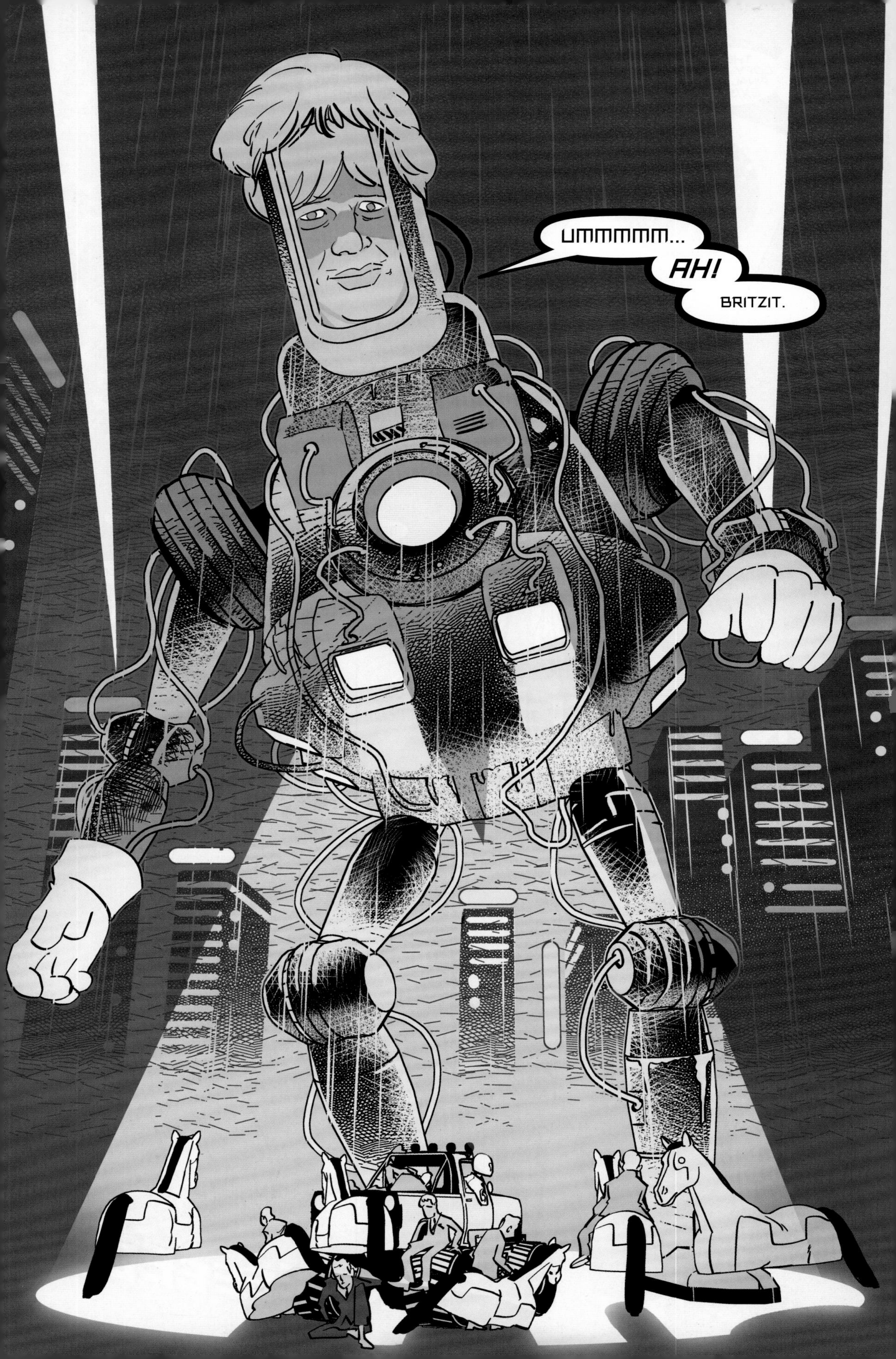
UMMMMM...
AH!
BRITZIT.

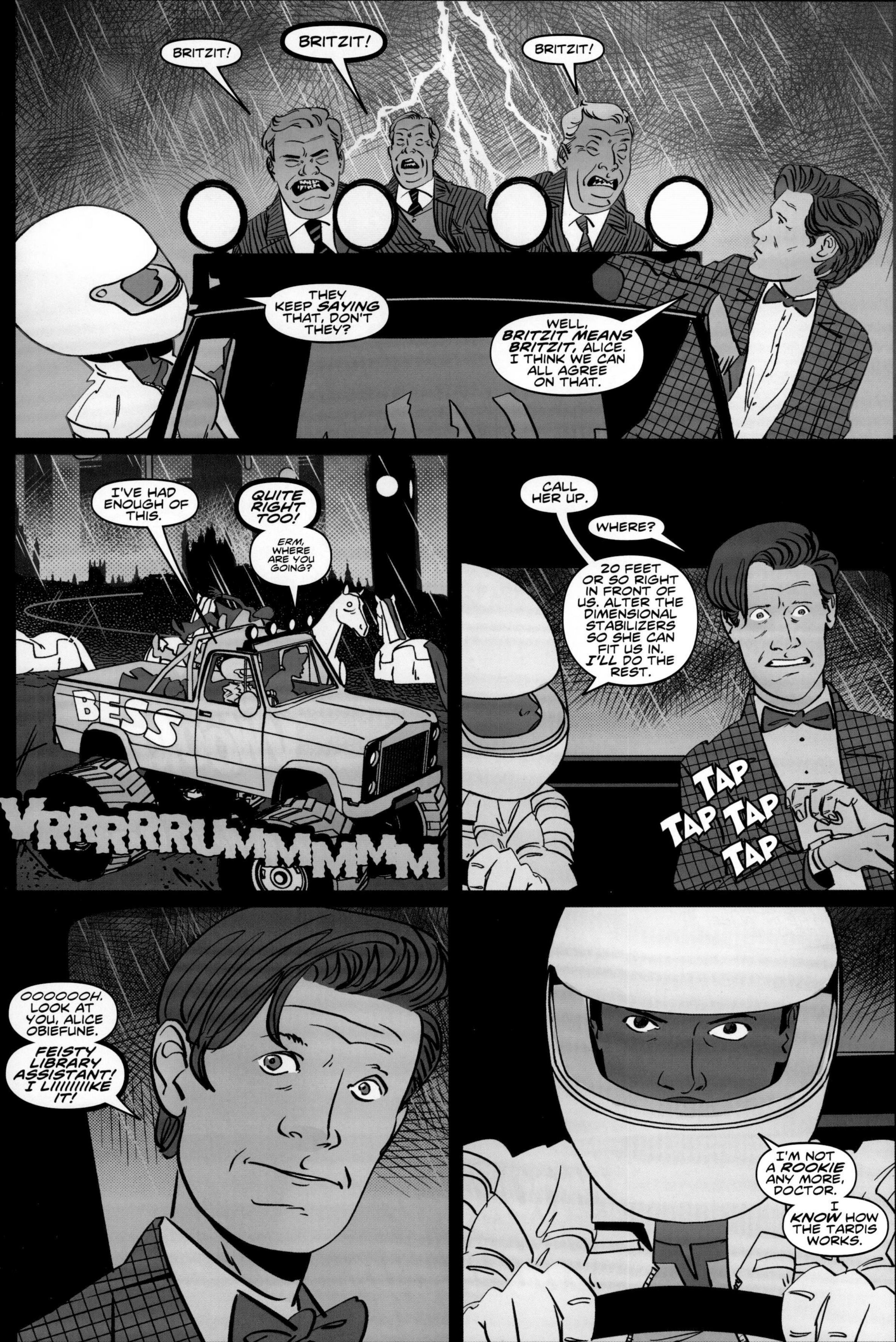
BRITZIT!
BRITZIT!
BRITZIT!
THEY KEEP SAYING THAT, DON'T THEY?
WELL, BRITZIT MEANS BRITZIT, ALICE. I THINK WE CAN ALL AGREE ON THAT.
I'VE HAD ENOUGH OF THIS.
QUITE RIGHT TOO!
ERM, WHERE ARE YOU GOING?
BESS
VRRRRRRUMMMMMM
CALL HER UP.
WHERE?
20 FEET OR SO RIGHT IN FRONT OF US. ALTER THE DIMENSIONAL STABILIZERS SO SHE CAN FIT US IN. I'LL DO THE REST.
TAP TAP TAP TAP
OOOOOOH. LOOK AT YOU, ALICE OBIEFUNE.
FEISTY LIBRARY ASSISTANT! I LIIIIIIIIKE IT!
I'M NOT A ROOKIE ANY MORE, DOCTOR.
I KNOW HOW THE TARDIS WORKS.

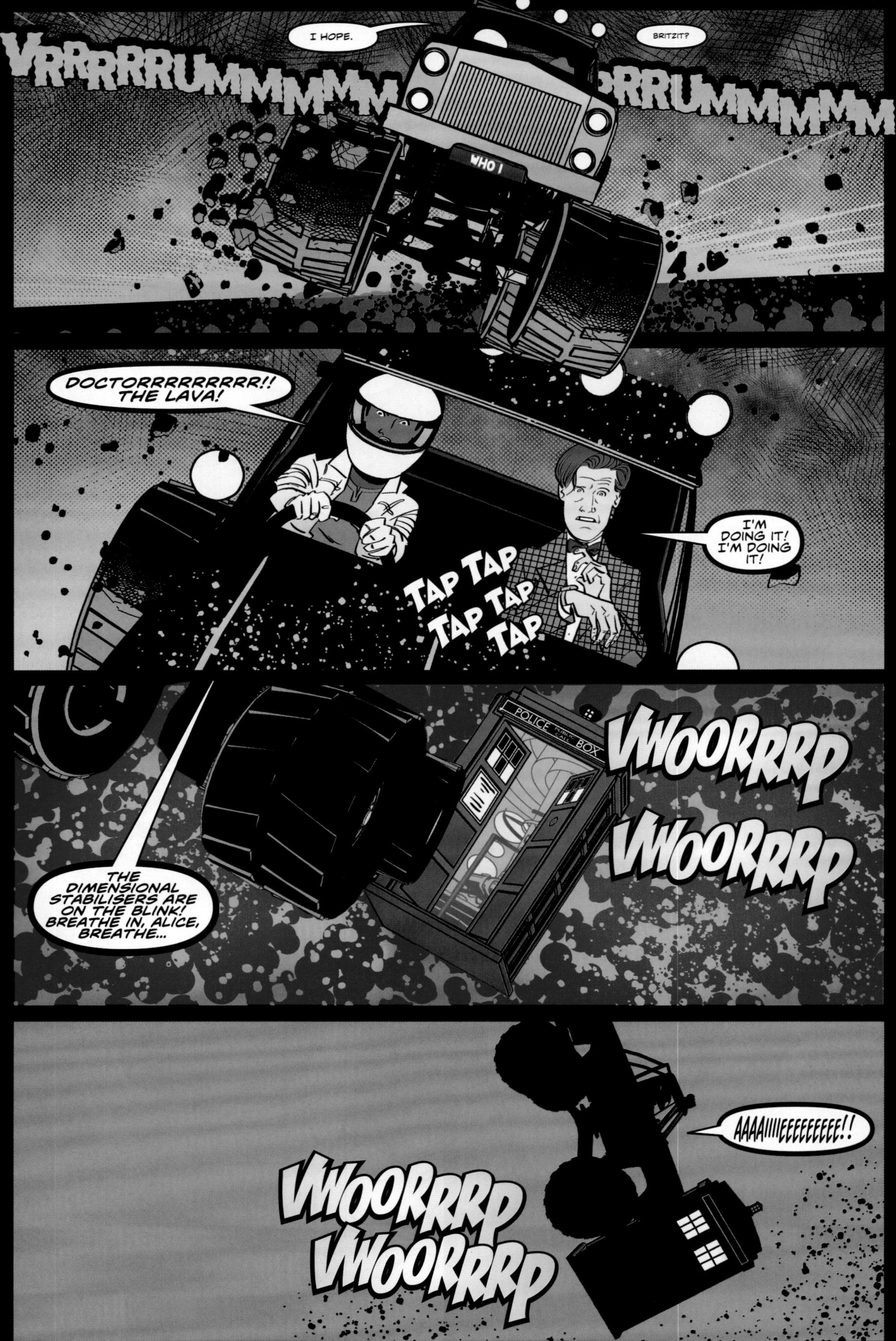
VRRRRRRUMMMMMM
I HOPE.
BRITZIT?
RRRUMMMMMM
WHO 1
DOCTORRRRRRRRR!! THE LAVA!
I'M DOING IT! I'M DOING IT!
TAP TAP TAP TAP TAP
POLICE PUBLIC CALL BOX
VWOORRRP
VWOORRRP
THE DIMENSIONAL STABILISERS ARE ON THE BLINK! BREATHE IN, ALICE, BREATHE...
AAAAIIIIEEEEEEEEE!!
VWOORRRP
VWOORRRP

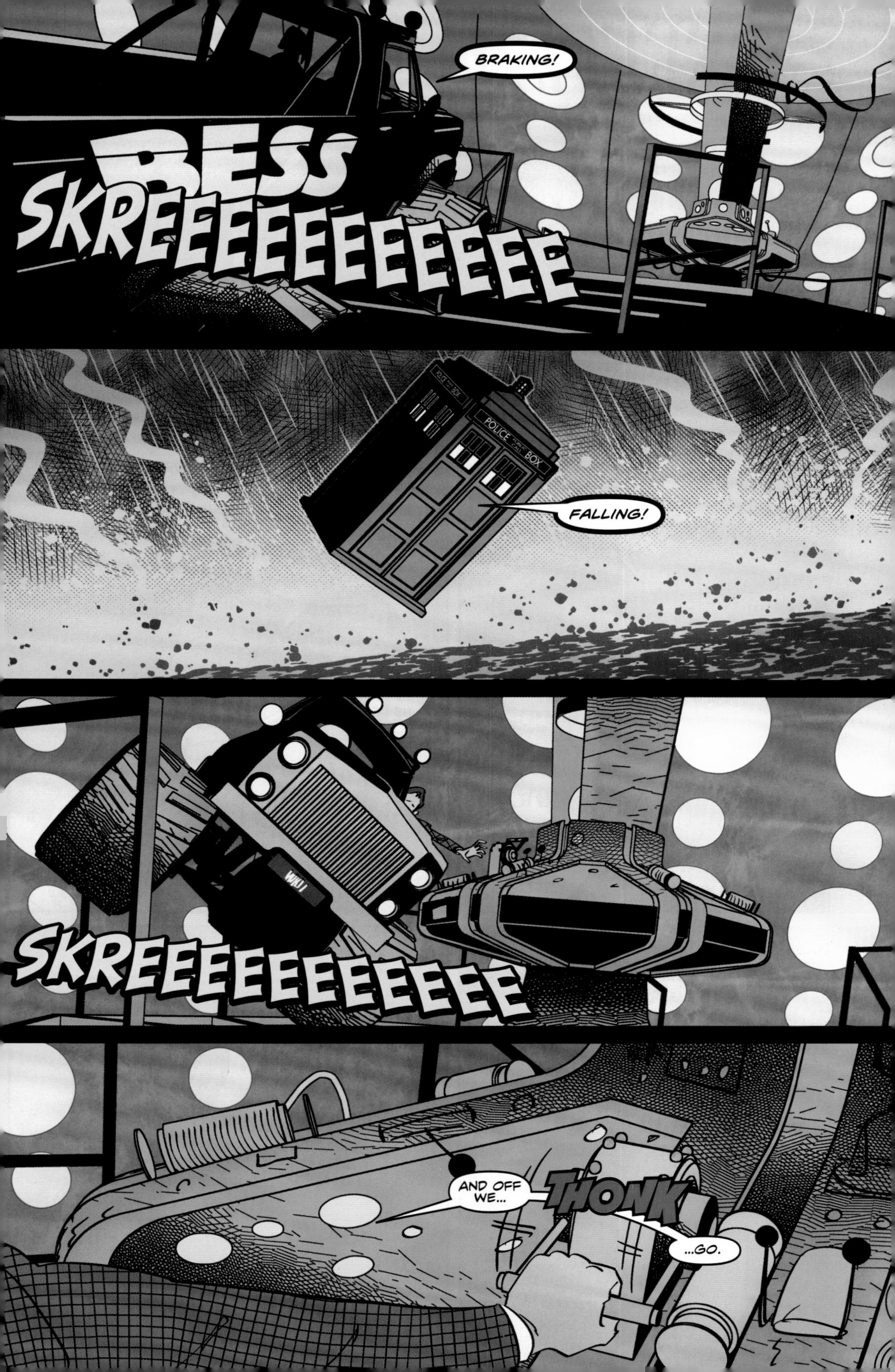
BRAKING!
BESS
SKREEEEEEEEEEE
FALLING!
SKREEEEEEEEEEE
AND OFF WE...
THONK
...GO.

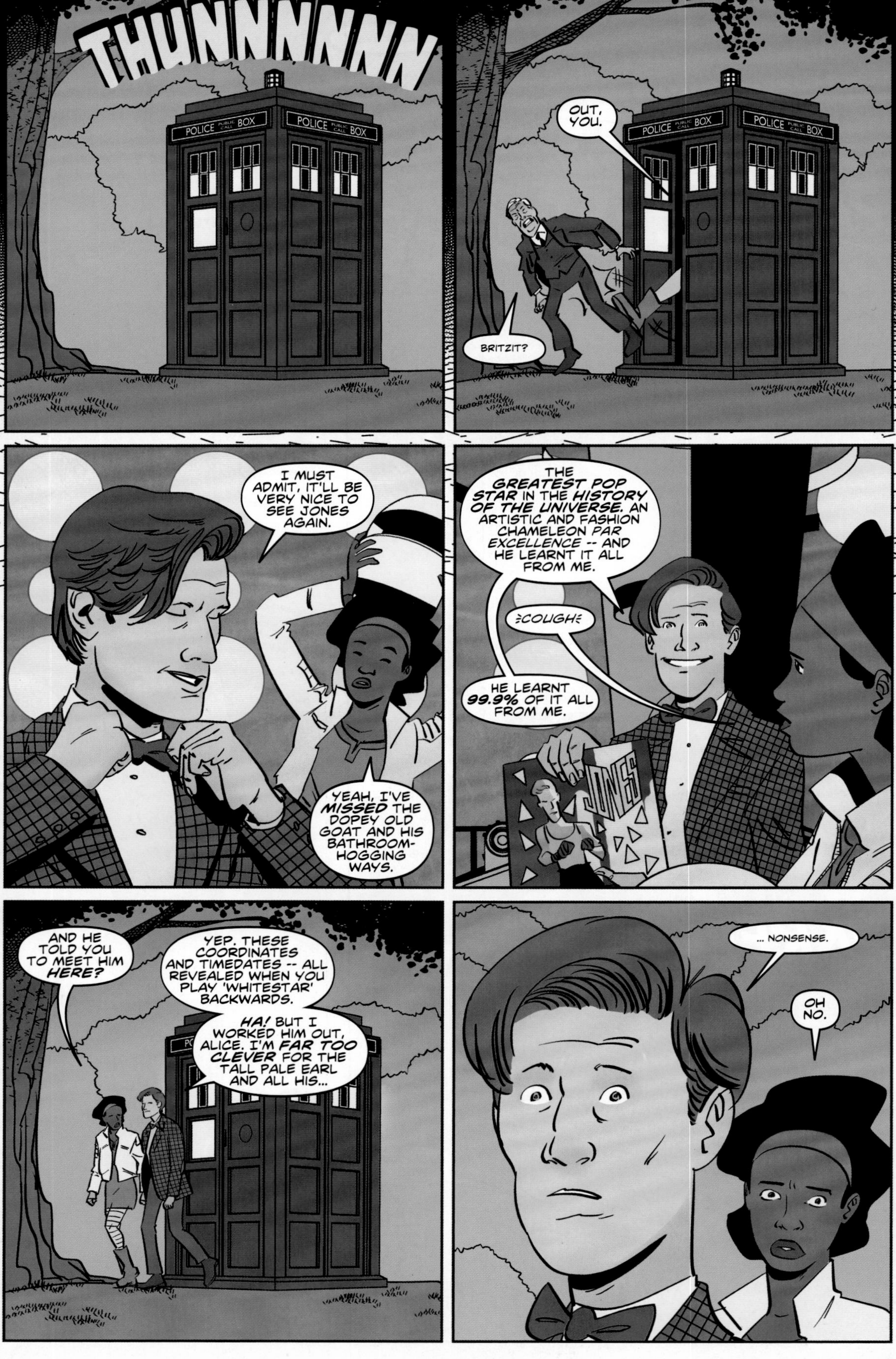

THUNNNNNN
POLICE PUBLIC CALL BOX
OUT, YOU.
BRITZIT?
I MUST ADMIT, IT'LL BE VERY NICE TO SEE JONES AGAIN.
YEAH, I'VE *MISSED* THE DOPEY OLD GOAT AND HIS BATHROOM-HOGGING WAYS.
THE *GREATEST POP STAR* IN THE *HISTORY OF THE UNIVERSE.* AN ARTISTIC AND FASHION CHAMELEON *PAR EXCELLENCE* -- AND HE LEARNT IT ALL FROM ME.
COUGH
HE LEARNT *99.9%* OF IT ALL FROM ME.
JONES
AND HE TOLD YOU TO MEET HIM *HERE?*
YEP. THESE COORDINATES AND TIMEDATES -- ALL REVEALED WHEN YOU PLAY 'WHITESTAR' BACKWARDS.
HA! BUT I WORKED HIM OUT, ALICE. I'M *FAR TOO CLEVER* FOR THE TALL PALE EARL AND ALL HIS...
... NONSENSE.
OH NO.

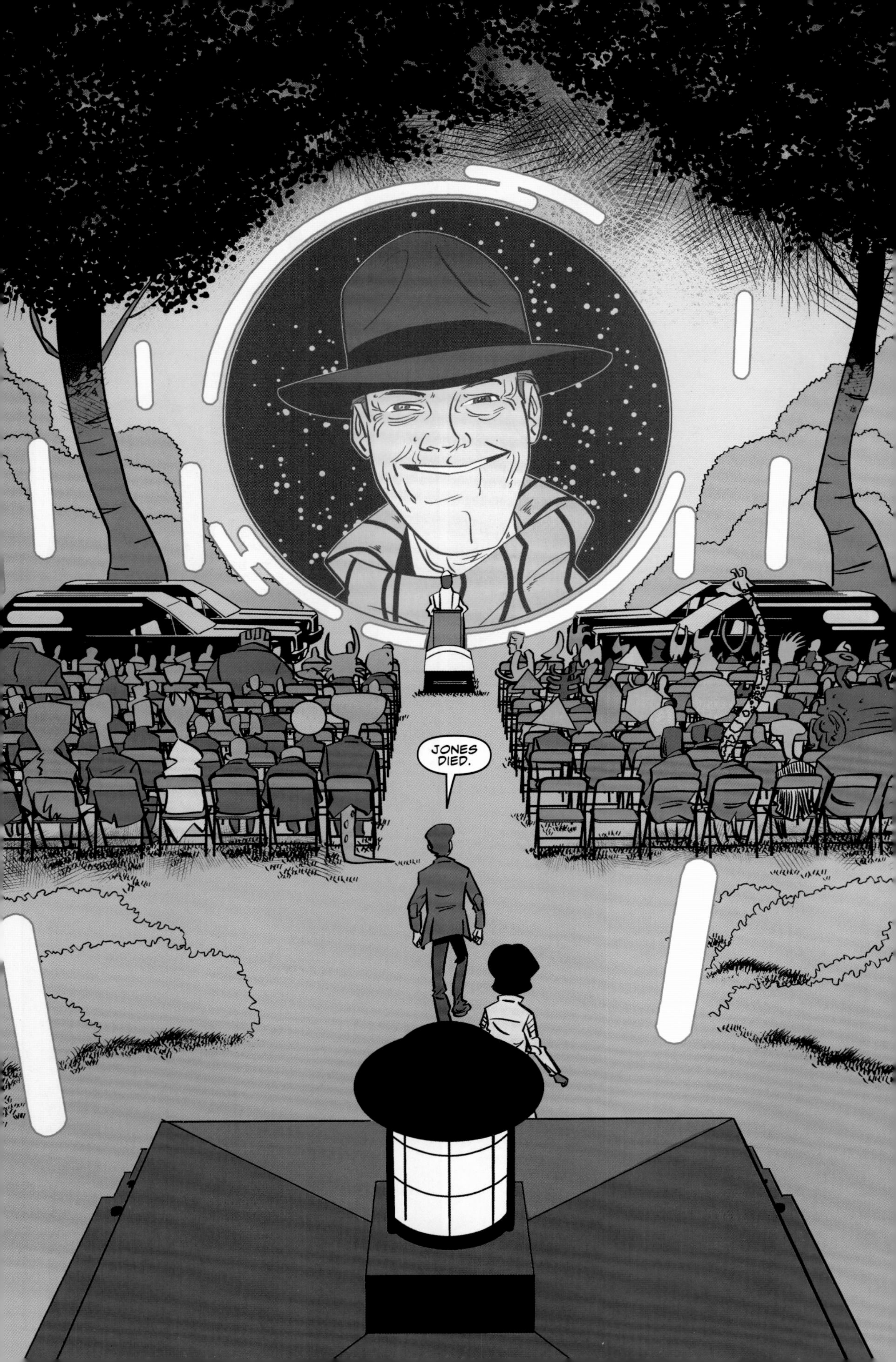
JONES DIED.

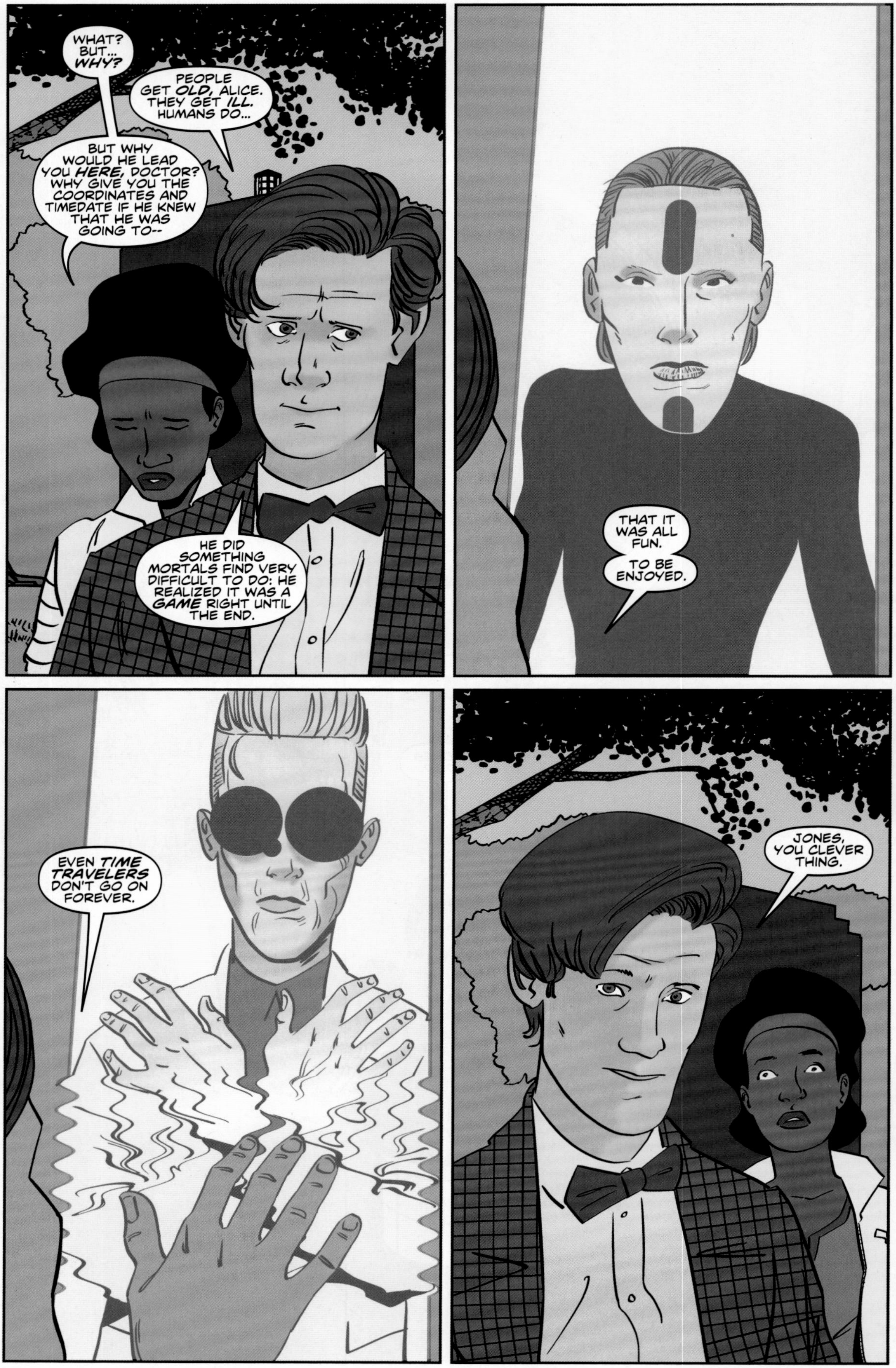

WHAT? BUT... *WHY?*
PEOPLE GET *OLD,* ALICE. THEY GET *ILL.* HUMANS DO...
BUT WHY WOULD HE LEAD YOU *HERE,* DOCTOR? WHY GIVE YOU THE COORDINATES AND TIMEDATE IF HE KNEW THAT HE WAS GOING TO--
HE DID SOMETHING MORTALS FIND VERY DIFFICULT TO DO: HE REALIZED IT WAS A *GAME* RIGHT UNTIL THE END.
THAT IT WAS ALL FUN.
TO BE ENJOYED.
EVEN *TIME TRAVELERS* DON'T GO ON FOREVER.
JONES, YOU CLEVER THING.

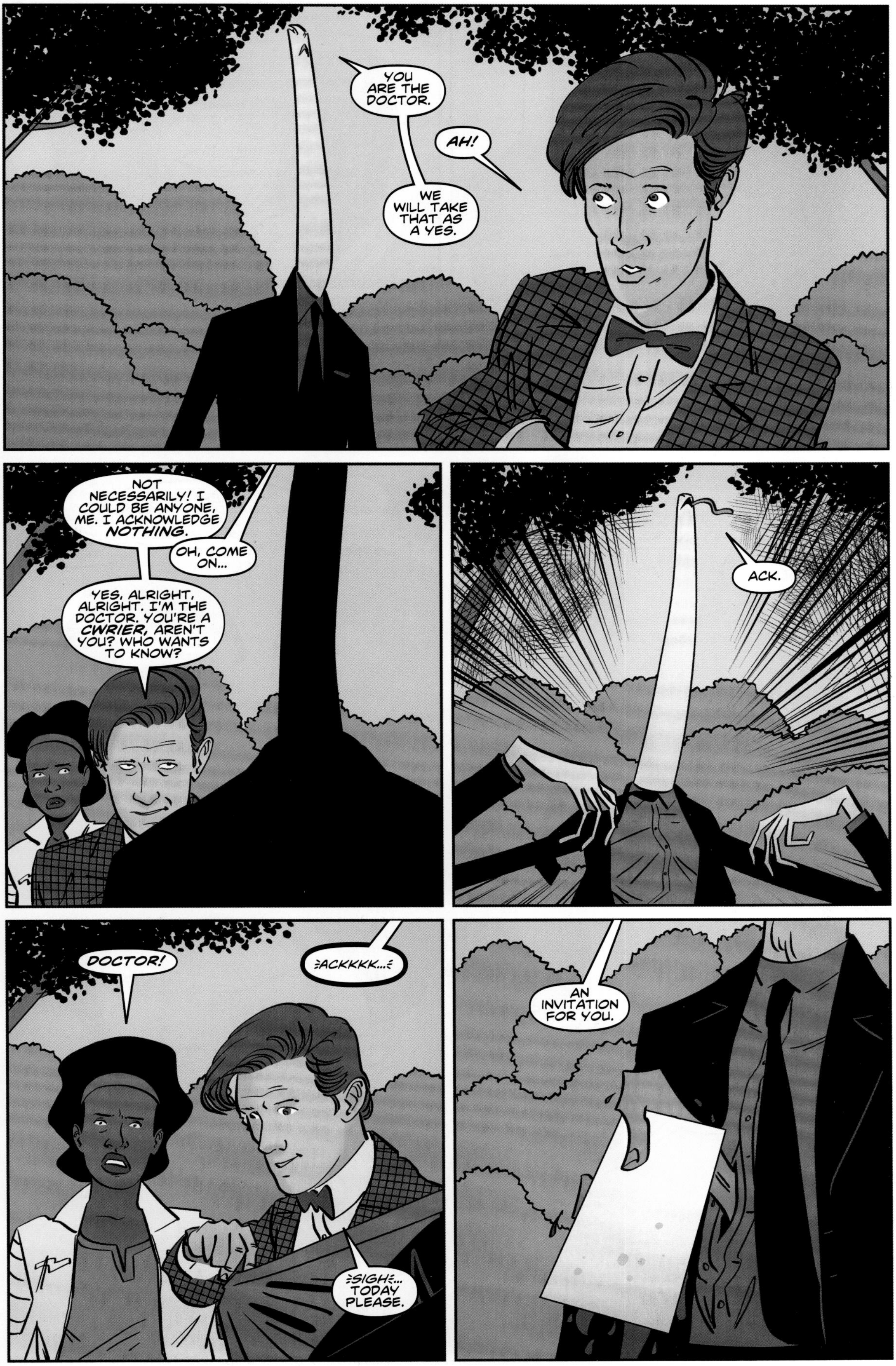
YOU ARE THE DOCTOR.
AH!
WE WILL TAKE THAT AS A YES.
NOT NECESSARILY! I COULD BE ANYONE, ME. I ACKNOWLEDGE NOTHING.
OH, COME ON...
YES, ALRIGHT, ALRIGHT. I'M THE DOCTOR. YOU'RE A CWRIER, AREN'T YOU? WHO WANTS TO KNOW?
ACK.
DOCTOR!
ACKKKK...
SIGH... TODAY PLEASE.
AN INVITATION FOR YOU.

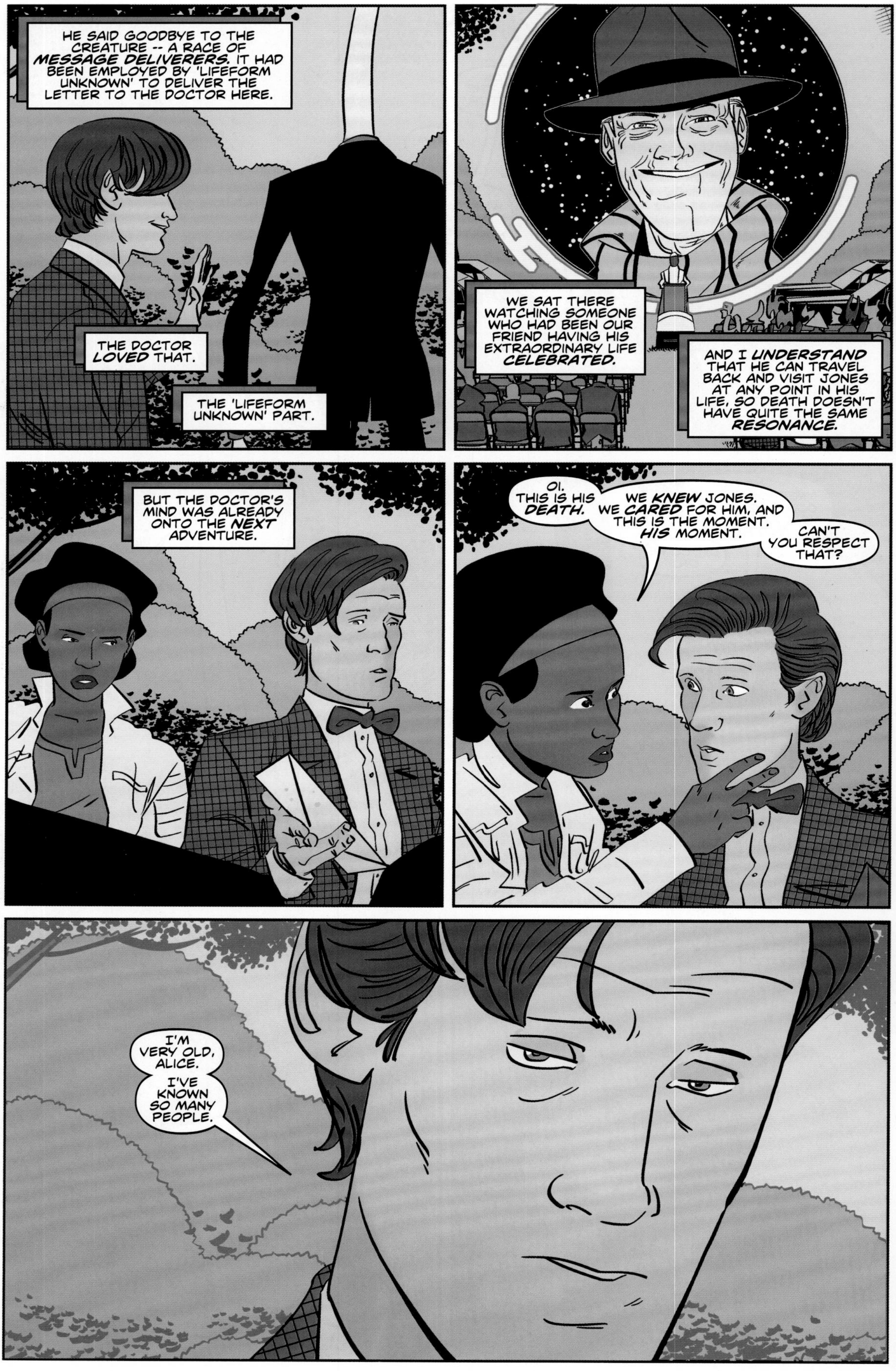
HE SAID GOODBYE TO THE CREATURE -- A RACE OF MESSAGE DELIVERERS. IT HAD BEEN EMPLOYED BY 'LIFEFORM UNKNOWN' TO DELIVER THE LETTER TO THE DOCTOR HERE.
THE DOCTOR LOVED THAT.
THE 'LIFEFORM UNKNOWN' PART.
WE SAT THERE WATCHING SOMEONE WHO HAD BEEN OUR FRIEND HAVING HIS EXTRAORDINARY LIFE CELEBRATED.
AND I UNDERSTAND THAT HE CAN TRAVEL BACK AND VISIT JONES AT ANY POINT IN HIS LIFE, SO DEATH DOESN'T HAVE QUITE THE SAME RESONANCE.
BUT THE DOCTOR'S MIND WAS ALREADY ONTO THE NEXT ADVENTURE.
OI. THIS IS HIS DEATH.
WE KNEW JONES. WE CARED FOR HIM, AND THIS IS THE MOMENT. HIS MOMENT.
CAN'T YOU RESPECT THAT?
I'M VERY OLD, ALICE.
I'VE KNOWN SO MANY PEOPLE.

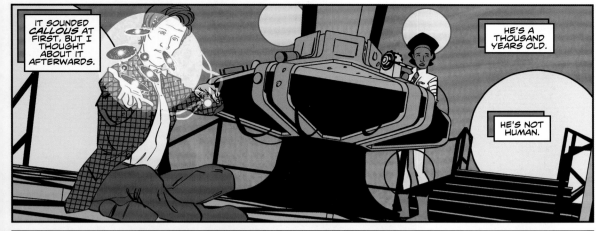

IT SOUNDED *CALLOUS* AT FIRST, BUT I THOUGHT ABOUT IT AFTERWARDS.

HE'S A THOUSAND YEARS OLD.

HE'S NOT HUMAN.

LOOK, IT'S NOT THAT I DON'T *CARE*, YOU KNOW. I DO. IT'S JUST... IT'S *DIFFERENT* FOR A TIME LORD.

JONES IS STILL OUT THERE, IN THE TIMESTREAM.

AND HE *ALWAYS* WILL BE. WE CAN GO VISIT HIM IF YOU LIKE.

LIFE IS *FINITE*. MUM. ME. EVEN. YOU.

SO LET'S HAVE SOME *FUN* WHILE WE CAN.

NO ONE SHOULD'VE KNOWN THAT I'D BE AT JONES' FUNERAL, ALICE. WHICH MEANS THAT WHOEVER SENT THIS IS *VERY* POWERFUL AND ALMOST CERTAINLY PROBABLY A MACHIAVELLIAN, UNIVERSE-ENDING PLAN-STYLE EVIL GENIUS.

RIIIIIP

SQUEEEEEE. EXCITED!

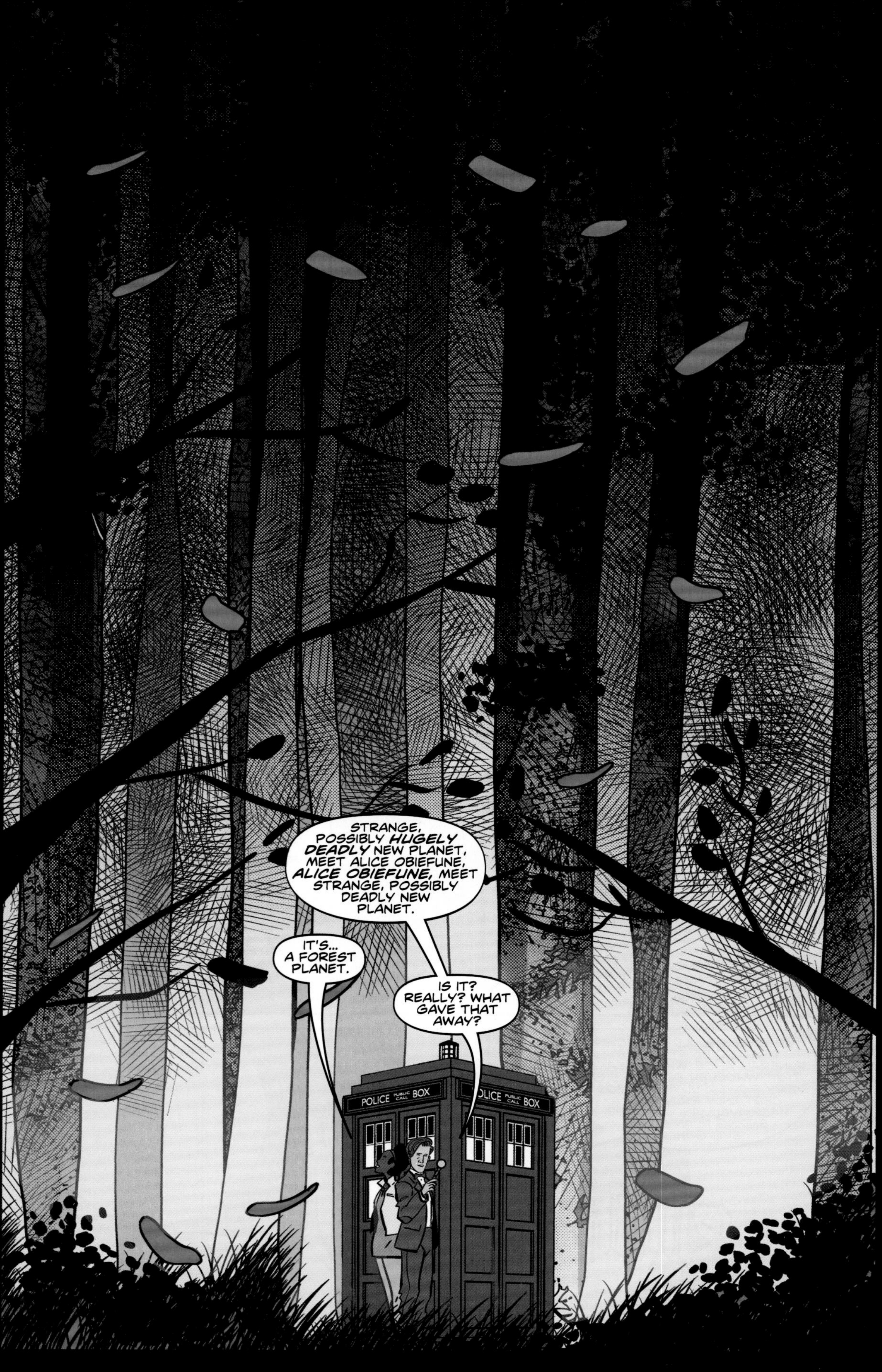
STRANGE, POSSIBLY HUGELY DEADLY NEW PLANET, MEET ALICE OBIEFUNE, ALICE OBIEFUNE, MEET STRANGE, POSSIBLY DEADLY NEW PLANET.
IT'S... A FOREST PLANET.
IS IT? REALLY? WHAT GAVE THAT AWAY?
POLICE PUBLIC CALL BOX
POLICE PUBLIC CALL BOX

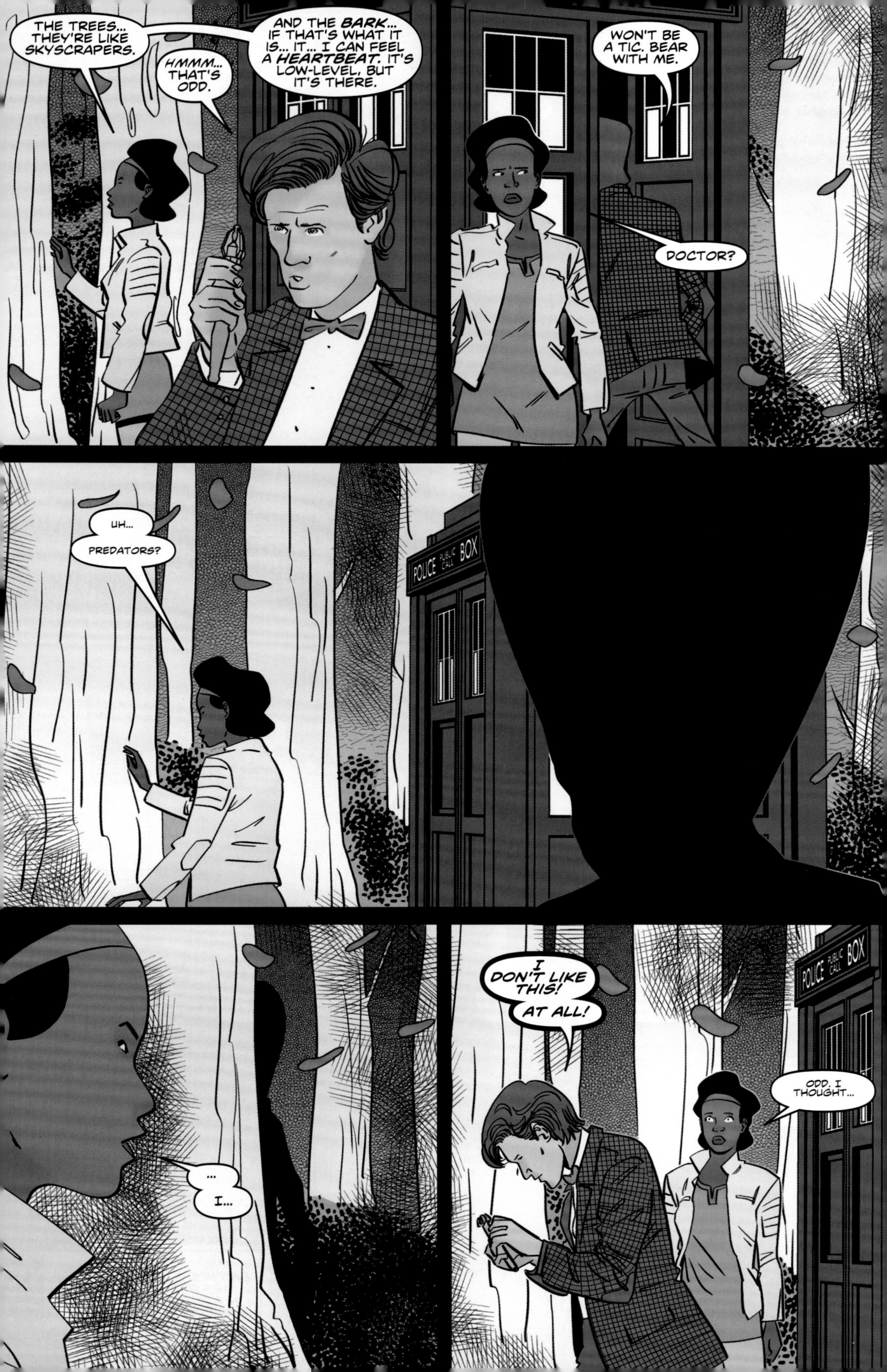
THE TREES... THEY'RE LIKE SKYSCRAPERS.
HMMM... THAT'S ODD.
AND THE BARK... IF THAT'S WHAT IT IS... IT... I CAN FEEL A HEARTBEAT. IT'S LOW-LEVEL, BUT IT'S THERE.
WON'T BE A TIC. BEAR WITH ME.
DOCTOR?
UH...
PREDATORS?
POLICE PUBLIC CALL BOX
...
I...
I DON'T LIKE THIS!
AT ALL!
POLICE PUBLIC CALL BOX
ODD. I THOUGHT...

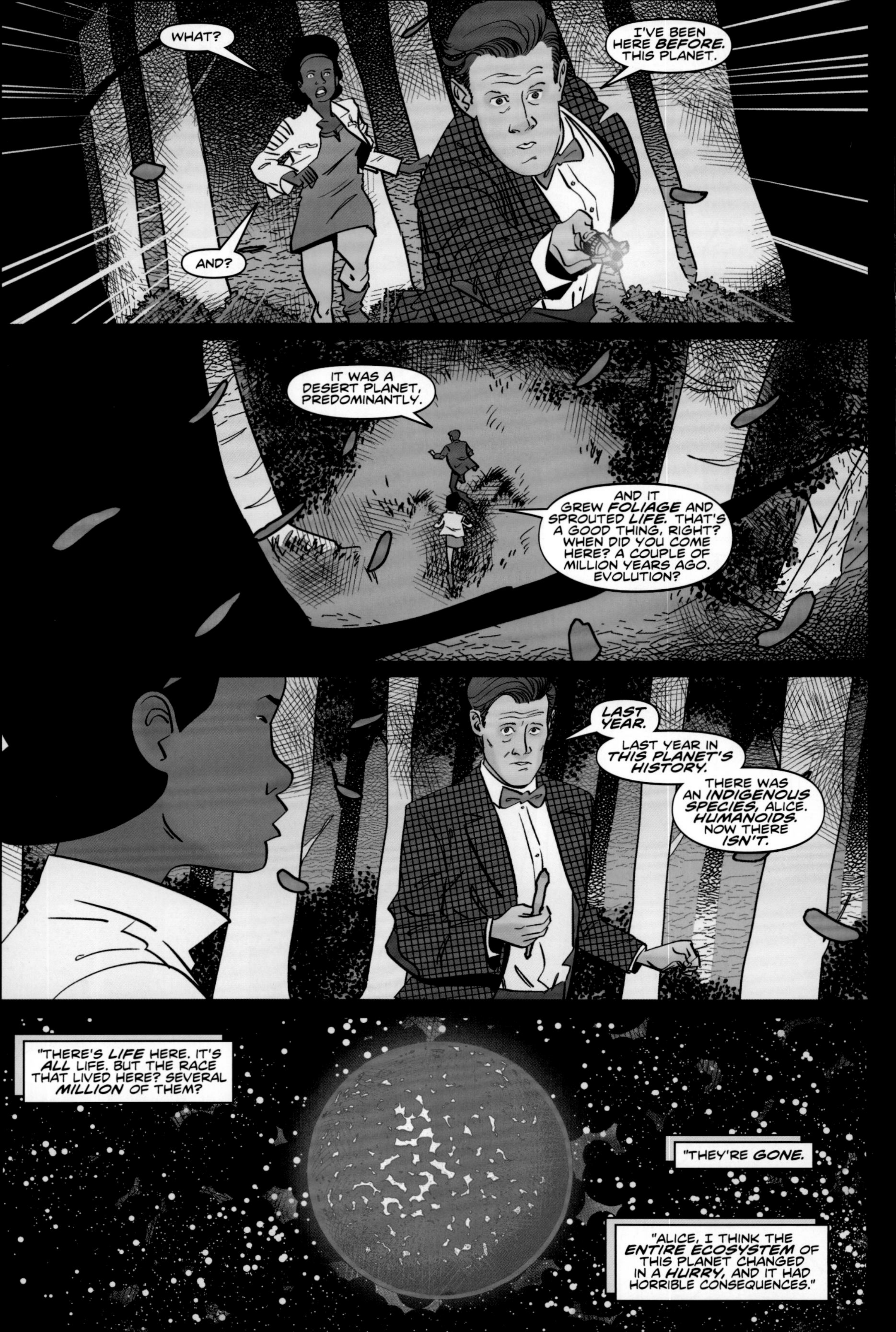
WHAT?
I'VE BEEN HERE BEFORE. THIS PLANET.
AND?
IT WAS A DESERT PLANET, PREDOMINANTLY.
AND IT GREW FOLIAGE AND SPROUTED LIFE. THAT'S A GOOD THING, RIGHT? WHEN DID YOU COME HERE? A COUPLE OF MILLION YEARS AGO. EVOLUTION?
LAST YEAR.
LAST YEAR IN THIS PLANET'S HISTORY.
THERE WAS AN INDIGENOUS SPECIES, ALICE. HUMANOIDS. NOW THERE ISN'T.
"THERE'S LIFE HERE. IT'S ALL LIFE. BUT THE RACE THAT LIVED HERE? SEVERAL MILLION OF THEM?
"THEY'RE GONE.
"ALICE, I THINK THE ENTIRE ECOSYSTEM OF THIS PLANET CHANGED IN A HURRY, AND IT HAD HORRIBLE CONSEQUENCES."

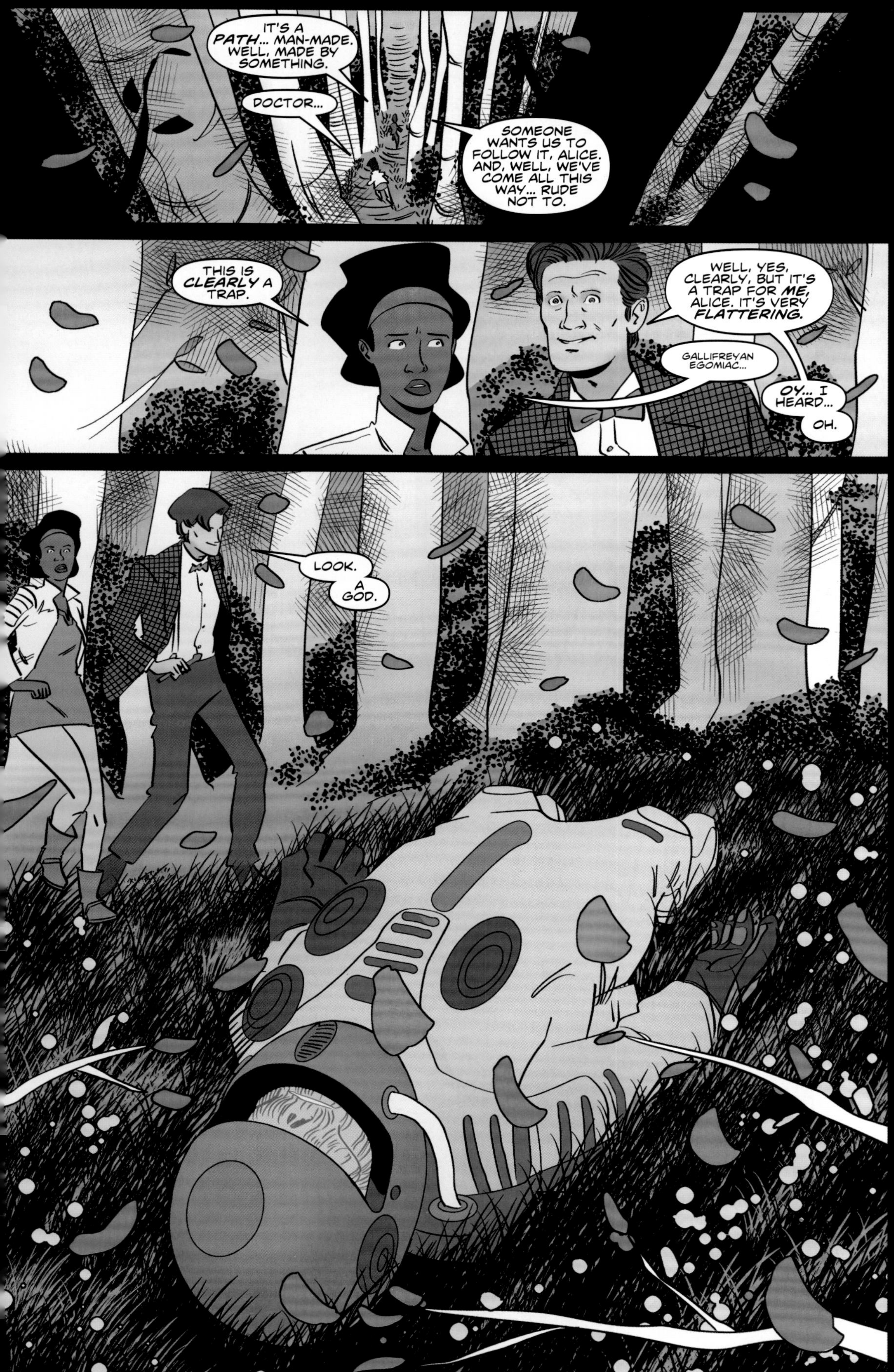
IT'S A PATH... MAN-MADE. WELL, MADE BY SOMETHING.
DOCTOR...
SOMEONE WANTS US TO FOLLOW IT, ALICE. AND, WELL, WE'VE COME ALL THIS WAY... RUDE NOT TO.
THIS IS CLEARLY A TRAP.
WELL, YES, CLEARLY, BUT IT'S A TRAP FOR ME, ALICE. IT'S VERY FLATTERING.
GALLIFREYAN EGOMIAC...
OY... I HEARD...
OH.
LOOK.
A GOD.

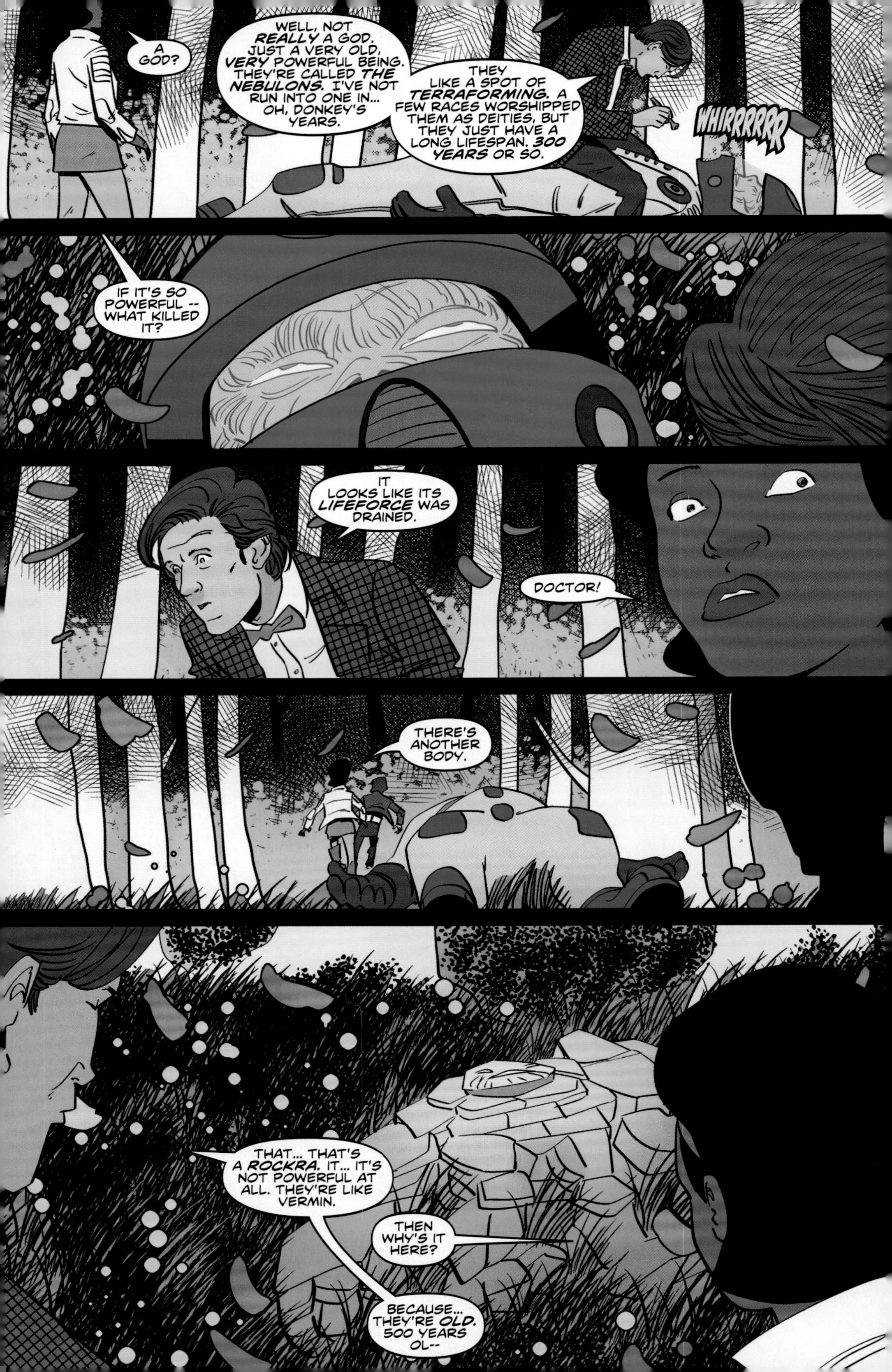

A GOD?
WELL, NOT REALLY A GOD. JUST A VERY OLD, VERY POWERFUL BEING. THEY'RE CALLED THE NEBULONS. I'VE NOT RUN INTO ONE IN... OH, DONKEY'S YEARS.
THEY LIKE A SPOT OF TERRAFORMING. A FEW RACES WORSHIPPED THEM AS DEITIES, BUT THEY JUST HAVE A LONG LIFESPAN. 300 YEARS OR SO.
WHIRRRRRR
IF IT'S SO POWERFUL -- WHAT KILLED IT?
IT LOOKS LIKE ITS LIFEFORCE WAS DRAINED.
DOCTOR!
THERE'S ANOTHER BODY.
THAT... THAT'S A ROCKRA. IT... IT'S NOT POWERFUL AT ALL. THEY'RE LIKE VERMIN.
THEN WHY'S IT HERE?
BECAUSE... THEY'RE OLD. 500 YEARS OL--

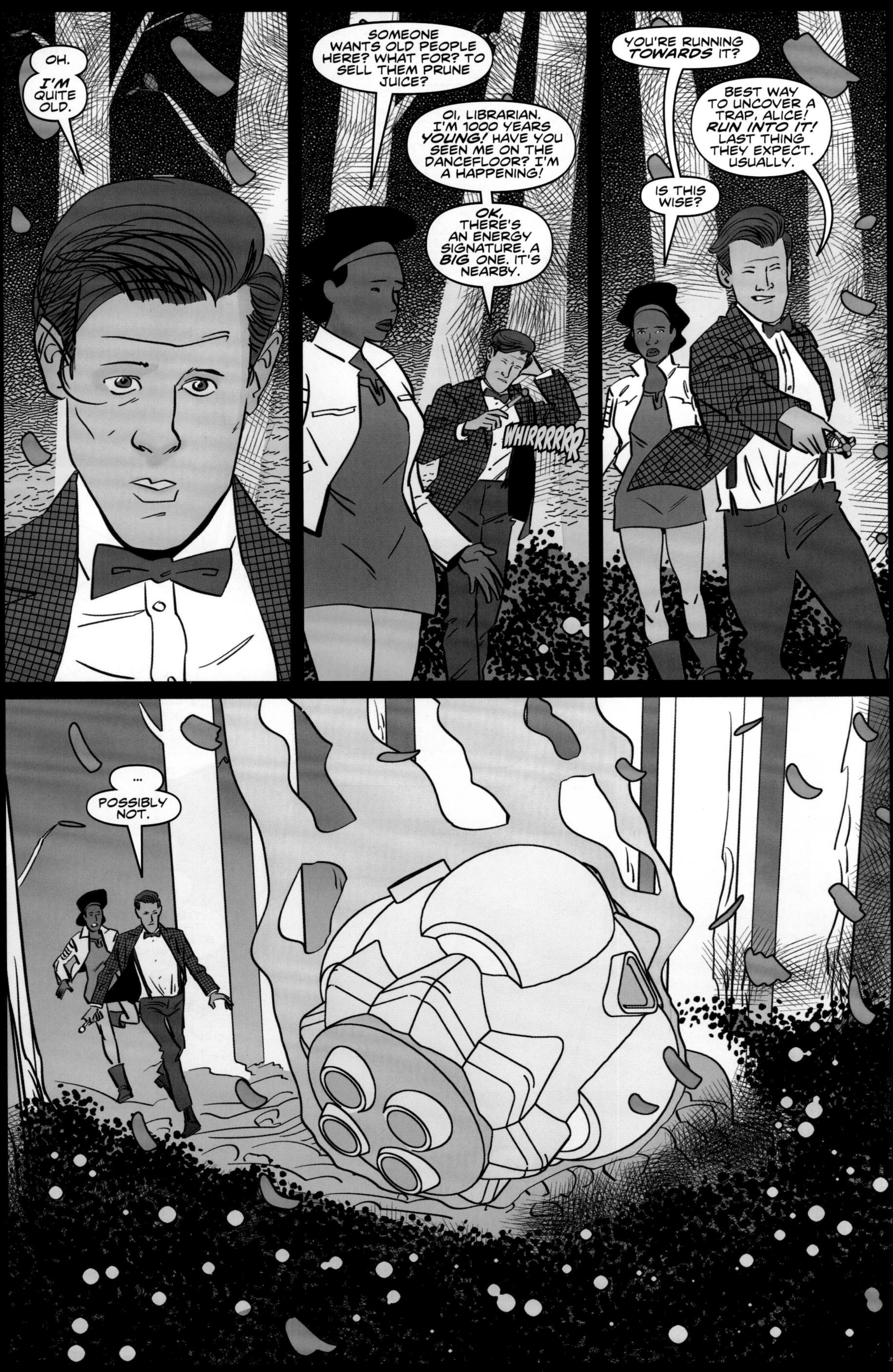
OH.
I'M QUITE OLD.
SOMEONE WANTS OLD PEOPLE HERE? WHAT FOR? TO SELL THEM PRUNE JUICE?
OI, LIBRARIAN. I'M 1000 YEARS YOUNG! HAVE YOU SEEN ME ON THE DANCEFLOOR? I'M A HAPPENING!
OK, THERE'S AN ENERGY SIGNATURE. A BIG ONE. IT'S NEARBY.
WHIRRRRRR
YOU'RE RUNNING TOWARDS IT?
BEST WAY TO UNCOVER A TRAP, ALICE! RUN INTO IT! LAST THING THEY EXPECT. USUALLY.
IS THIS WISE?
...
POSSIBLY NOT.

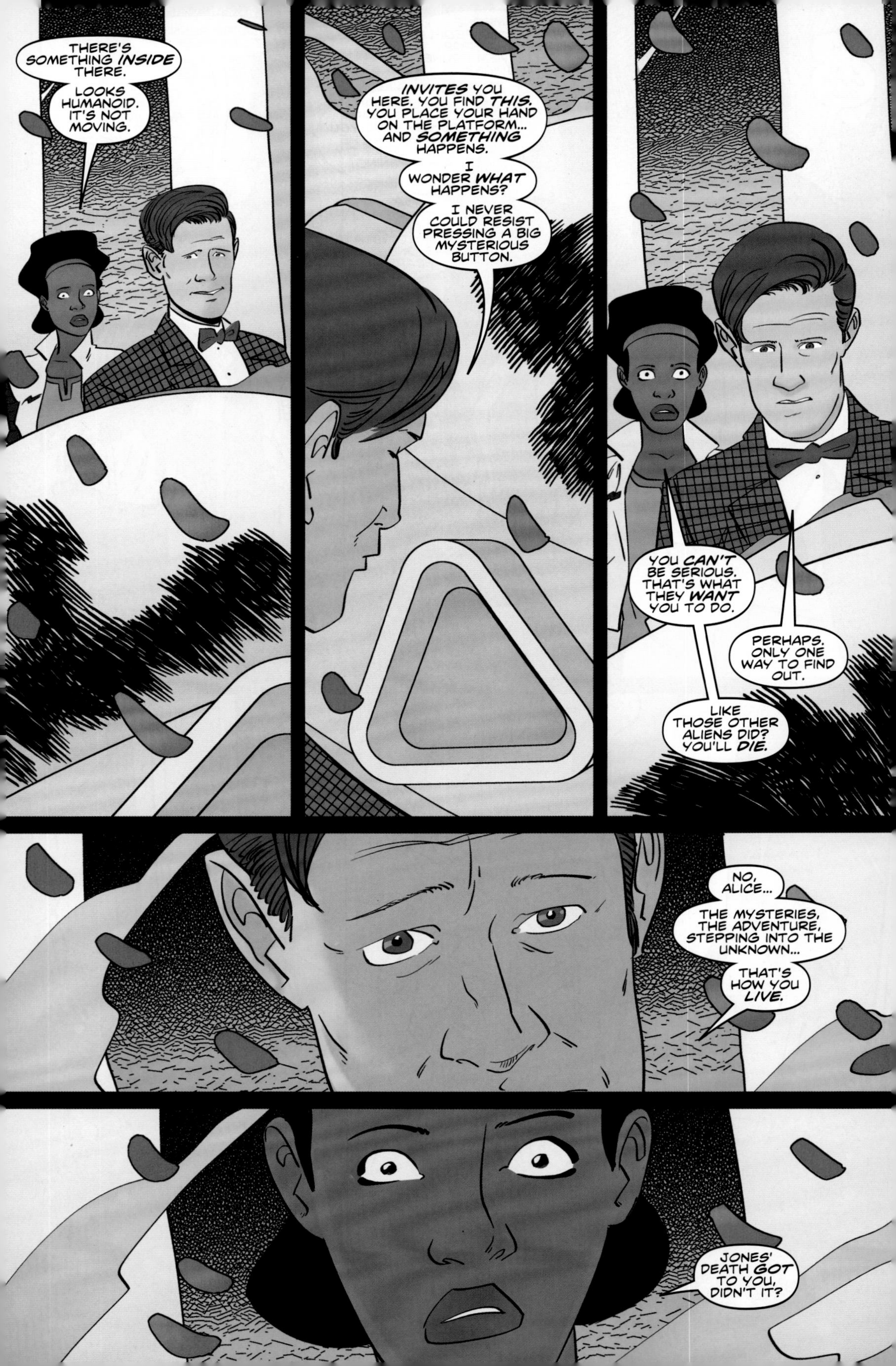
THERE'S SOMETHING INSIDE THERE.
LOOKS HUMANOID. IT'S NOT MOVING.
INVITES YOU HERE. YOU FIND THIS. YOU PLACE YOUR HAND ON THE PLATFORM... AND SOMETHING HAPPENS.
I WONDER WHAT HAPPENS?
I NEVER COULD RESIST PRESSING A BIG MYSTERIOUS BUTTON.
YOU CAN'T BE SERIOUS. THAT'S WHAT THEY WANT YOU TO DO.
PERHAPS. ONLY ONE WAY TO FIND OUT.
LIKE THOSE OTHER ALIENS DID? YOU'LL DIE.
NO, ALICE...
THE MYSTERIES, THE ADVENTURE, STEPPING INTO THE UNKNOWN...
THAT'S HOW YOU LIVE.
JONES' DEATH GOT TO YOU, DIDN'T IT?

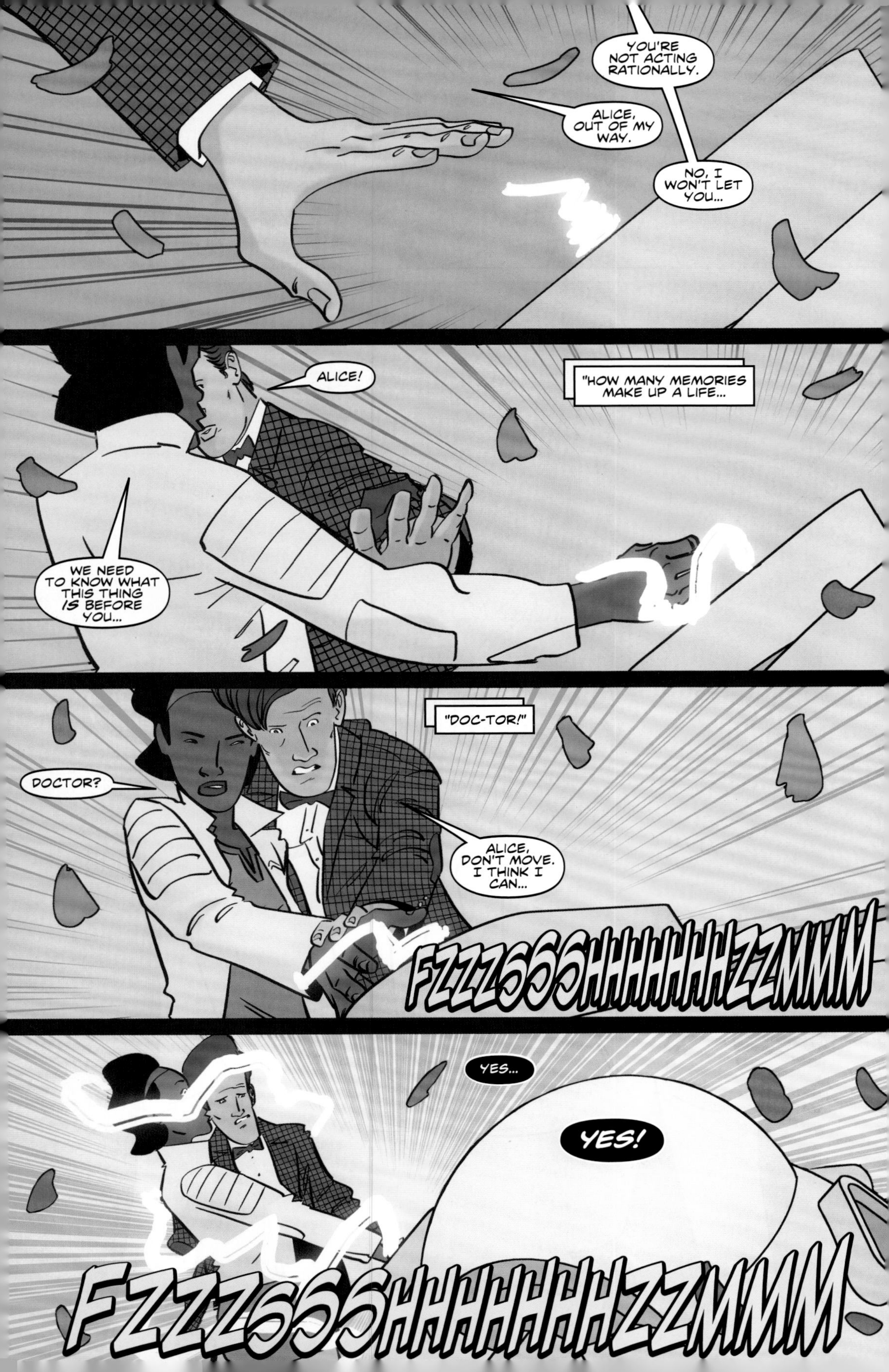
YOU'RE NOT ACTING RATIONALLY.
ALICE, OUT OF MY WAY.
NO, I WON'T LET YOU...
ALICE!
"HOW MANY MEMORIES MAKE UP A LIFE...
WE NEED TO KNOW WHAT THIS THING IS BEFORE YOU...
"DOC-TOR!"
DOCTOR?
ALICE, DON'T MOVE. I THINK I CAN...
FZZZGGSHHHHHHZZMMM
YES...
YES!
FZZZGGGSHHHHHHHZZMMM

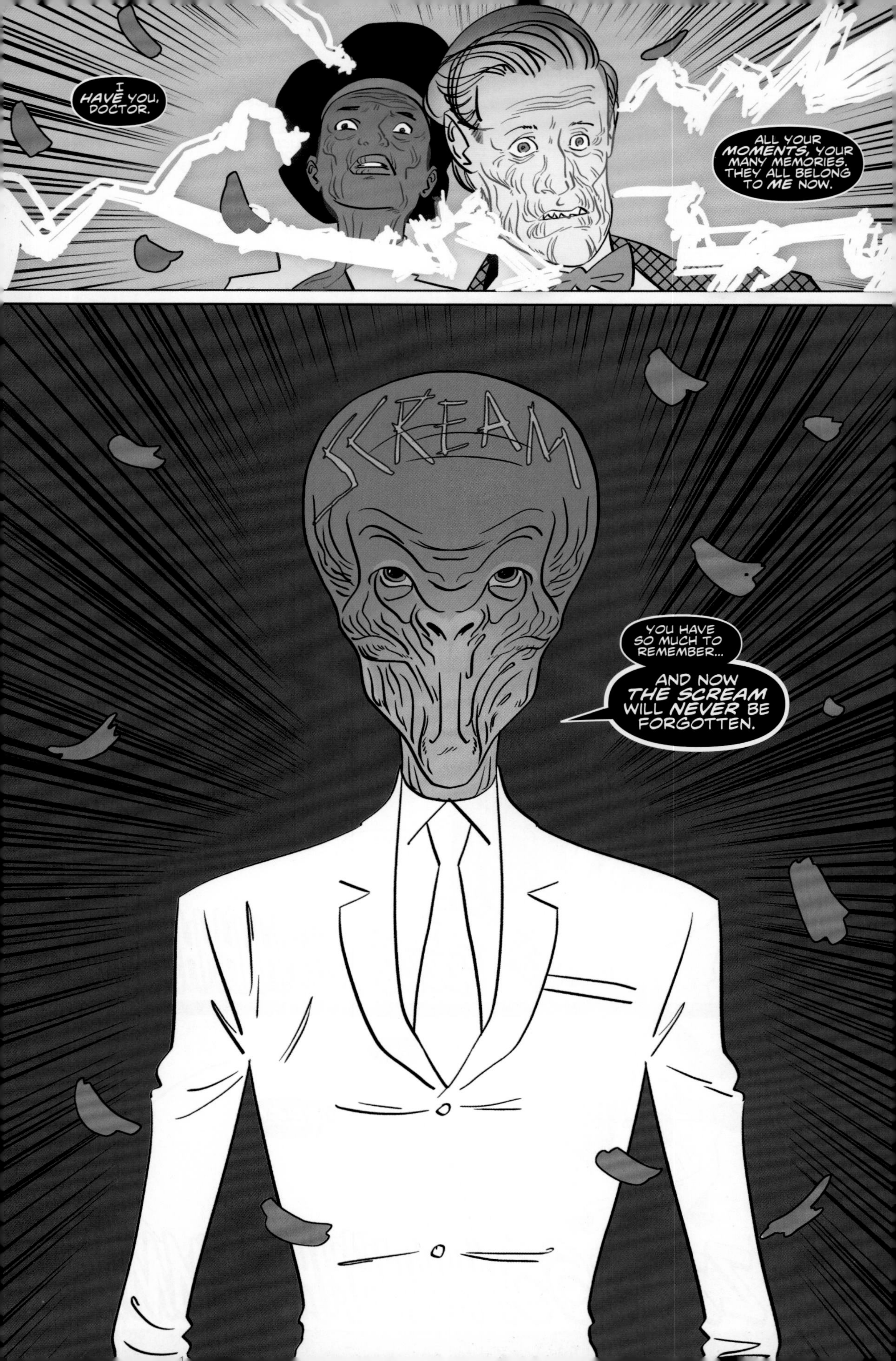
I HAVE YOU, DOCTOR.
ALL YOUR MOMENTS, YOUR MANY MEMORIES. THEY ALL BELONG TO ME NOW.
SCREAM
YOU HAVE SO MUCH TO REMEMBER...
AND NOW THE SCREAM WILL NEVER BE FORGOTTEN.

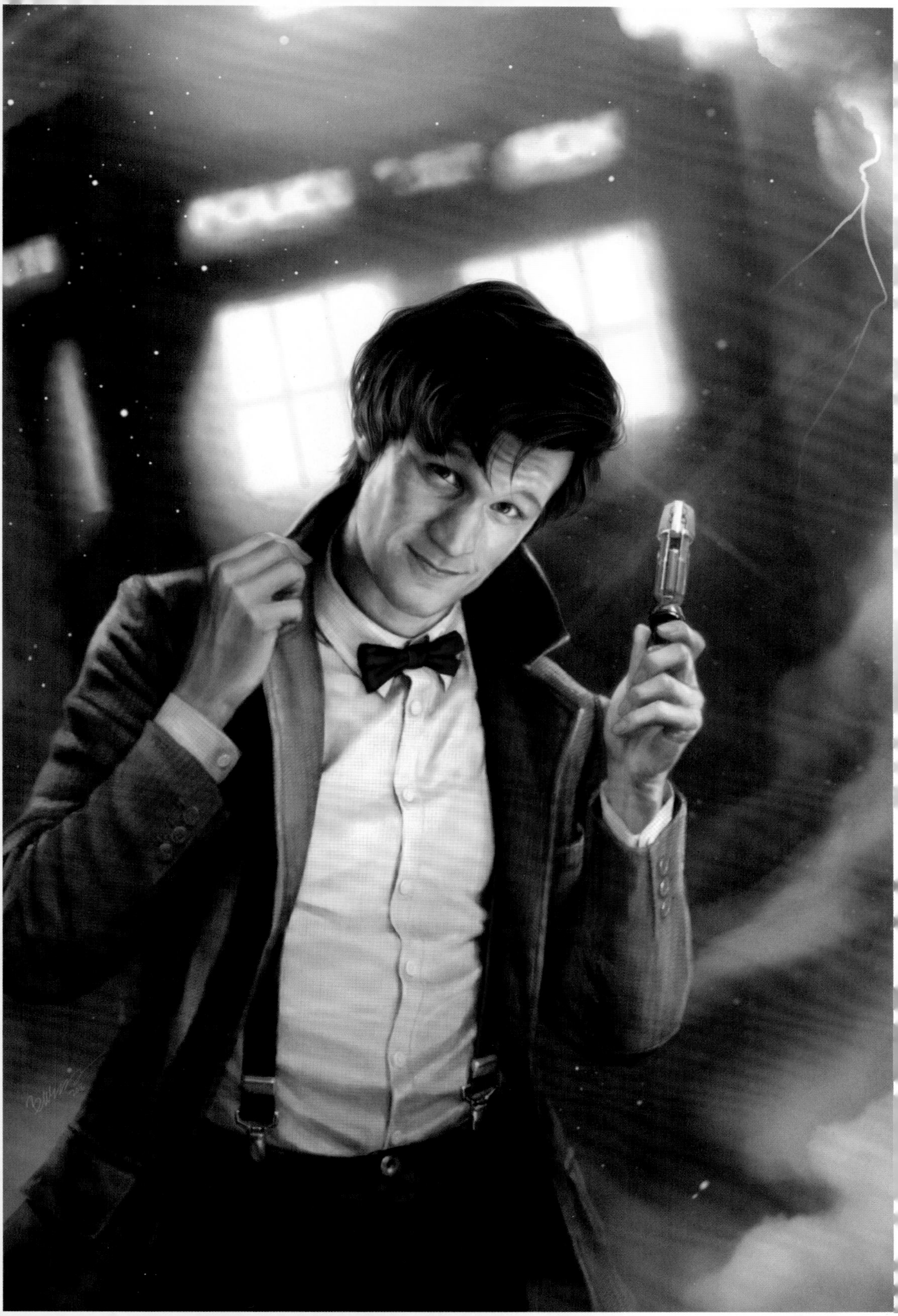

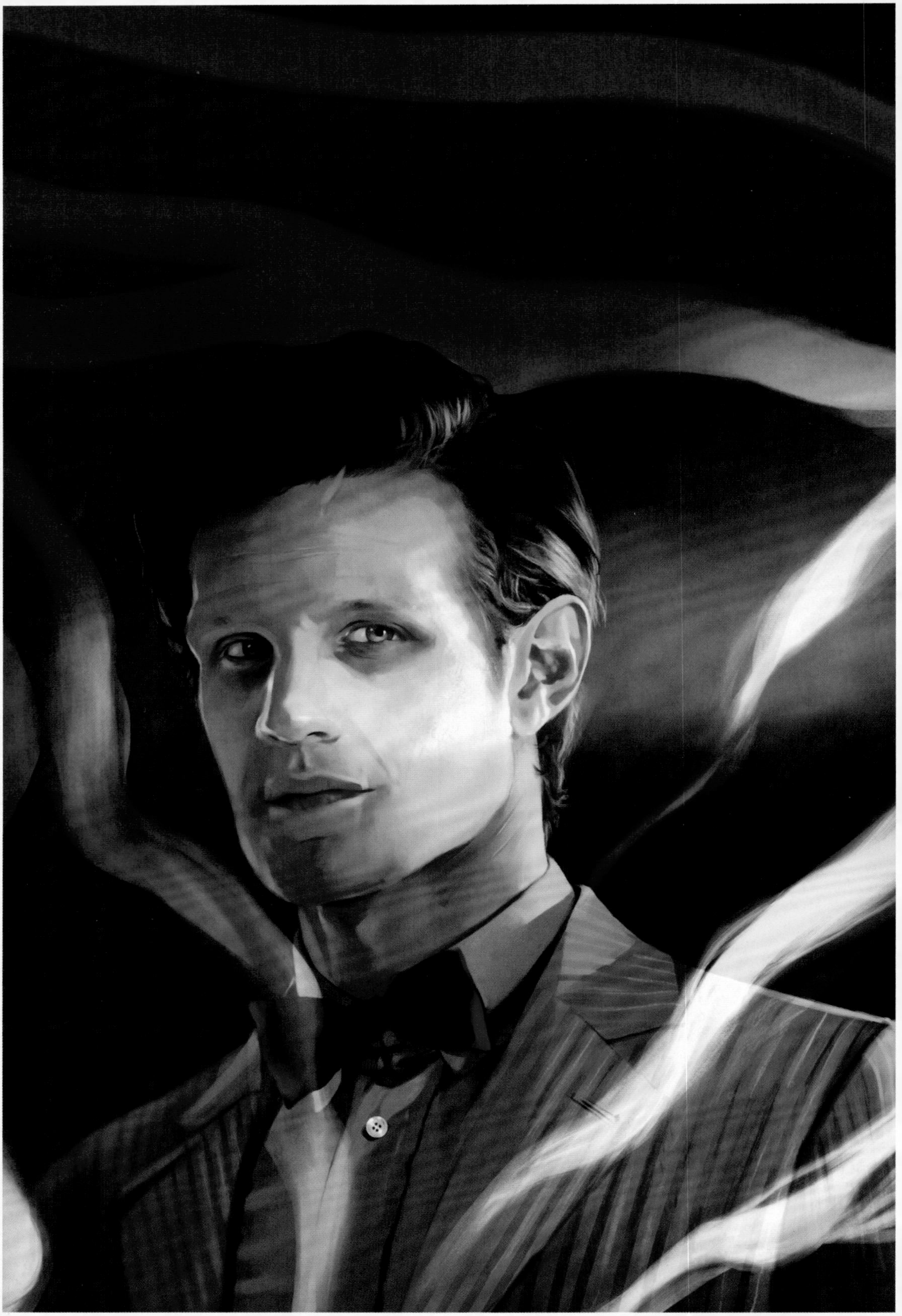

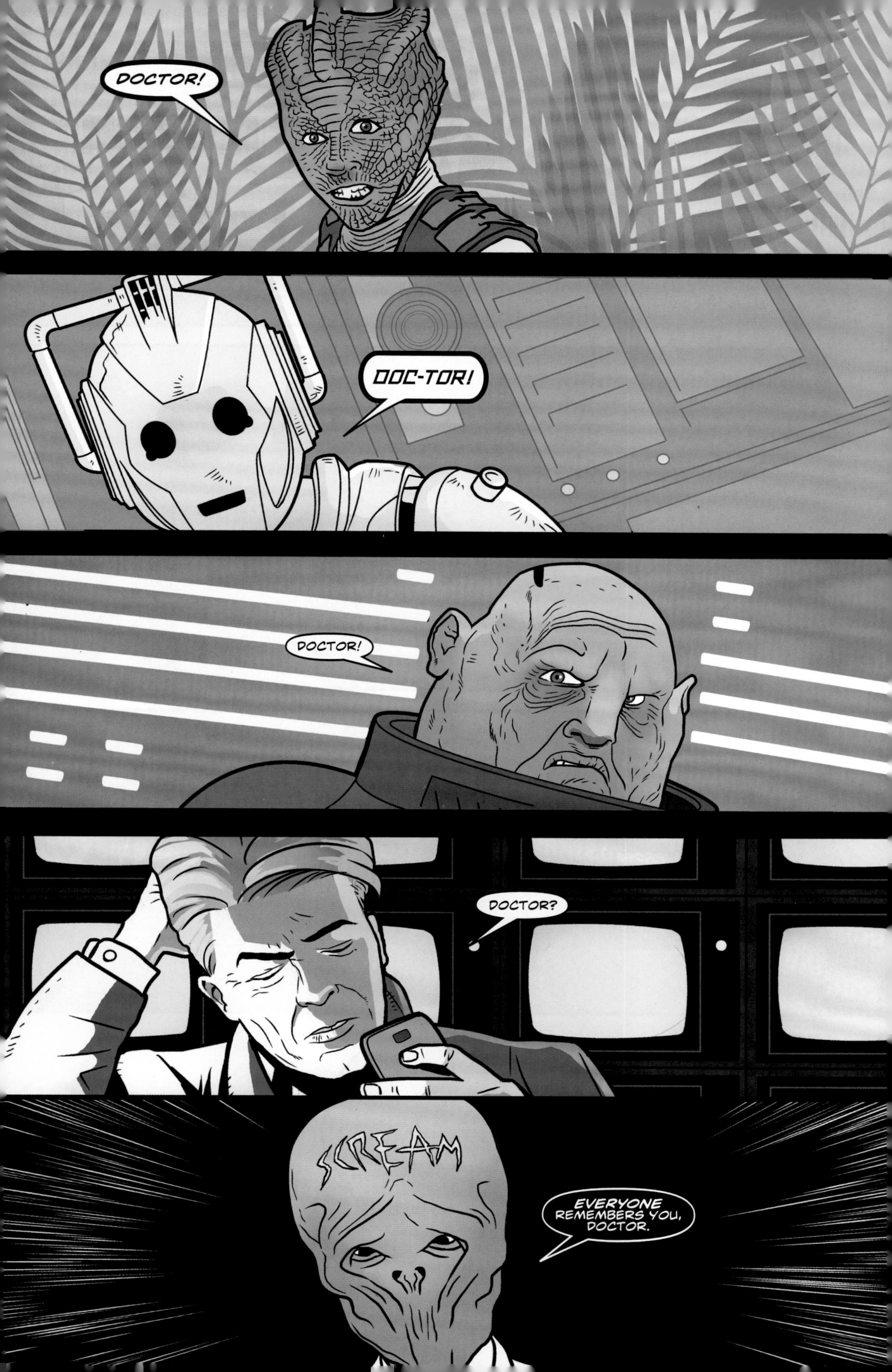
DOCTOR!
DOC-TOR!
DOCTOR!
DOCTOR?
SCREAM
EVERYONE REMEMBERS YOU, DOCTOR.

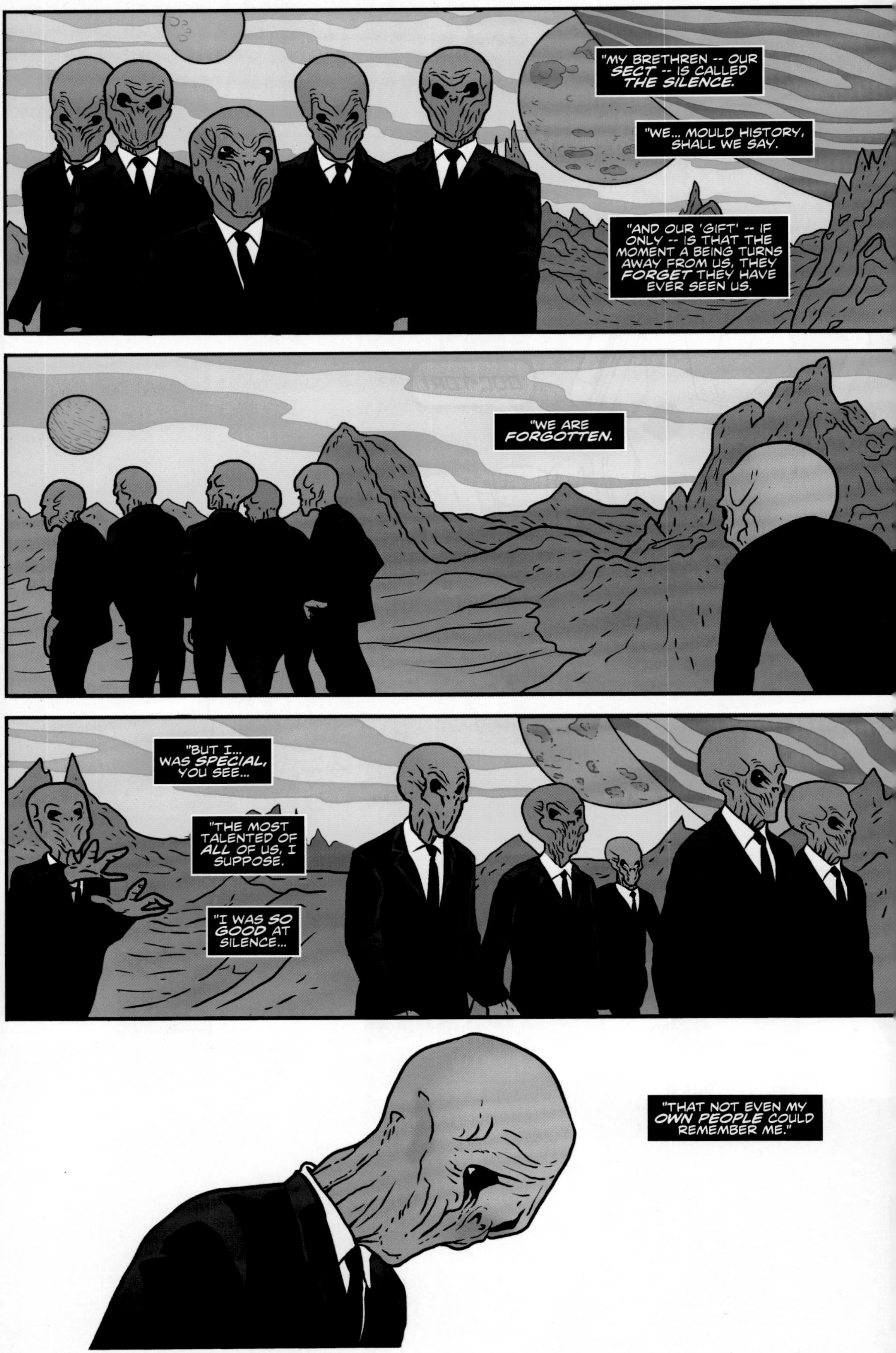
"MY BRETHREN -- OUR SECT -- IS CALLED THE SILENCE.
"WE... MOULD HISTORY, SHALL WE SAY.
"AND OUR 'GIFT' -- IF ONLY -- IS THAT THE MOMENT A BEING TURNS AWAY FROM US, THEY FORGET THEY HAVE EVER SEEN US.
"WE ARE FORGOTTEN.
"BUT I... WAS SPECIAL, YOU SEE...
"THE MOST TALENTED OF ALL OF US, I SUPPOSE.
"I WAS SO GOOD AT SILENCE...
"THAT NOT EVEN MY OWN PEOPLE COULD REMEMBER ME."

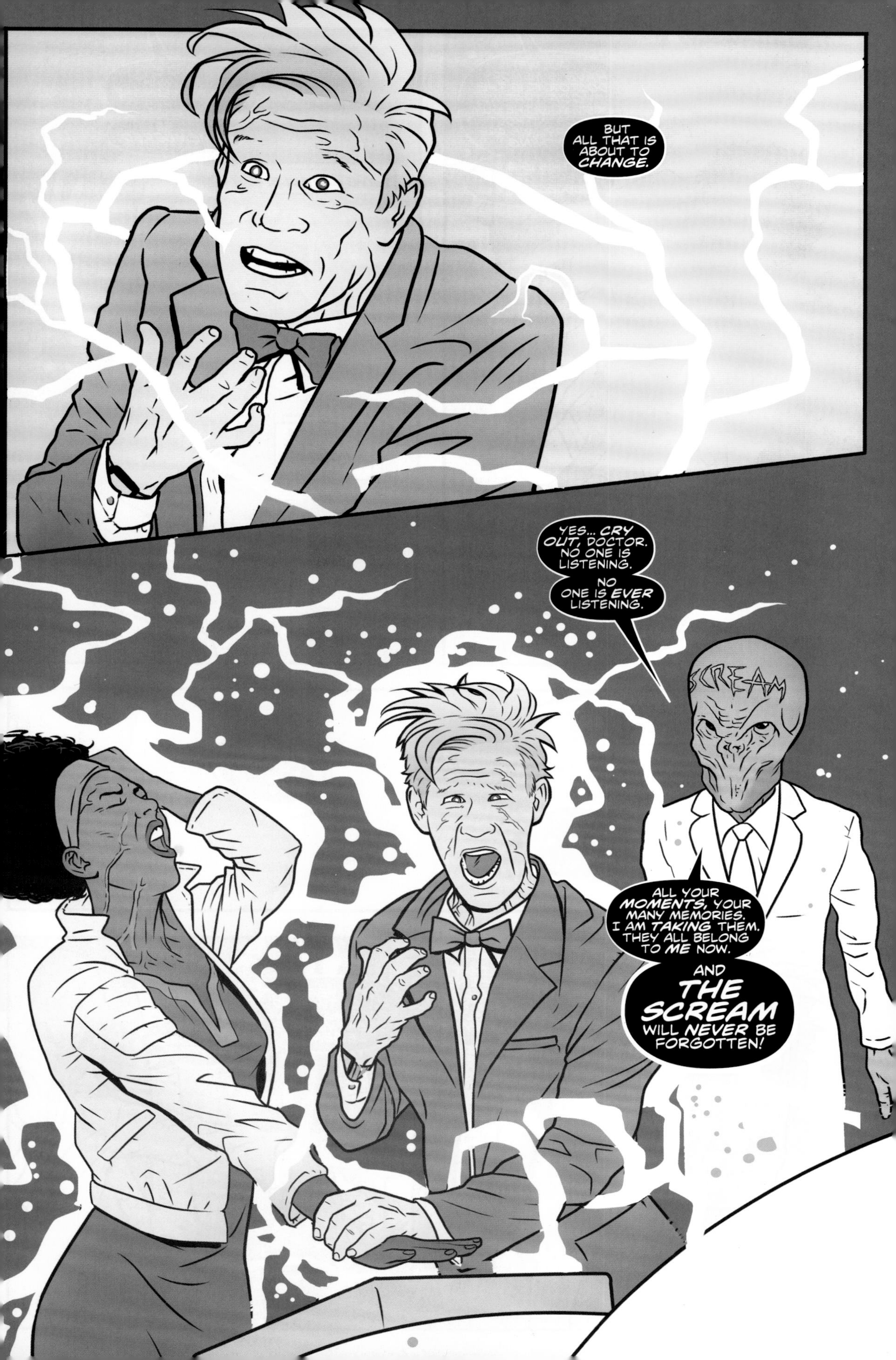
BUT ALL THAT IS ABOUT TO *CHANGE.*
YES... *CRY OUT,* DOCTOR. NO ONE IS LISTENING.
NO ONE IS *EVER* LISTENING.
SCREAM
ALL YOUR *MOMENTS,* YOUR MANY MEMORIES. I AM *TAKING* THEM. THEY ALL BELONG TO *ME* NOW.
AND *THE SCREAM* WILL *NEVER* BE FORGOTTEN!

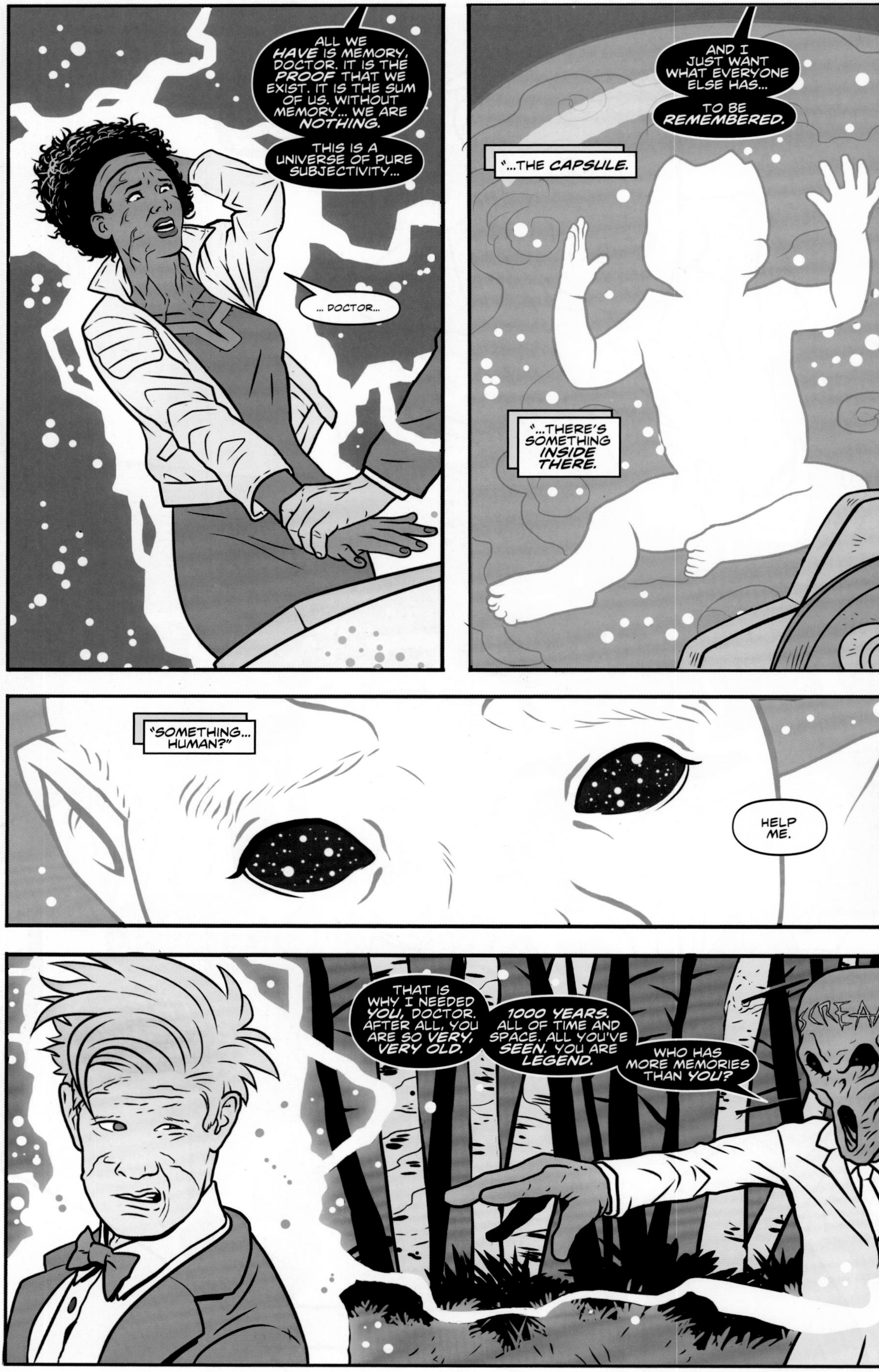
ALL WE *HAVE* IS MEMORY, DOCTOR. IT IS THE *PROOF* THAT WE EXIST. IT IS THE SUM OF US. WITHOUT MEMORY... WE ARE *NOTHING*.
THIS IS A UNIVERSE OF PURE SUBJECTIVITY...
... DOCTOR...
AND I JUST WANT WHAT EVERYONE ELSE HAS...
TO BE *REMEMBERED*.
"...THE *CAPSULE*.
"...THERE'S SOMETHING *INSIDE THERE*.
"SOMETHING... HUMAN?"
HELP ME.
THAT IS WHY I NEEDED *YOU*, DOCTOR. AFTER ALL, YOU ARE SO *VERY, VERY OLD*.
1000 YEARS. ALL OF TIME AND SPACE. ALL YOU'VE *SEEN*. YOU ARE *LEGEND*.
WHO HAS MORE MEMORIES THAN *YOU*?
SCREAM

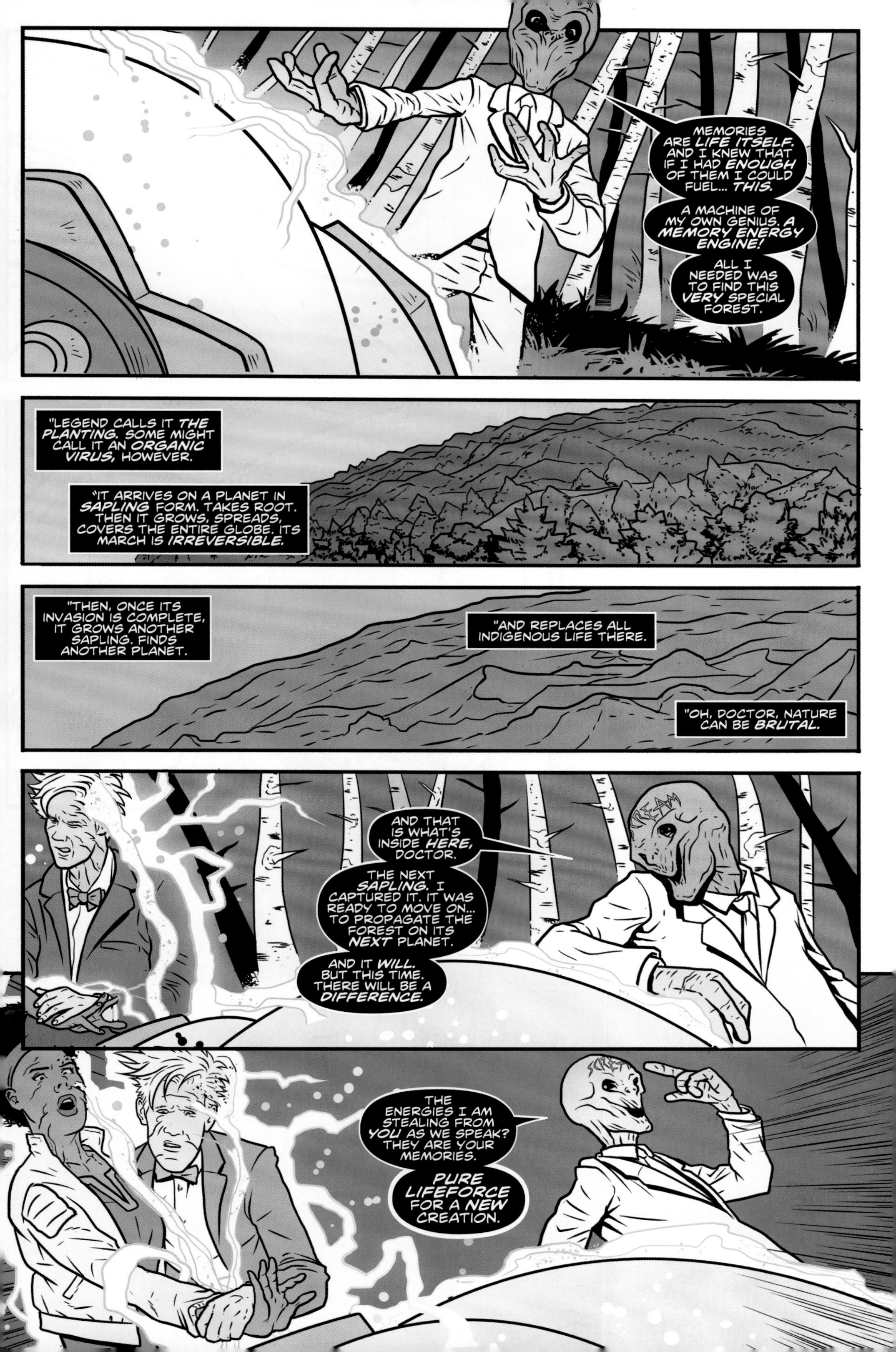

MEMORIES ARE LIFE ITSELF. AND I KNEW THAT IF I HAD ENOUGH OF THEM I COULD FUEL... THIS.
A MACHINE OF MY OWN GENIUS. A MEMORY ENERGY ENGINE!
ALL I NEEDED WAS TO FIND THIS VERY SPECIAL FOREST.
"LEGEND CALLS IT THE PLANTING. SOME MIGHT CALL IT AN ORGANIC VIRUS, HOWEVER.
"IT ARRIVES ON A PLANET IN SAPLING FORM. TAKES ROOT. THEN IT GROWS, SPREADS, COVERS THE ENTIRE GLOBE. ITS MARCH IS IRREVERSIBLE.
"THEN, ONCE ITS INVASION IS COMPLETE, IT GROWS ANOTHER SAPLING. FINDS ANOTHER PLANET.
"AND REPLACES ALL INDIGENOUS LIFE THERE.
"OH, DOCTOR, NATURE CAN BE BRUTAL.
AND THAT IS WHAT'S INSIDE HERE, DOCTOR.
THE NEXT SAPLING. I CAPTURED IT. IT WAS READY TO MOVE ON... TO PROPAGATE THE FOREST ON ITS NEXT PLANET.
AND IT WILL. BUT THIS TIME. THERE WILL BE A DIFFERENCE.
THE ENERGIES I AM STEALING FROM YOU AS WE SPEAK? THEY ARE YOUR MEMORIES.
PURE LIFEFORCE FOR A NEW CREATION.

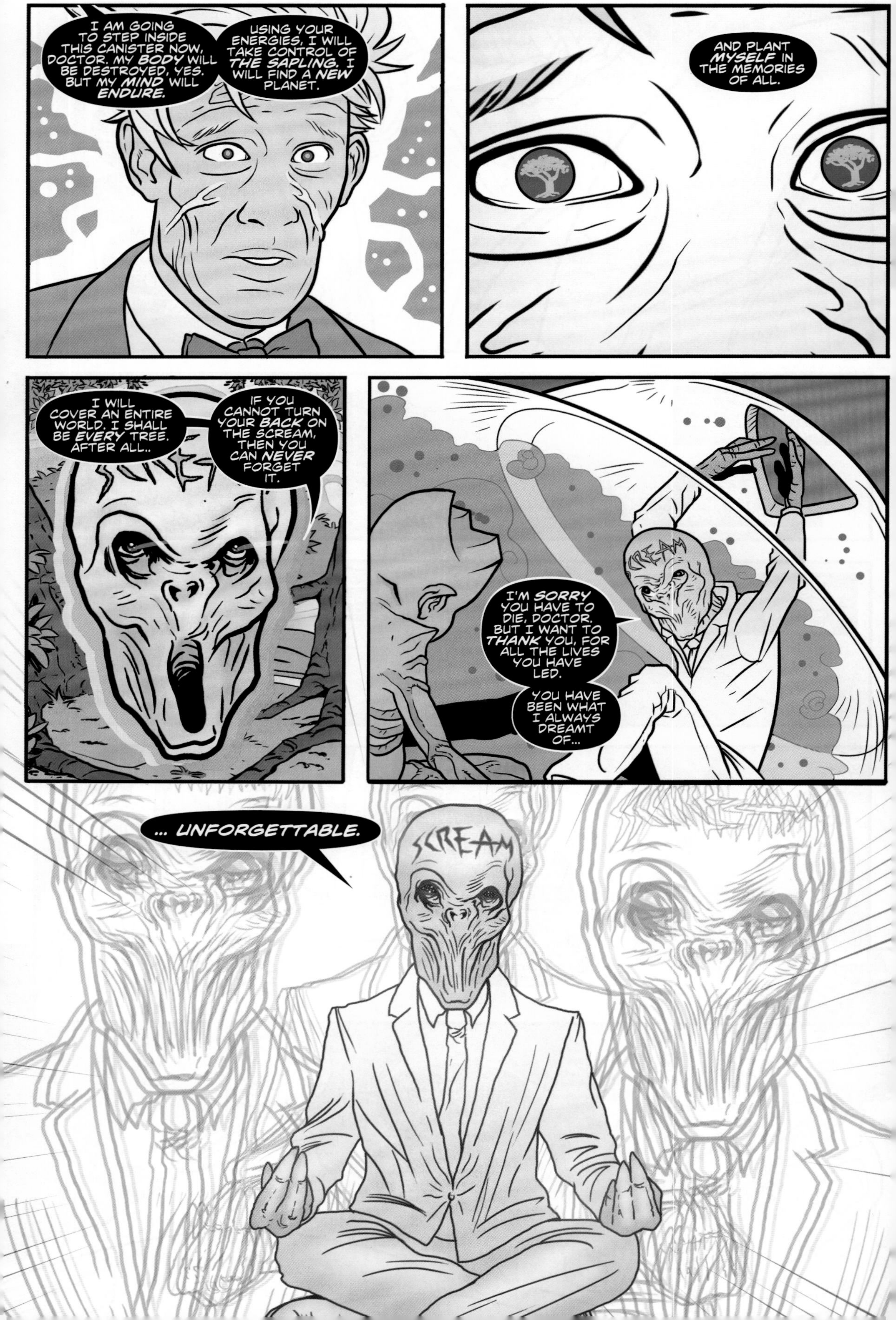
I AM GOING TO STEP INSIDE THIS CANISTER NOW, DOCTOR. MY BODY WILL BE DESTROYED, YES. BUT MY MIND WILL ENDURE.
USING YOUR ENERGIES, I WILL TAKE CONTROL OF THE SAPLING. I WILL FIND A NEW PLANET.
AND PLANT MYSELF IN THE MEMORIES OF ALL.
I WILL COVER AN ENTIRE WORLD. I SHALL BE EVERY TREE. AFTER ALL..
IF YOU CANNOT TURN YOUR BACK ON THE SCREAM, THEN YOU CAN NEVER FORGET IT.
I'M SORRY YOU HAVE TO DIE, DOCTOR. BUT I WANT TO THANK YOU, FOR ALL THE LIVES YOU HAVE LED.
YOU HAVE BEEN WHAT I ALWAYS DREAMT OF...
CREAM
... UNFORGETTABLE.
SCREAM

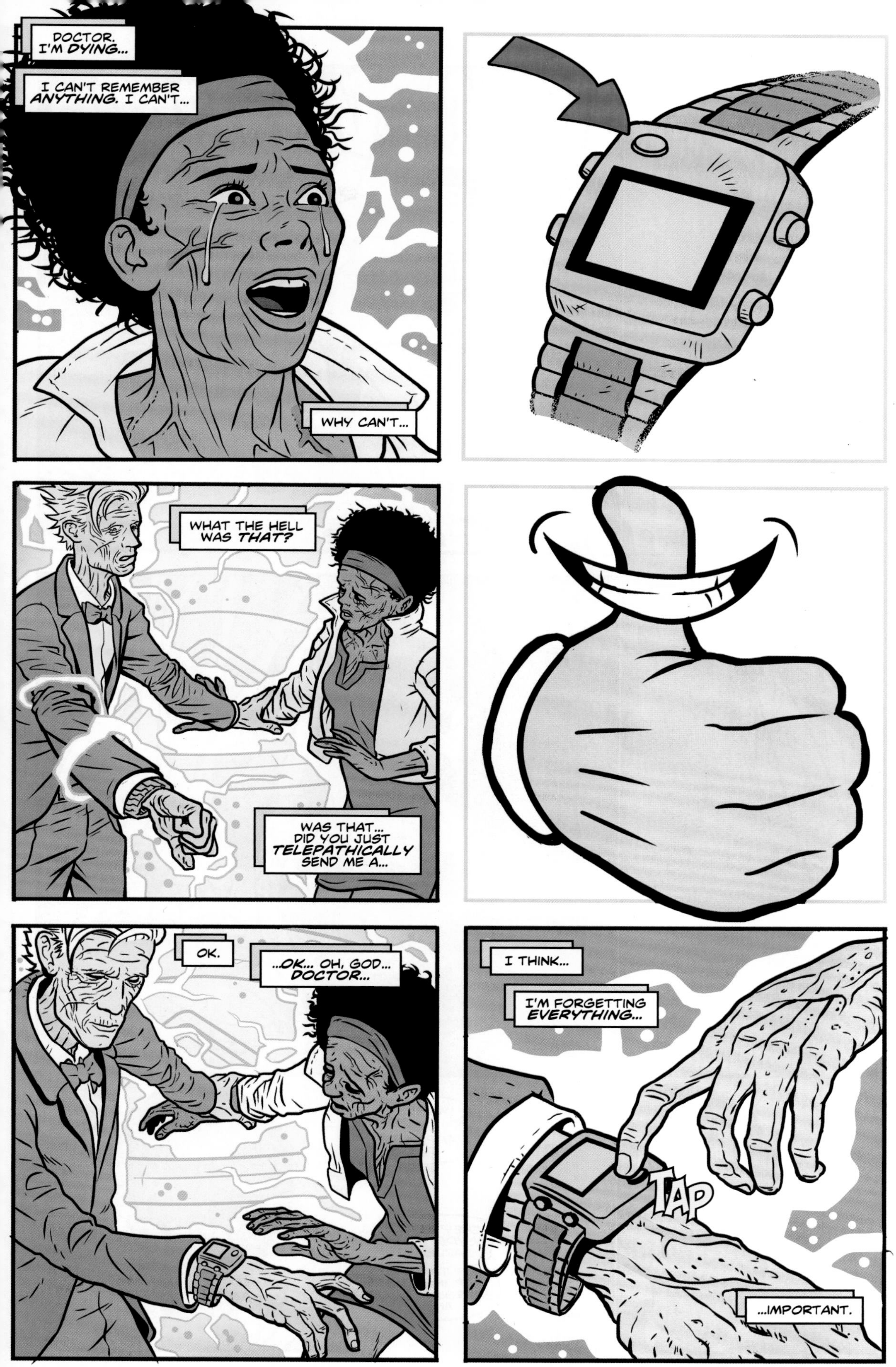
DOCTOR. I'M DYING...
I CAN'T REMEMBER ANYTHING. I CAN'T...
WHY CAN'T...
WHAT THE HELL WAS THAT?
WAS THAT... DID YOU JUST TELEPATHICALLY SEND ME A...
OK.
...OK... OH, GOD... DOCTOR...
I THINK...
I'M FORGETTING EVERYTHING...
TAP
...IMPORTANT.

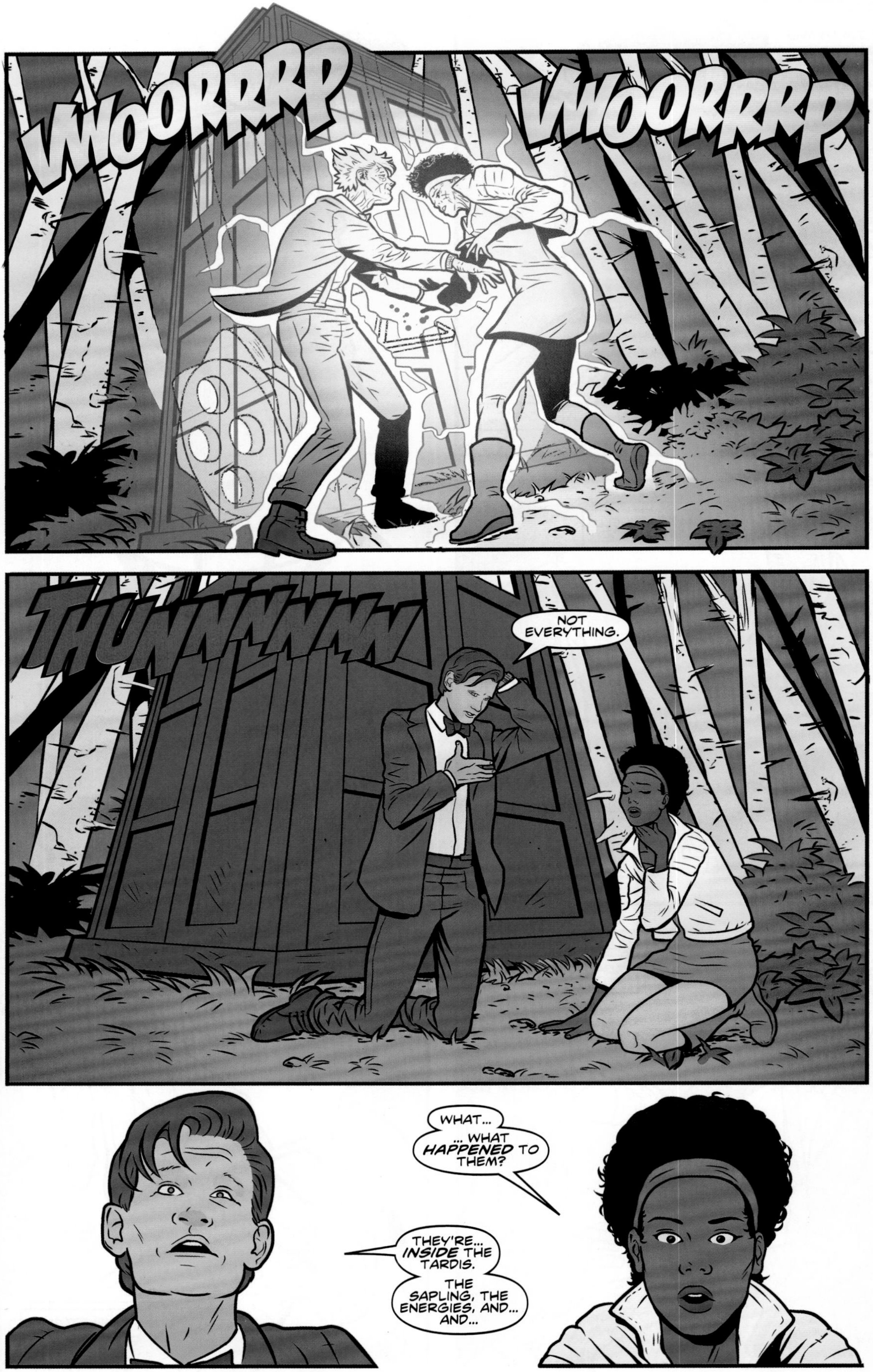
VWOORRRP
VWOORRRP
THUNNNNNN
NOT EVERYTHING.
WHAT...
... WHAT HAPPENED TO THEM?
THEY'RE... INSIDE THE TARDIS.
THE SAPLING, THE ENERGIES, AND... AND...

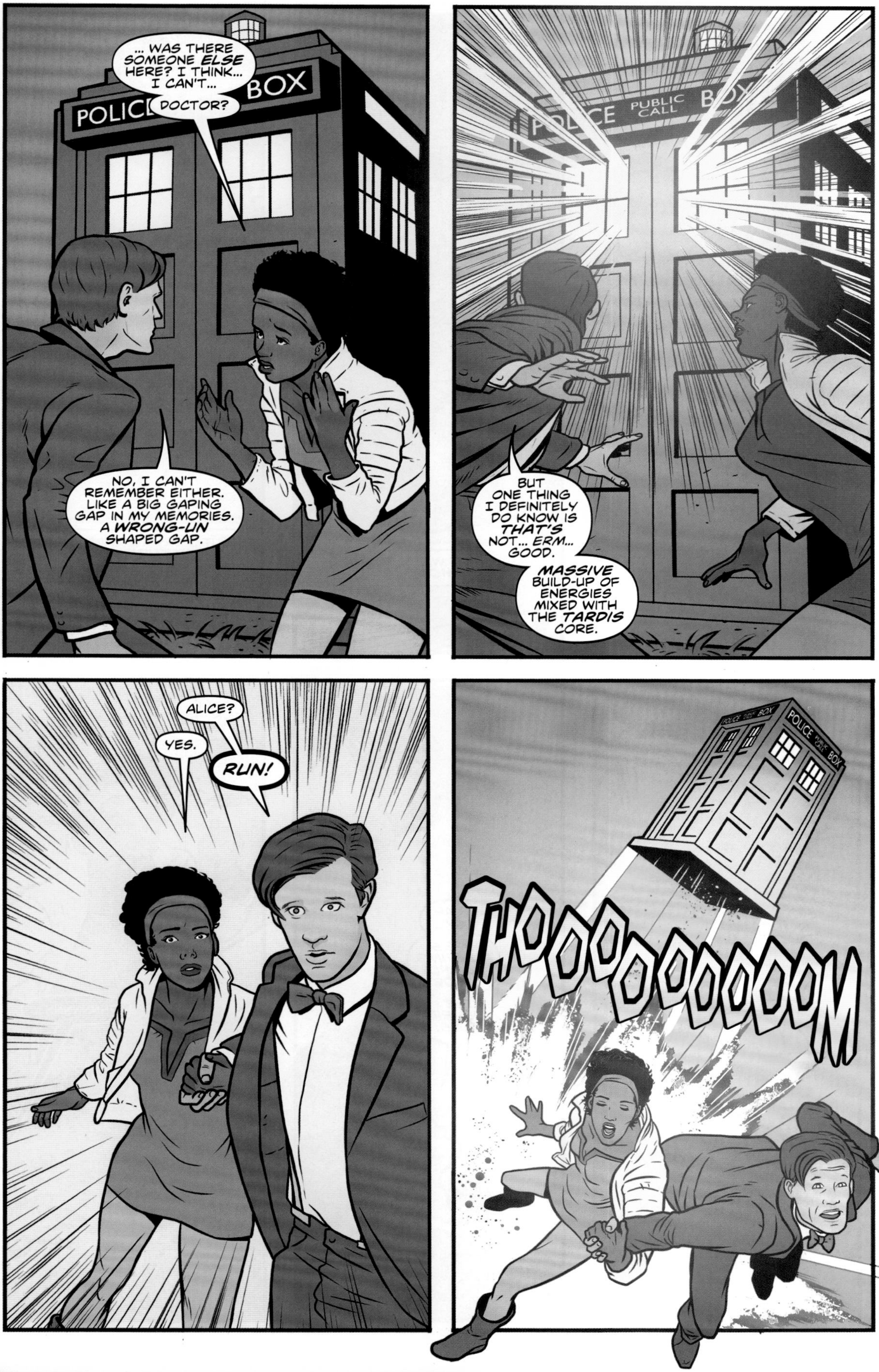
... WAS THERE SOMEONE ELSE HERE? I THINK... I CAN'T...
POLICE BOX
DOCTOR?
NO, I CAN'T REMEMBER EITHER. LIKE A BIG GAPING GAP IN MY MEMORIES. A WRONG-UN SHAPED GAP.
POLICE PUBLIC CALL BOX
BUT ONE THING I DEFINITELY DO KNOW IS THAT'S NOT... ERM... GOOD.
MASSIVE BUILD-UP OF ENERGIES MIXED WITH THE TARDIS CORE.
ALICE?
YES.
RUN!
POLICE PUBLIC CALL BOX
THOOOOOOOOOM

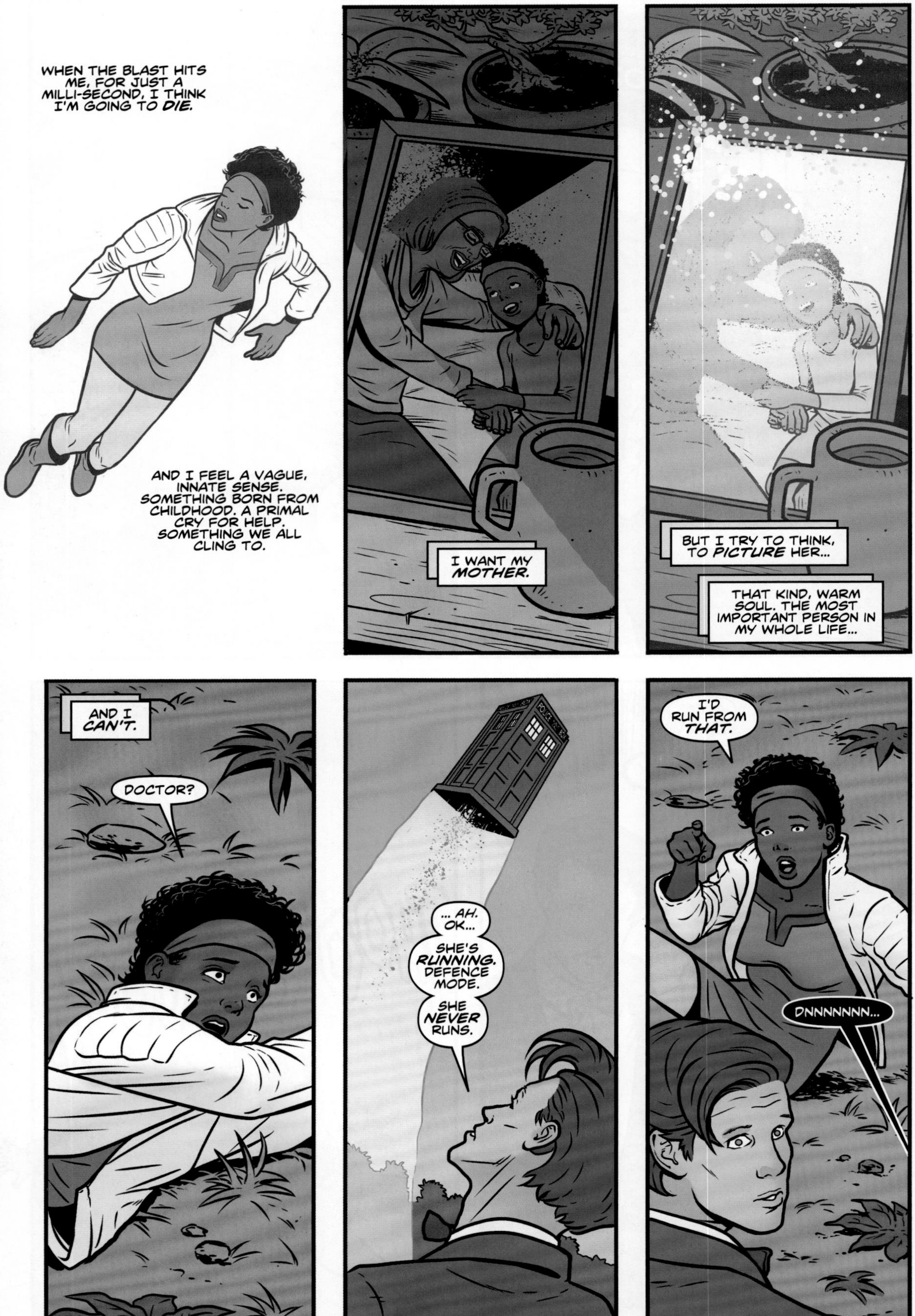
WHEN THE BLAST HITS ME, FOR JUST A MILLI-SECOND, I THINK I'M GOING TO *DIE*.
AND I FEEL A VAGUE, INNATE SENSE. SOMETHING BORN FROM CHILDHOOD. A PRIMAL CRY FOR HELP. SOMETHING WE ALL CLING TO.
I WANT MY *MOTHER*.
BUT I TRY TO THINK, TO *PICTURE* HER...
THAT KIND, WARM SOUL. THE MOST IMPORTANT PERSON IN MY WHOLE LIFE...
AND I *CAN'T*.
DOCTOR?
... AH. OK...
SHE'S *RUNNING*. DEFENCE MODE.
SHE *NEVER* RUNS.
I'D RUN FROM *THAT*.
DNNNNNNN...

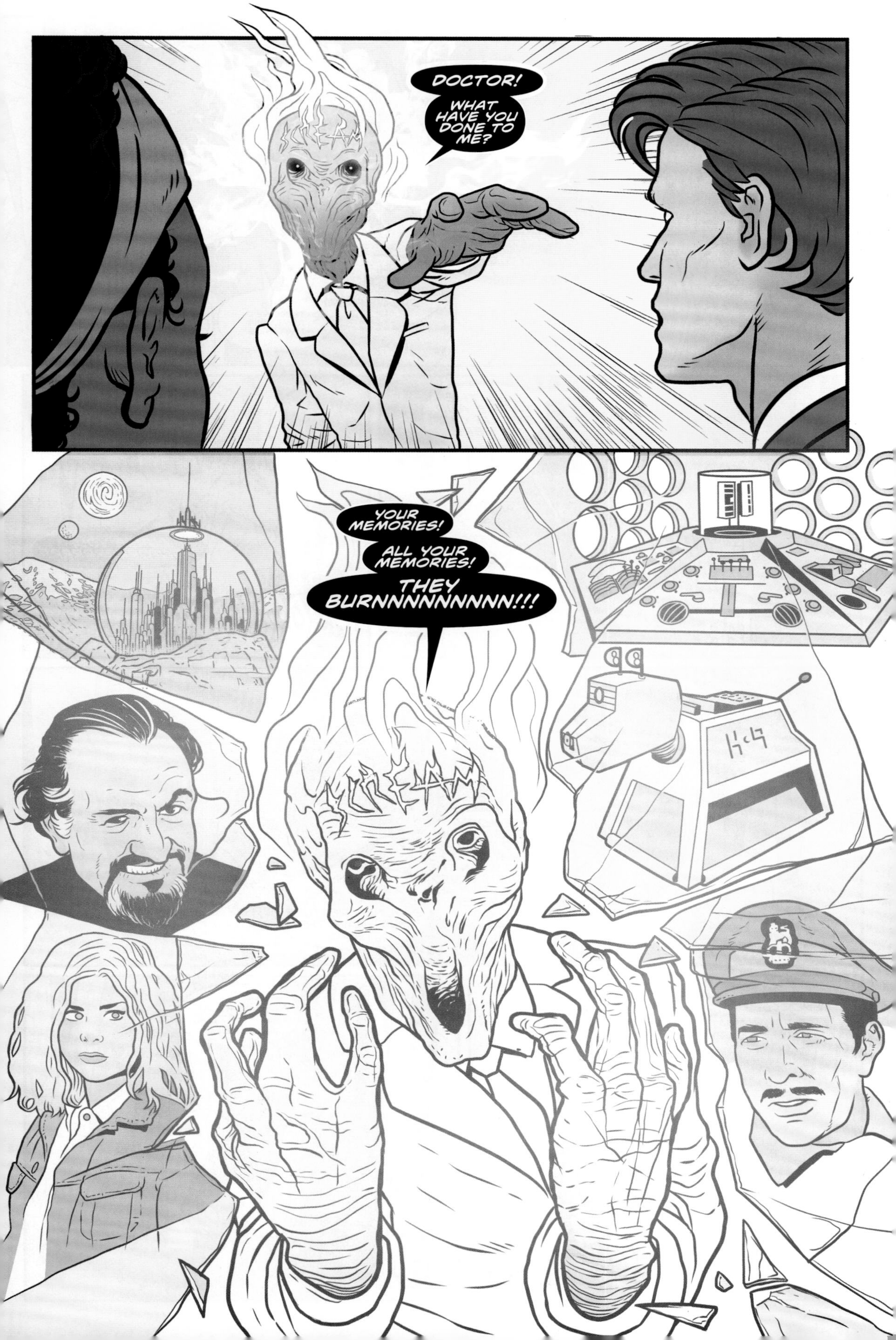
DOCTOR!
WHAT HAVE YOU DONE TO ME?
YOUR MEMORIES!
ALL YOUR MEMORIES!
THEY BURNNNNNNNNN!!!

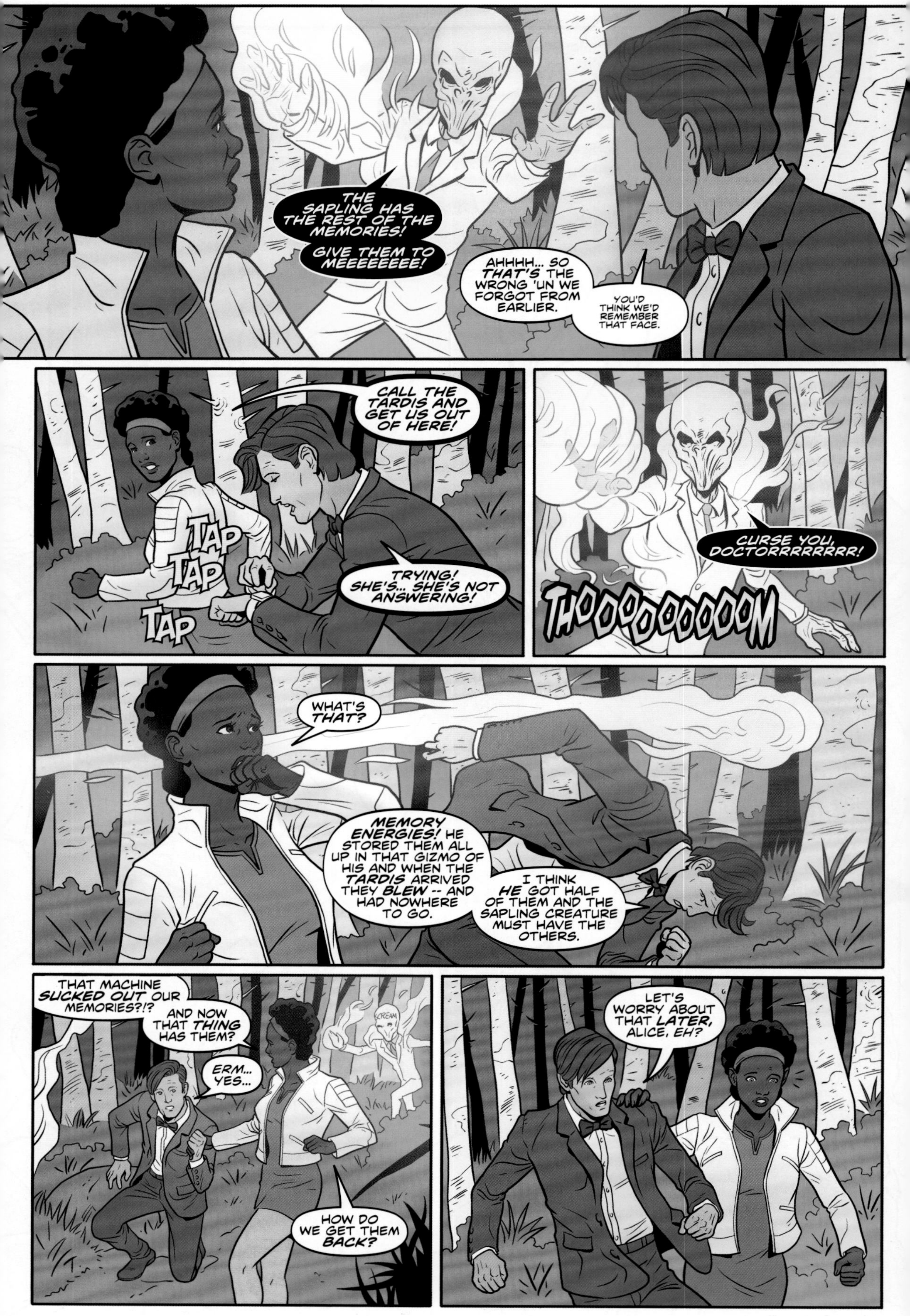
THE SAPLING HAS THE REST OF THE MEMORIES!
GIVE THEM TO MEEEEEEEE!
AHHHH... SO THAT'S THE WRONG 'UN WE FORGOT FROM EARLIER.
YOU'D THINK WE'D REMEMBER THAT FACE.
CALL THE TARDIS AND GET US OUT OF HERE!
TAP
TAP
TAP
TRYING! SHE'S... SHE'S NOT ANSWERING!
CURSE YOU, DOCTORRRRRRRR!
THOOOOOOOOOM
WHAT'S THAT?
MEMORY ENERGIES! HE STORED THEM ALL UP IN THAT GIZMO OF HIS AND WHEN THE TARDIS ARRIVED THEY BLEW -- AND HAD NOWHERE TO GO.
I THINK HE GOT HALF OF THEM AND THE SAPLING CREATURE MUST HAVE THE OTHERS.
THAT MACHINE SUCKED OUT OUR MEMORIES?!?
AND NOW THAT THING HAS THEM?
ERM... YES...
SCREAM
HOW DO WE GET THEM BACK?
LET'S WORRY ABOUT THAT LATER, ALICE, EH?

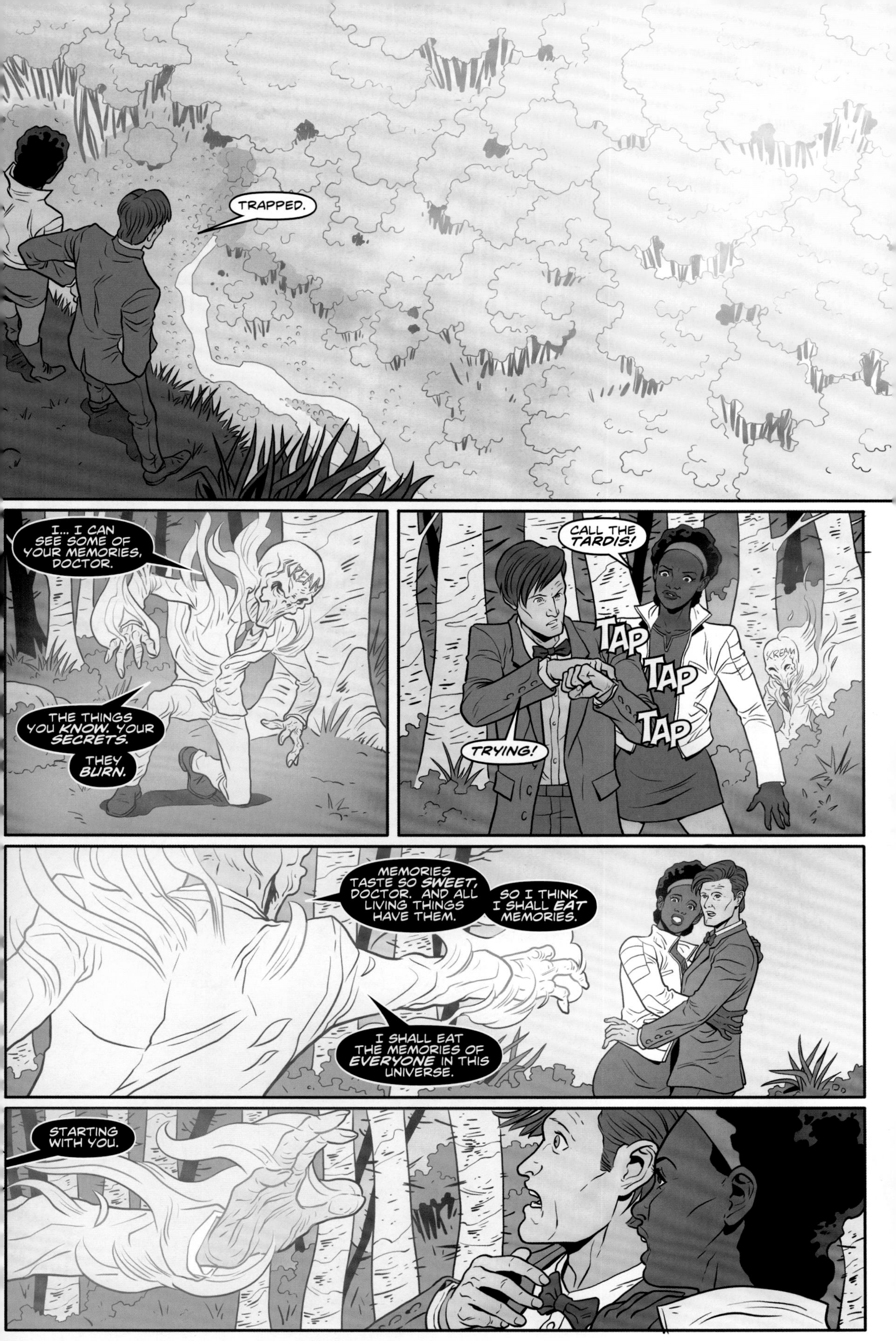
TRAPPED.
I... I CAN SEE SOME OF YOUR MEMORIES, DOCTOR.
THE THINGS YOU KNOW. YOUR SECRETS.
THEY BURN.
CALL THE TARDIS!
TAP
TAP
TAP
TRYING!
MEMORIES TASTE SO SWEET, DOCTOR. AND ALL LIVING THINGS HAVE THEM.
SO I THINK I SHALL EAT MEMORIES.
I SHALL EAT THE MEMORIES OF EVERYONE IN THIS UNIVERSE.
STARTING WITH YOU.

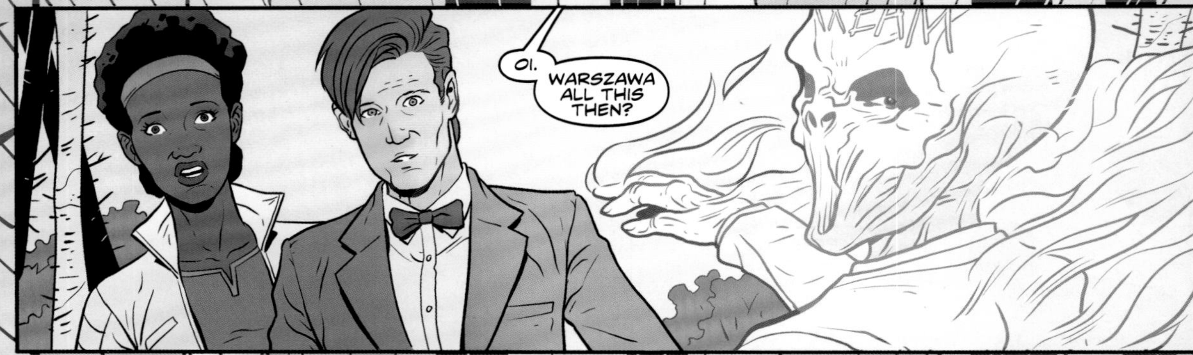
OI.
WARSZAWA ALL THIS THEN?

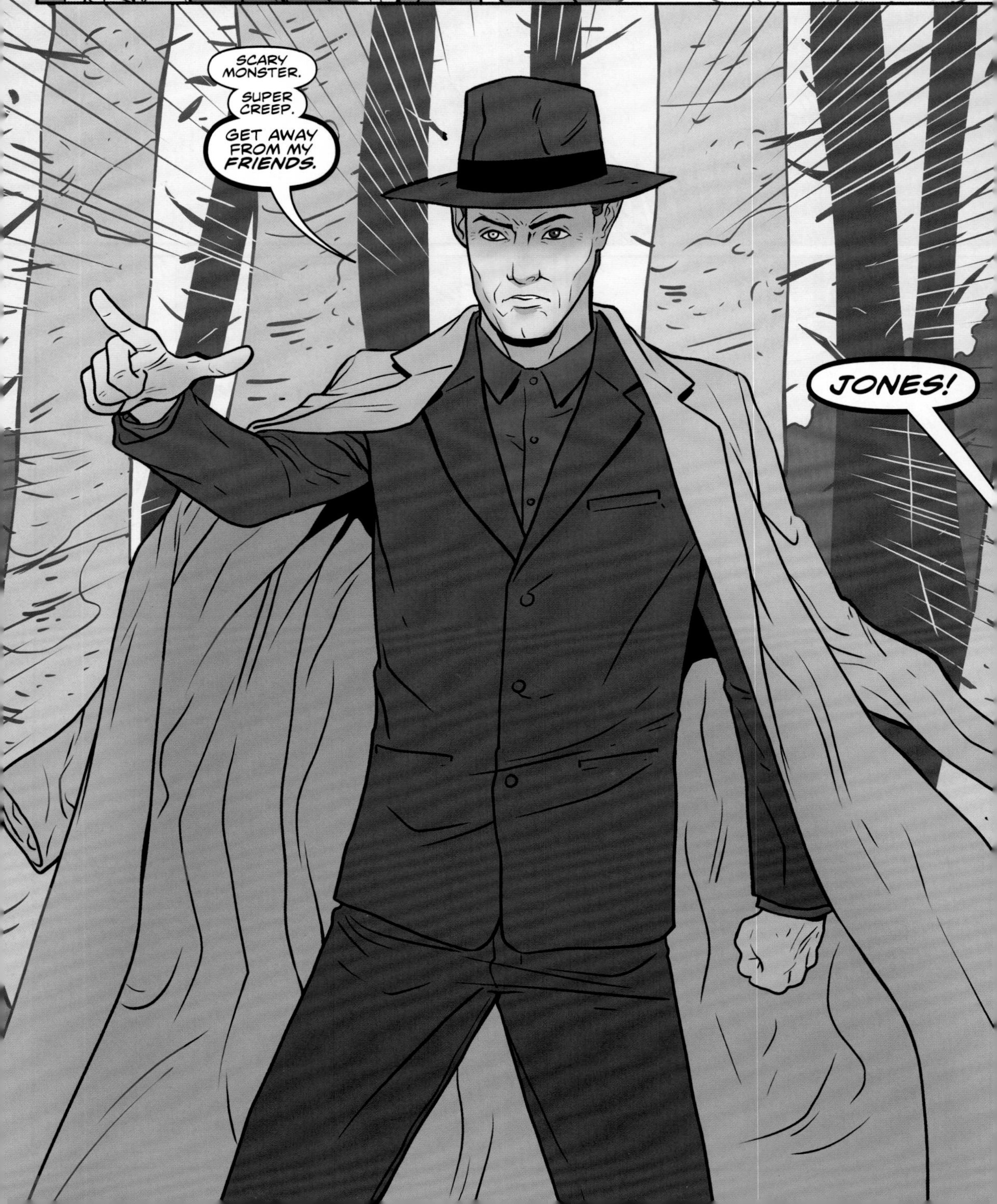
SCARY MONSTER.
SUPER CREEP.
GET AWAY FROM MY FRIENDS.
JONES!

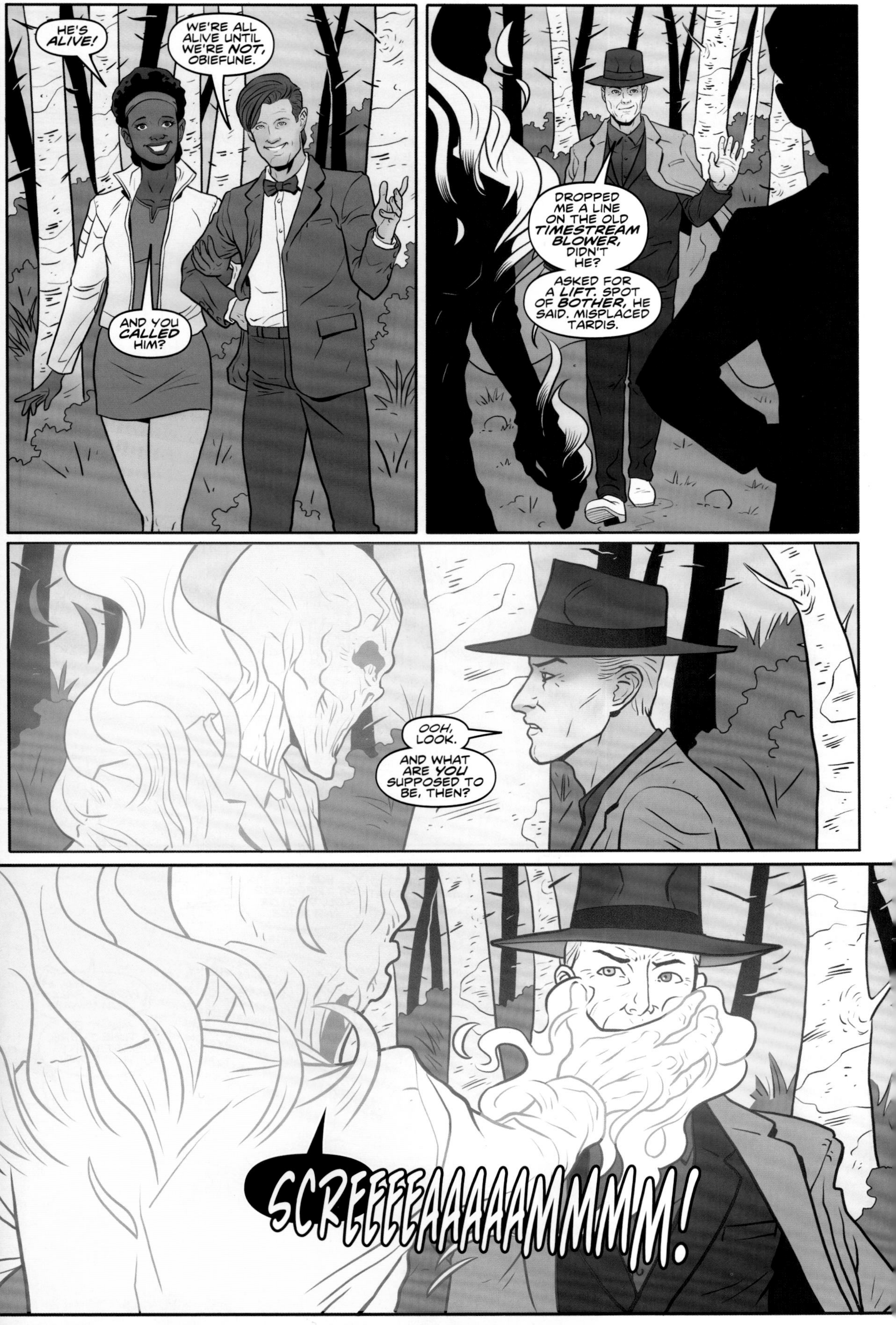
HE'S ALIVE!
WE'RE ALL ALIVE UNTIL WE'RE NOT, OBIEFUNE.
AND YOU CALLED HIM?
DROPPED ME A LINE ON THE OLD TIMESTREAM BLOWER, DIDN'T HE?
ASKED FOR A LIFT. SPOT OF BOTHER, HE SAID. MISPLACED TARDIS.
OOH, LOOK.
AND WHAT ARE YOU SUPPOSED TO BE, THEN?
SCREEEEAAAAAMMMMM!

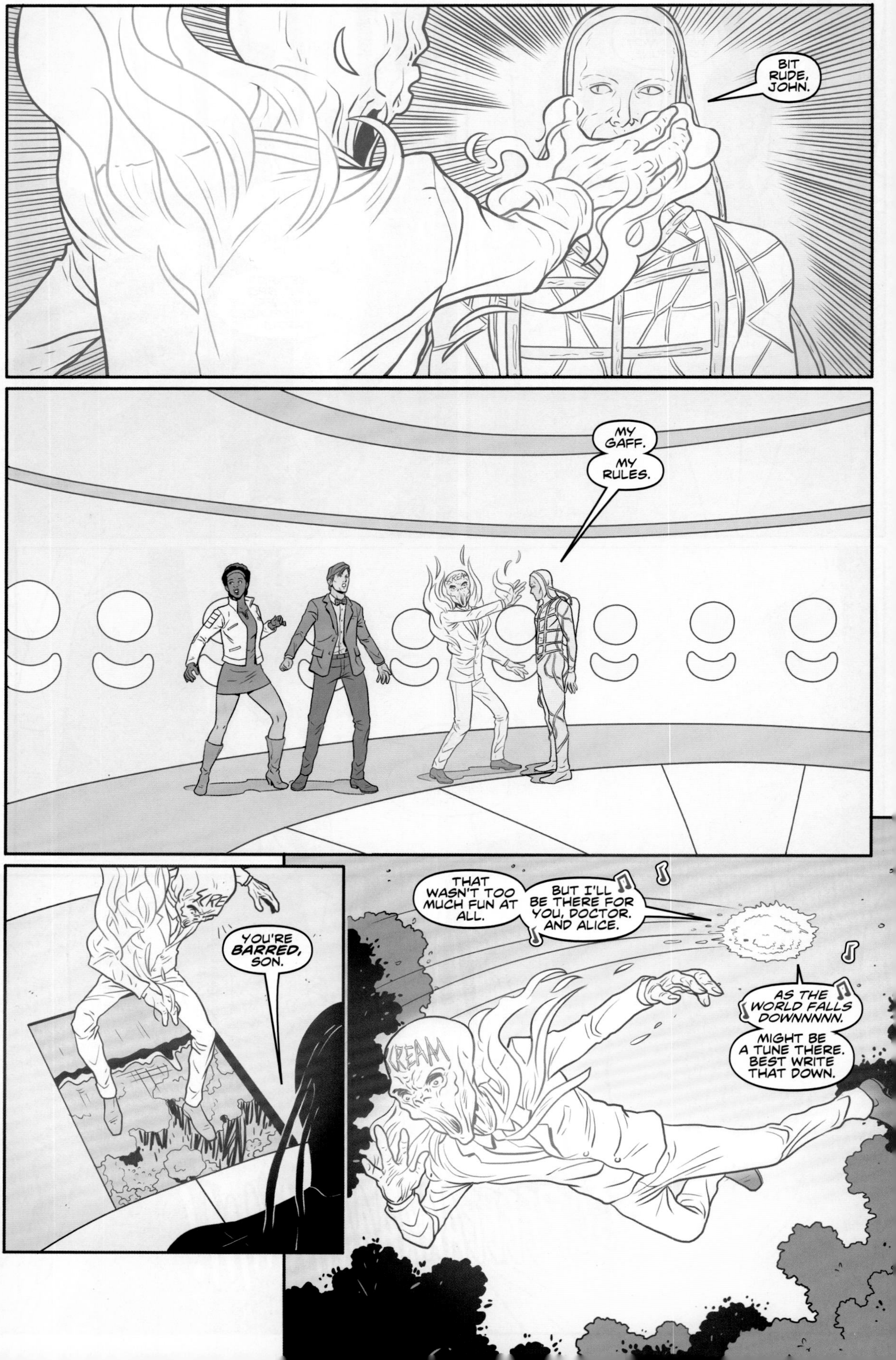
BIT RUDE, JOHN.
MY GAFF. MY RULES.
YOU'RE BARRED, SON.
THAT WASN'T TOO MUCH FUN AT ALL.
BUT I'LL BE THERE FOR YOU, DOCTOR. AND ALICE.
AS THE WORLD FALLS DOWNNNNNN.
MIGHT BE A TUNE THERE. BEST WRITE THAT DOWN.

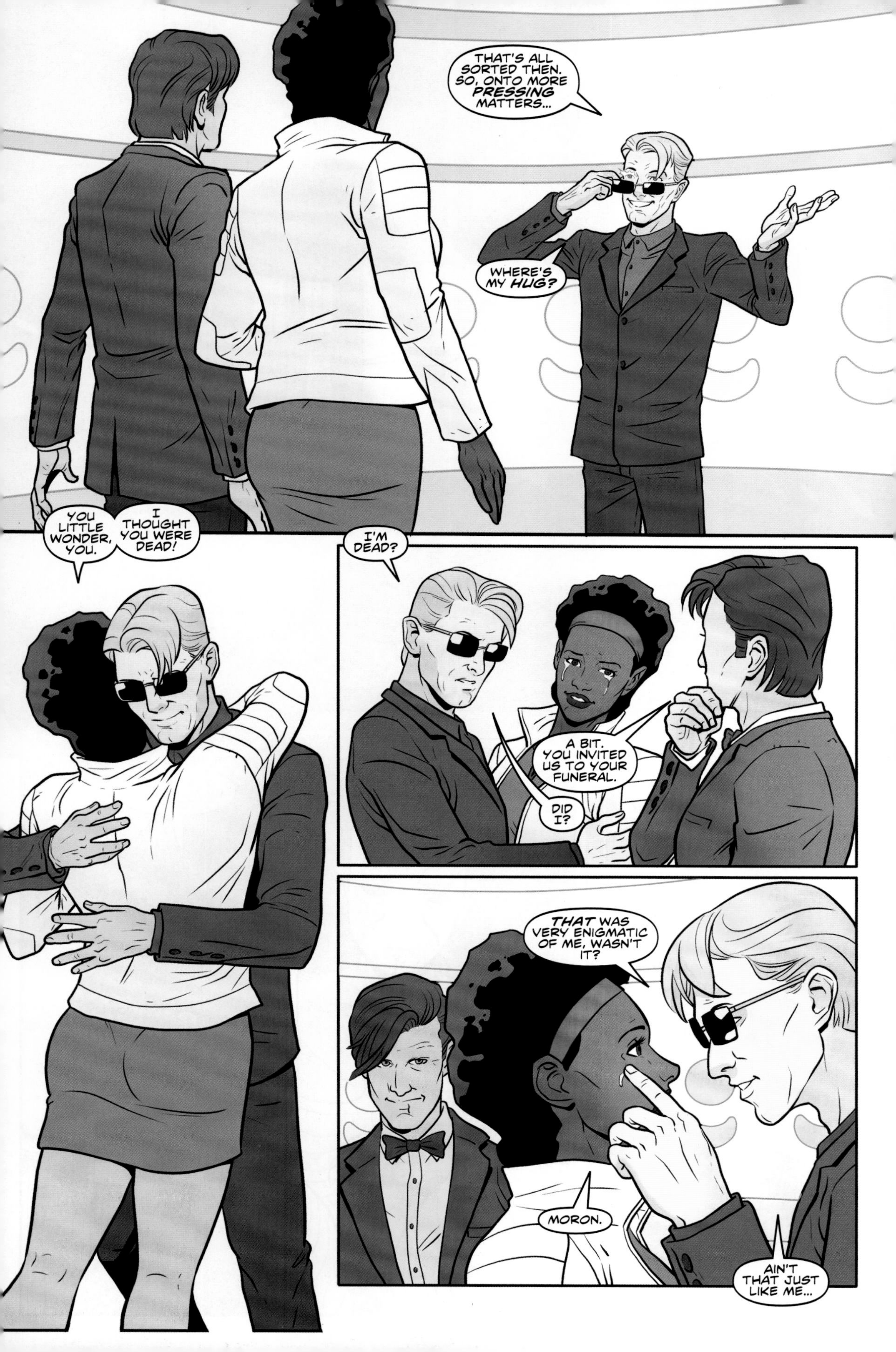
THAT'S ALL SORTED THEN. SO, ONTO MORE *PRESSING* MATTERS...
WHERE'S MY *HUG*?
YOU LITTLE WONDER, YOU.
I THOUGHT YOU WERE DEAD!
I'M DEAD?
A BIT. YOU INVITED US TO YOUR FUNERAL.
DID I?
THAT WAS VERY ENIGMATIC OF ME, WASN'T IT?
MORON.
AIN'T THAT JUST LIKE ME...

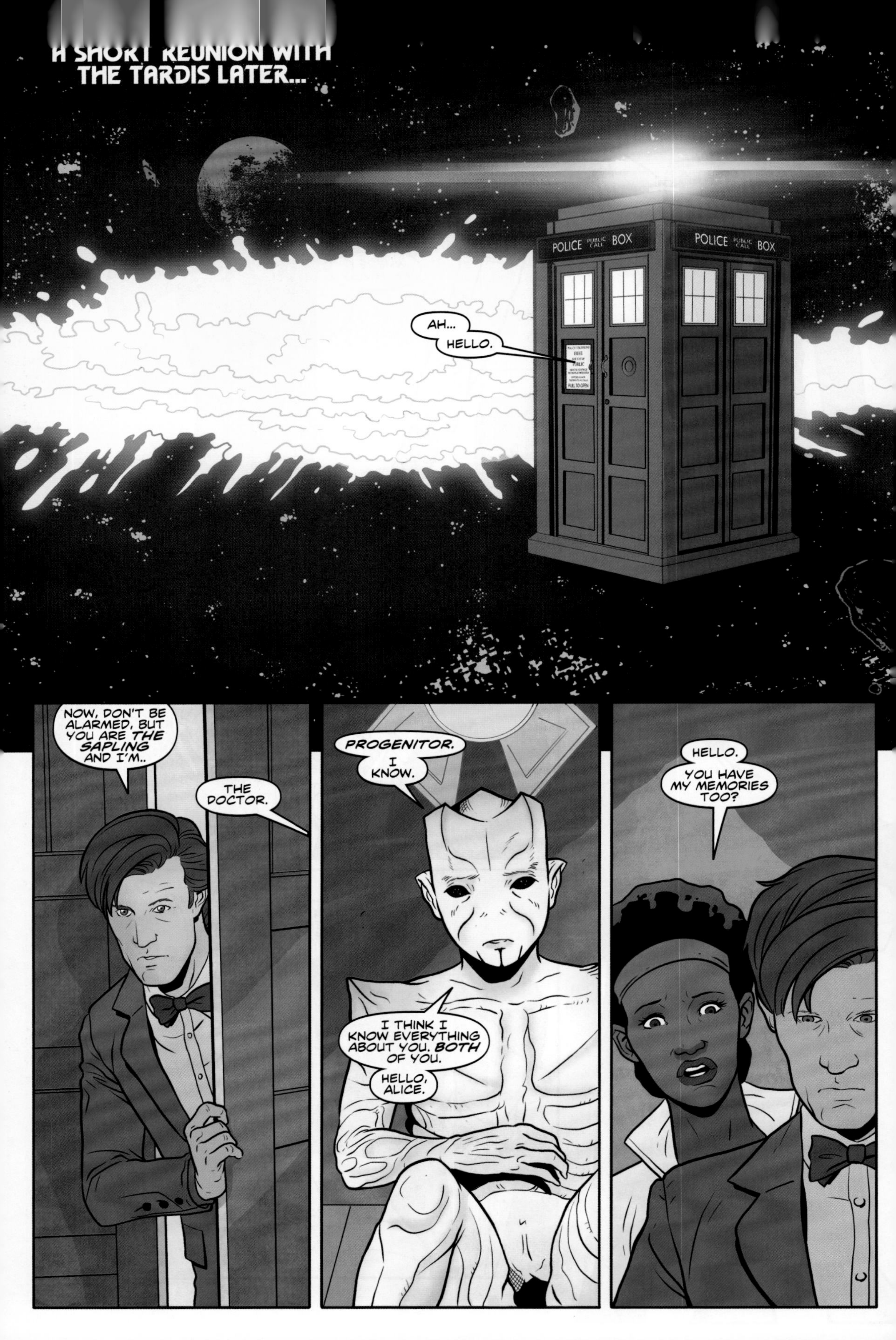

A SHORT REUNION WITH THE TARDIS LATER...
POLICE PUBLIC CALL BOX
AH...
HELLO.
NOW, DON'T BE ALARMED, BUT YOU ARE *THE SAPLING* AND I'M..
THE DOCTOR.
PROGENITOR.
I KNOW.
I THINK I KNOW EVERYTHING ABOUT YOU. *BOTH* OF YOU.
HELLO, ALICE.
HELLO.
YOU HAVE MY MEMORIES TOO?

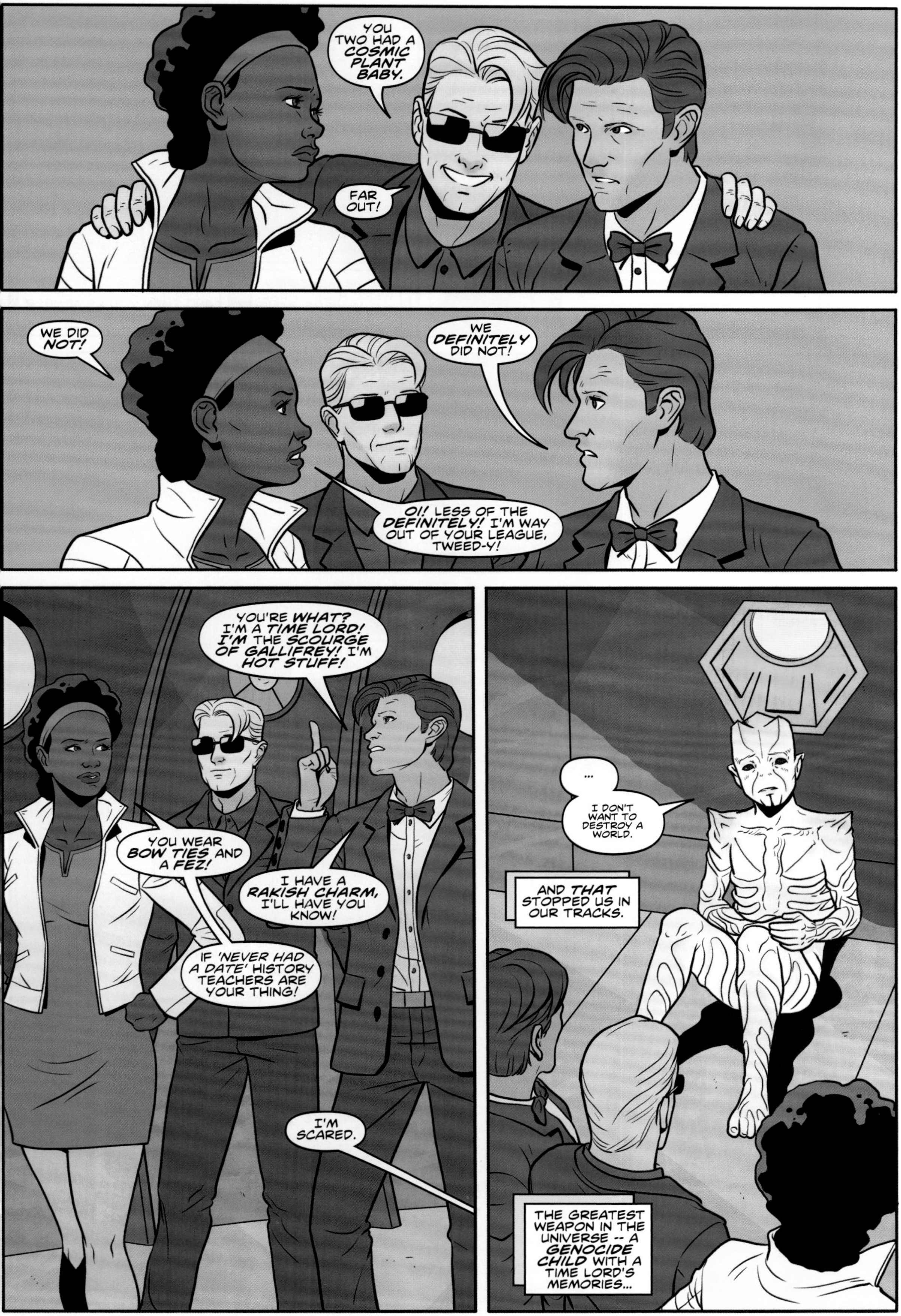
YOU TWO HAD A COSMIC PLANT BABY.
FAR OUT!
WE DID NOT!
WE DEFINITELY DID NOT!
OI! LESS OF THE DEFINITELY! I'M WAY OUT OF YOUR LEAGUE, TWEED-Y!
YOU'RE WHAT? I'M A TIME LORD! I'M THE SCOURGE OF GALLIFREY! I'M HOT STUFF!
YOU WEAR BOW TIES AND A FEZ!
I HAVE A RAKISH CHARM, I'LL HAVE YOU KNOW!
IF 'NEVER HAD A DATE' HISTORY TEACHERS ARE YOUR THING!
I'M SCARED.
...
I DON'T WANT TO DESTROY A WORLD.
AND THAT STOPPED US IN OUR TRACKS.
THE GREATEST WEAPON IN THE UNIVERSE -- A GENOCIDE CHILD WITH A TIME LORD'S MEMORIES...

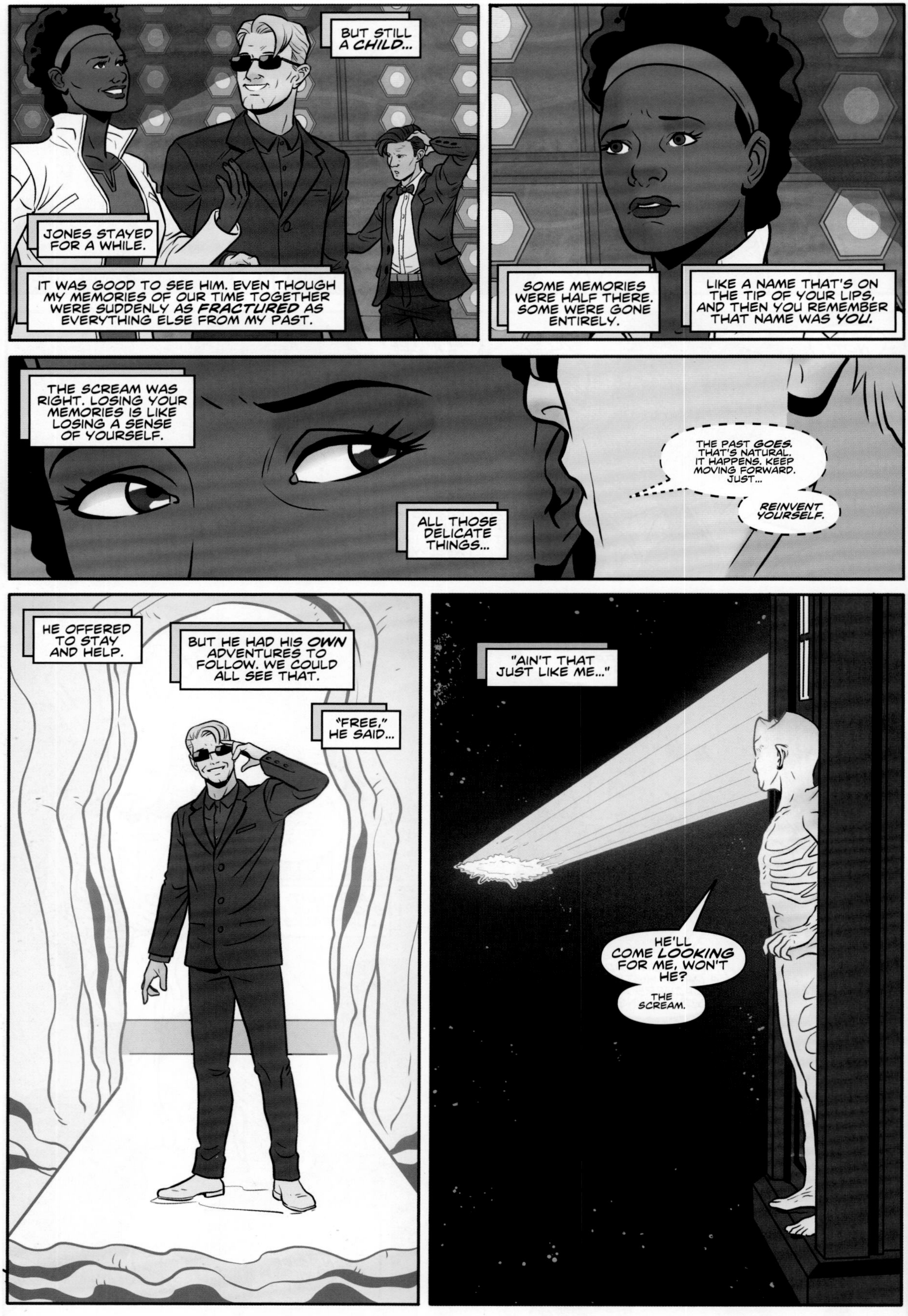
BUT STILL A *CHILD*...
JONES STAYED FOR A WHILE.
IT WAS GOOD TO SEE HIM. EVEN THOUGH MY MEMORIES OF OUR TIME TOGETHER WERE SUDDENLY AS *FRACTURED* AS EVERYTHING ELSE FROM MY PAST.
SOME MEMORIES WERE HALF THERE. SOME WERE GONE ENTIRELY.
LIKE A NAME THAT'S ON THE TIP OF YOUR LIPS, AND THEN YOU REMEMBER THAT NAME WAS *YOU*.
THE SCREAM WAS RIGHT. LOSING YOUR MEMORIES IS LIKE LOSING A SENSE OF YOURSELF.
THE PAST *GOES*. THAT'S NATURAL. IT HAPPENS. KEEP MOVING FORWARD. JUST...
REINVENT YOURSELF.
ALL THOSE DELICATE THINGS...
HE OFFERED TO STAY AND HELP.
BUT HE HAD HIS *OWN* ADVENTURES TO FOLLOW. WE COULD ALL SEE THAT.
"FREE," HE SAID...
"AIN'T THAT JUST LIKE ME..."
HE'LL COME *LOOKING* FOR ME, WON'T HE?
THE SCREAM.

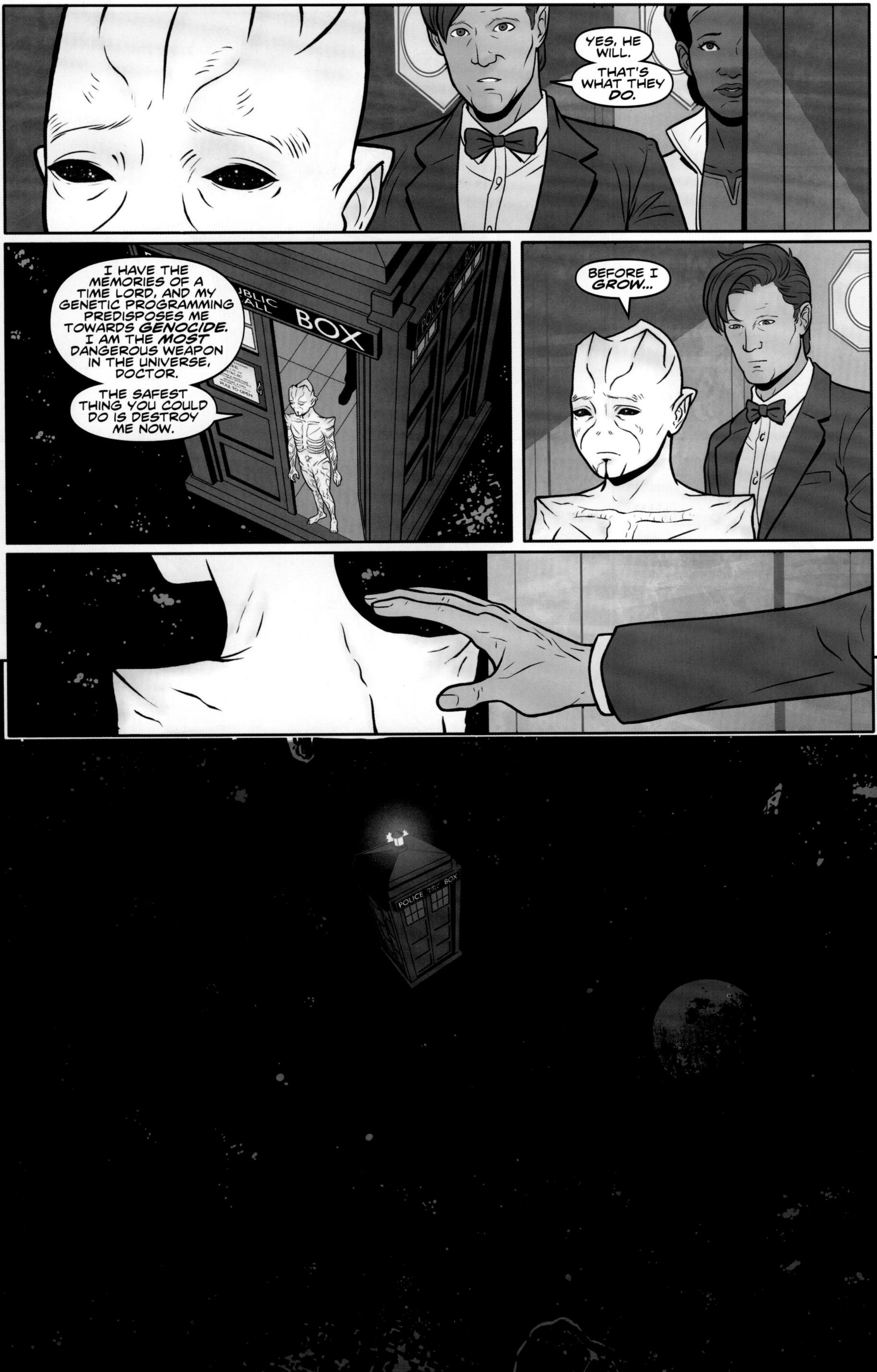

YES, HE WILL.
THAT'S WHAT THEY DO.
I HAVE THE MEMORIES OF A TIME LORD, AND MY GENETIC PROGRAMMING PREDISPOSES ME TOWARDS GENOCIDE. I AM THE MOST DANGEROUS WEAPON IN THE UNIVERSE, DOCTOR.
THE SAFEST THING YOU COULD DO IS DESTROY ME NOW.
POLICE PUBLIC CALL BOX
PULL TO OPEN
BEFORE I GROW...
POLICE BOX

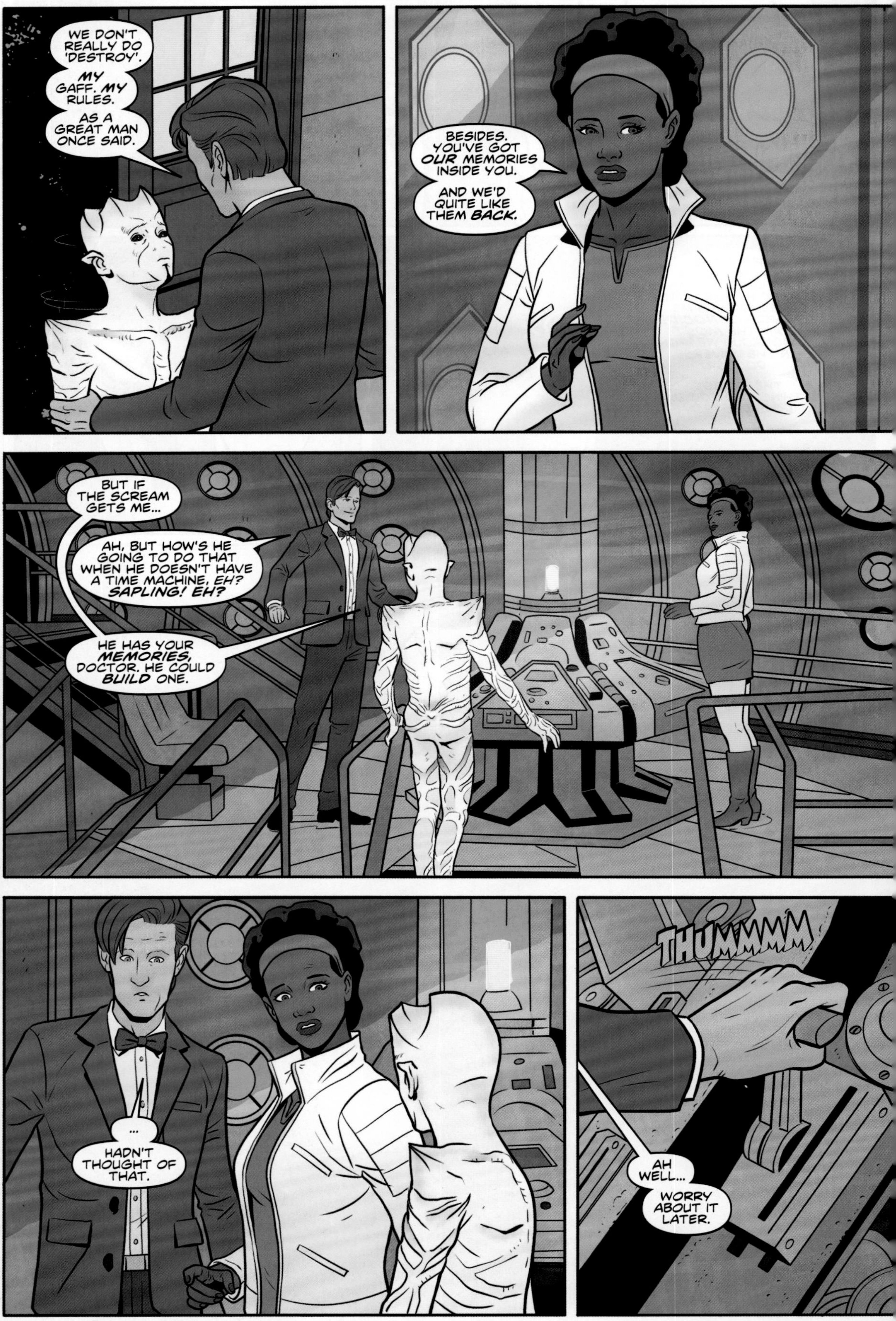

WE DON'T REALLY DO 'DESTROY'.
MY GAFF. MY RULES.
AS A GREAT MAN ONCE SAID.
BESIDES. YOU'VE GOT OUR MEMORIES INSIDE YOU.
AND WE'D QUITE LIKE THEM BACK.
BUT IF THE SCREAM GETS ME...
AH, BUT HOW'S HE GOING TO DO THAT WHEN HE DOESN'T HAVE A TIME MACHINE, EH? SAPLING! EH?
HE HAS YOUR MEMORIES, DOCTOR. HE COULD BUILD ONE.
...
HADN'T THOUGHT OF THAT.
THUMMMM
AH WELL...
WORRY ABOUT IT LATER.

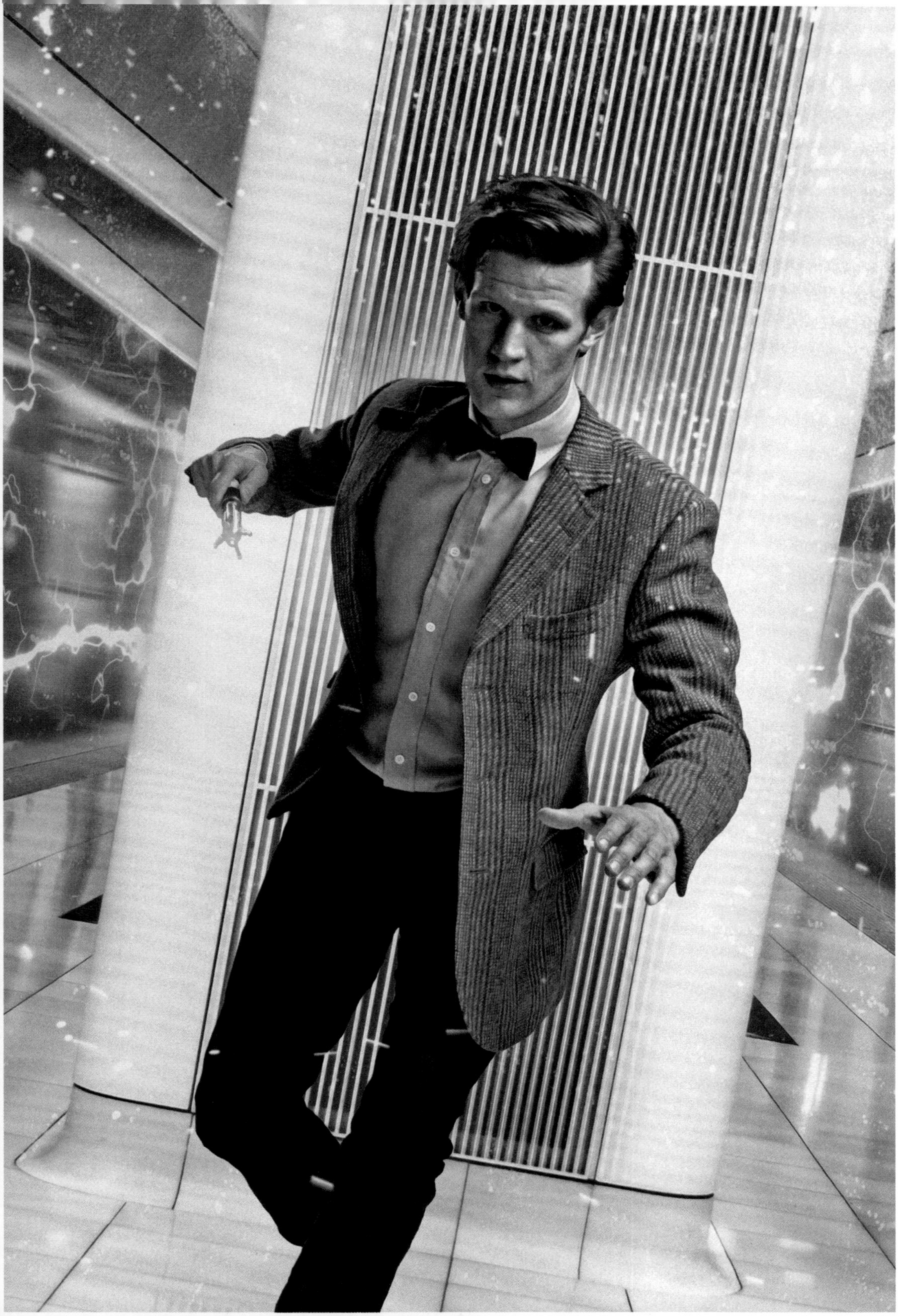

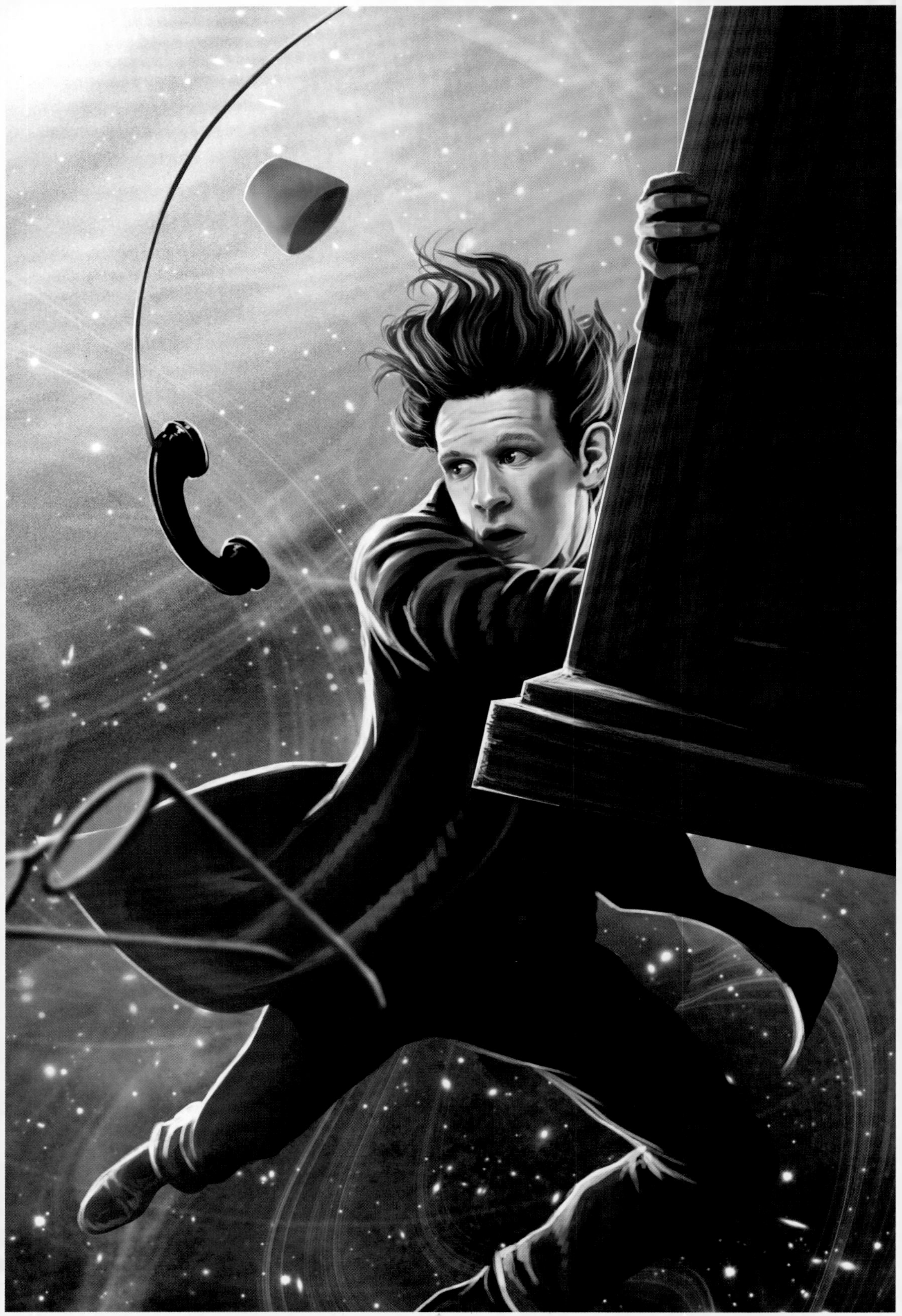

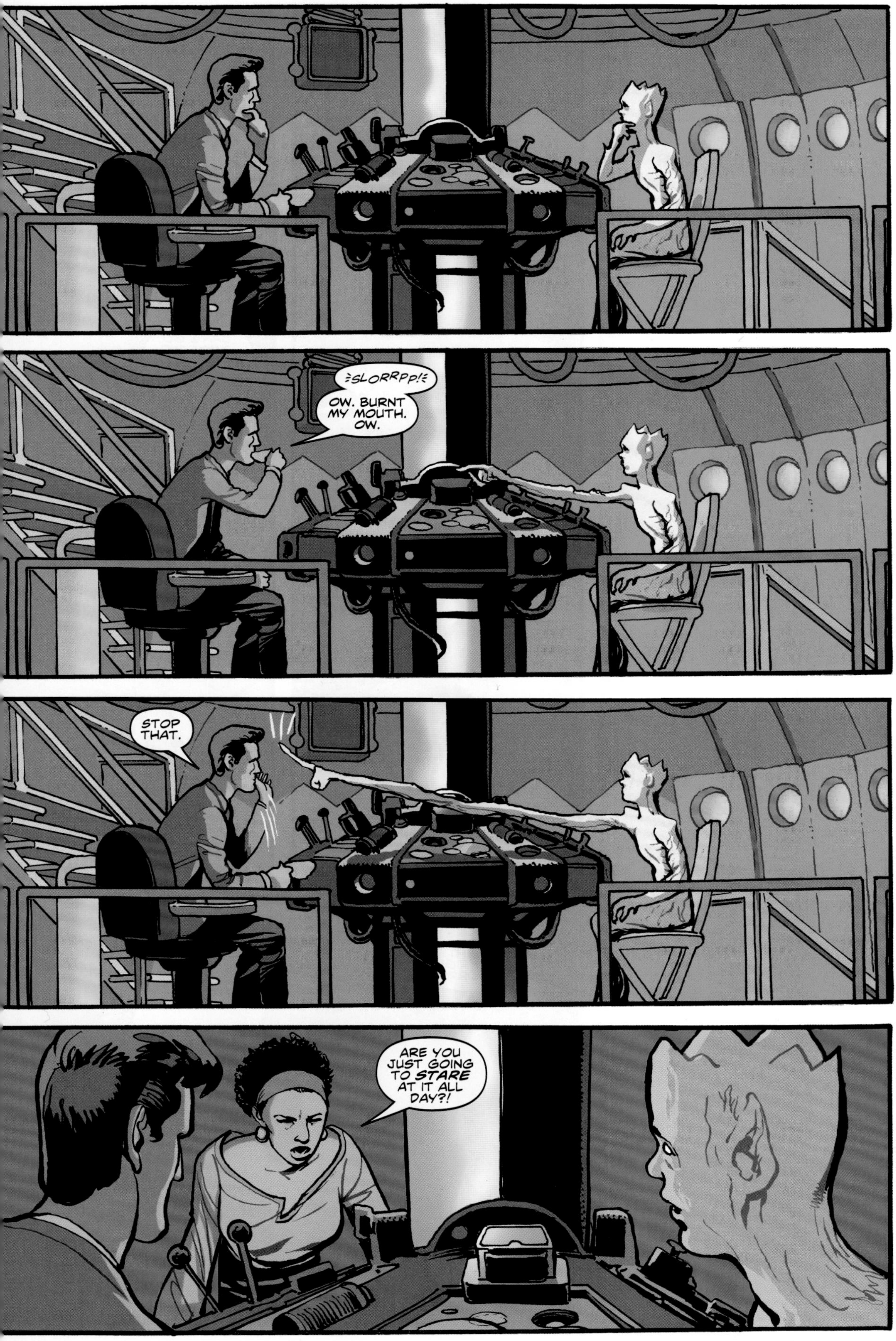
SLORRPP!
OW. BURNT MY MOUTH. OW.
STOP THAT.
ARE YOU JUST GOING TO STARE AT IT ALL DAY?!

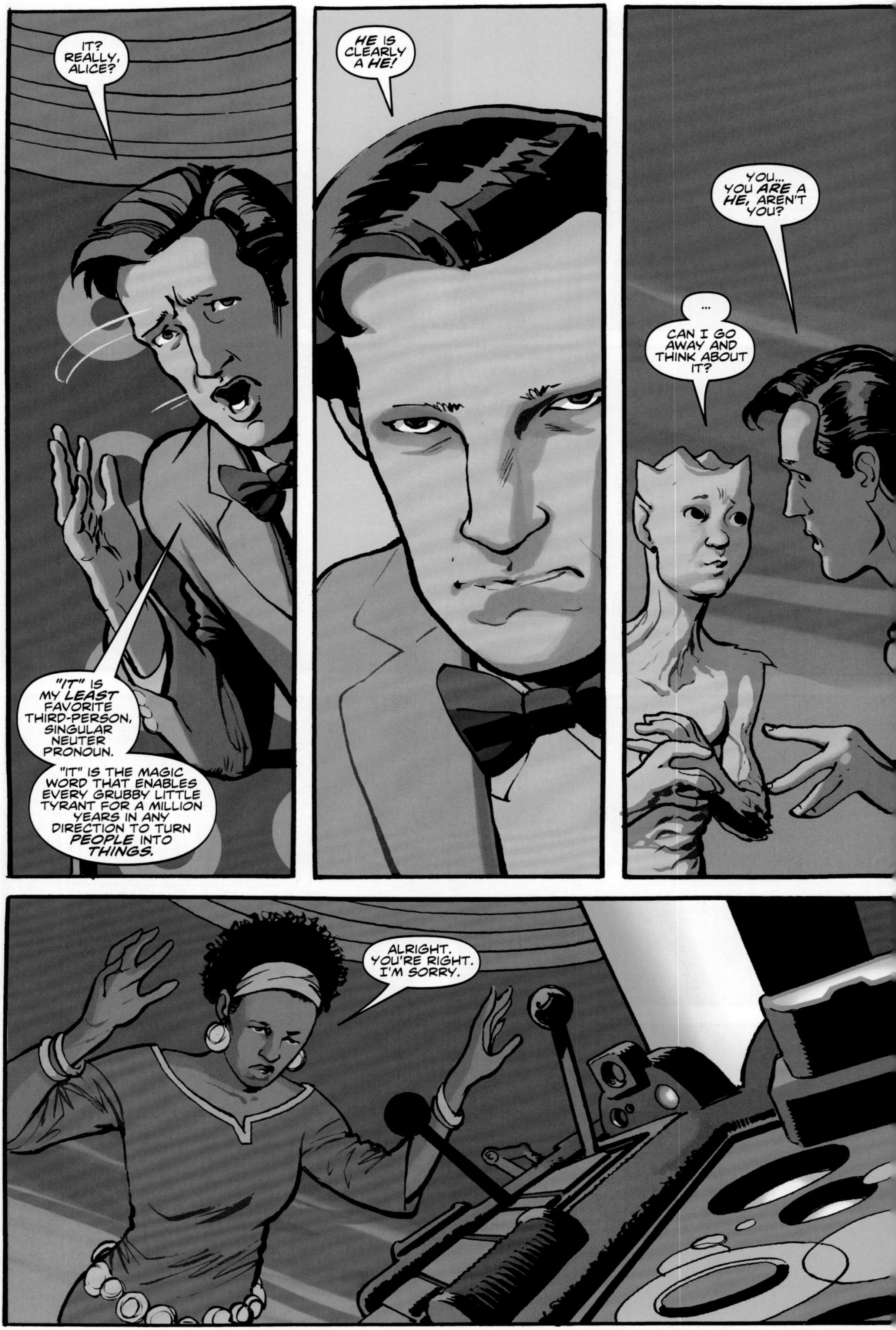
IT? REALLY, ALICE?
"IT" IS MY LEAST FAVORITE THIRD-PERSON, SINGULAR NEUTER PRONOUN.
"IT" IS THE MAGIC WORD THAT ENABLES EVERY GRUBBY LITTLE TYRANT FOR A MILLION YEARS IN ANY DIRECTION TO TURN PEOPLE INTO THINGS.
HE IS CLEARLY A HE!
YOU... YOU ARE A HE, AREN'T YOU?
...
CAN I GO AWAY AND THINK ABOUT IT?
ALRIGHT. YOU'RE RIGHT. I'M SORRY.

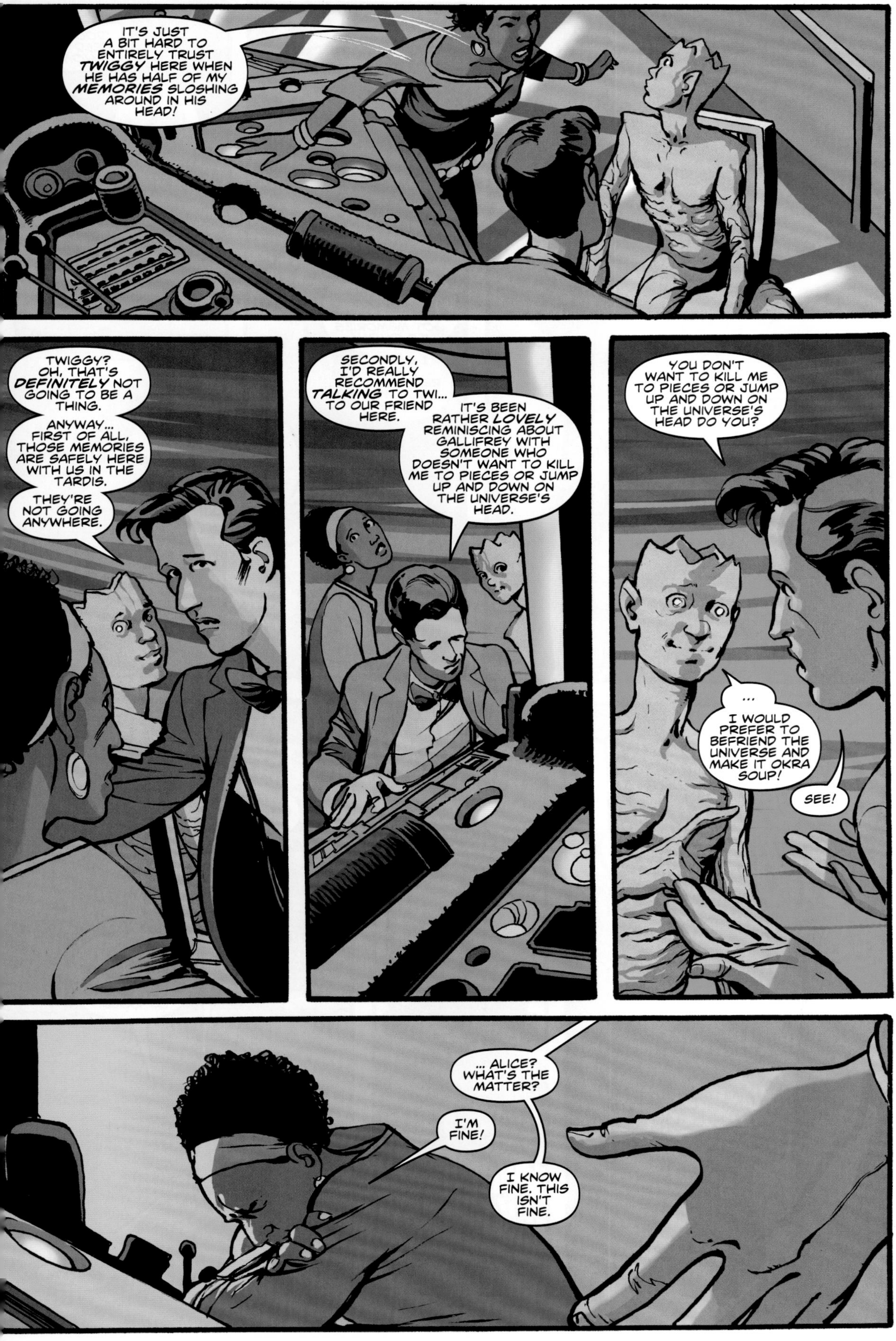
IT'S JUST A BIT HARD TO ENTIRELY TRUST TWIGGY HERE WHEN HE HAS HALF OF MY MEMORIES SLOSHING AROUND IN HIS HEAD!
TWIGGY? OH, THAT'S DEFINITELY NOT GOING TO BE A THING.
ANYWAY... FIRST OF ALL, THOSE MEMORIES ARE SAFELY HERE WITH US IN THE TARDIS.
THEY'RE NOT GOING ANYWHERE.
SECONDLY, I'D REALLY RECOMMEND TALKING TO TWI... TO OUR FRIEND HERE.
IT'S BEEN RATHER LOVELY REMINISCING ABOUT GALLIFREY WITH SOMEONE WHO DOESN'T WANT TO KILL ME TO PIECES OR JUMP UP AND DOWN ON THE UNIVERSE'S HEAD.
YOU DON'T WANT TO KILL ME TO PIECES OR JUMP UP AND DOWN ON THE UNIVERSE'S HEAD DO YOU?
...
I WOULD PREFER TO BEFRIEND THE UNIVERSE AND MAKE IT OKRA SOUP!
SEE!
... ALICE? WHAT'S THE MATTER?
I'M FINE!
I KNOW FINE. THIS ISN'T FINE.

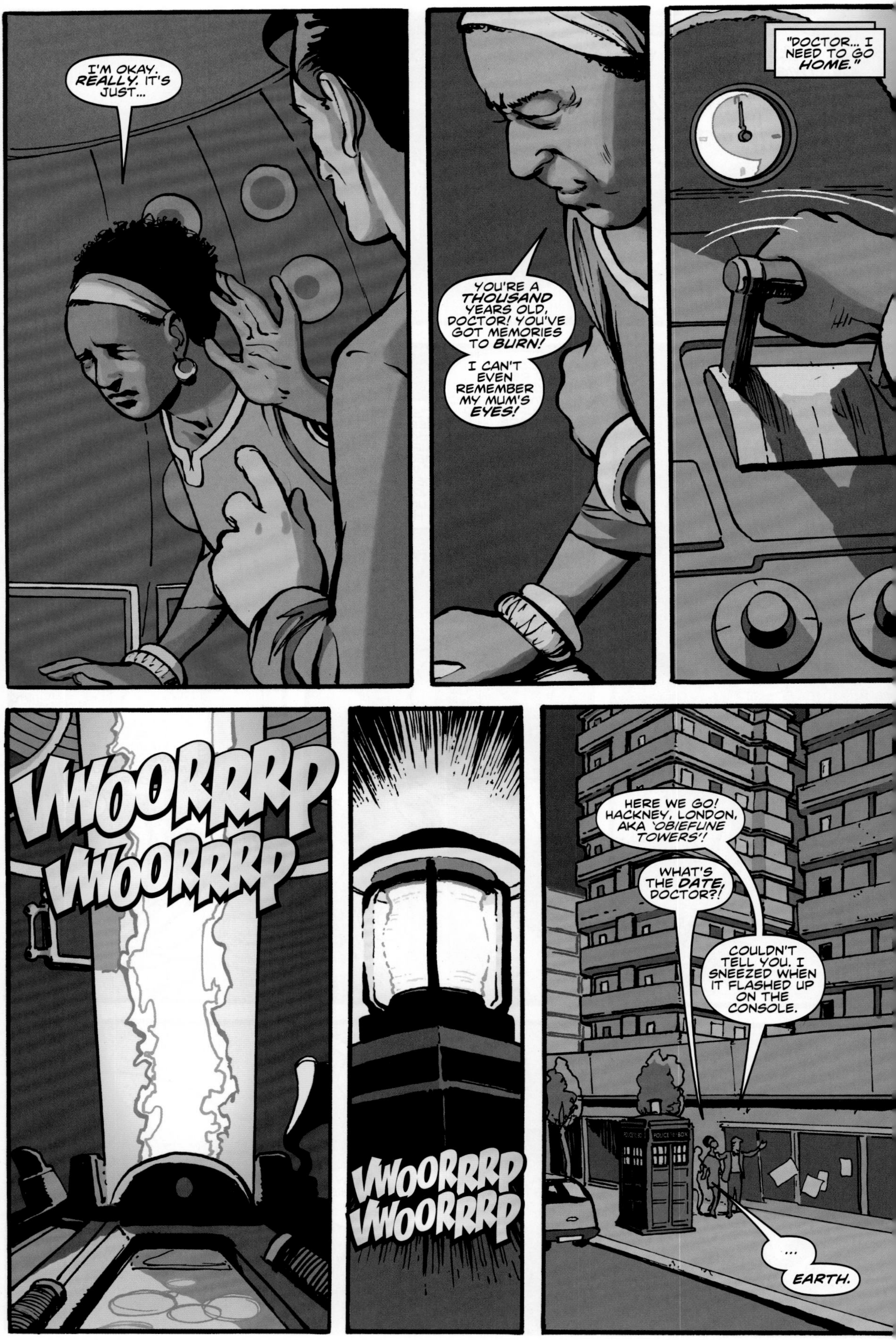
I'M OKAY. REALLY. IT'S JUST...
YOU'RE A THOUSAND YEARS OLD, DOCTOR! YOU'VE GOT MEMORIES TO BURN!
I CAN'T EVEN REMEMBER MY MUM'S EYES!
"DOCTOR... I NEED TO GO HOME."
VWOORRRP VWOORRRP
VWOORRRP VWOORRRP
HERE WE GO! HACKNEY, LONDON, AKA 'OBIEFUNE TOWERS'!
WHAT'S THE DATE, DOCTOR?!
COULDN'T TELL YOU. I SNEEZED WHEN IT FLASHED UP ON THE CONSOLE.
...
EARTH.

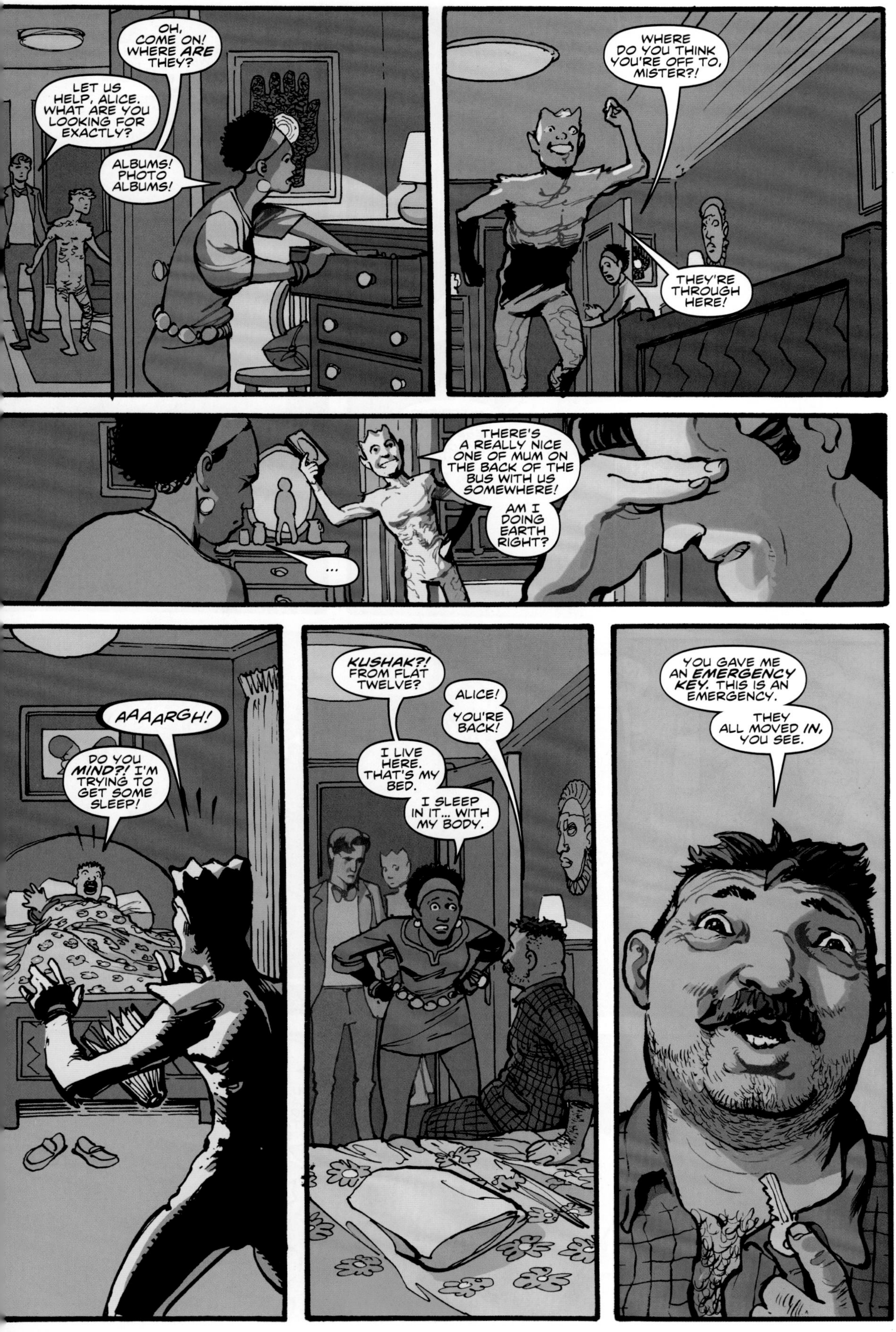
OH, COME ON! WHERE *ARE* THEY?
LET US HELP, ALICE. WHAT ARE YOU LOOKING FOR EXACTLY?
ALBUMS! PHOTO ALBUMS!
WHERE DO YOU THINK YOU'RE OFF TO, MISTER?!
THEY'RE THROUGH HERE!
THERE'S A REALLY NICE ONE OF MUM ON THE BACK OF THE BUS WITH US SOMEWHERE!
AM I DOING EARTH RIGHT?
...
AAAARGH!
DO YOU *MIND?!* I'M TRYING TO GET SOME SLEEP!
KUSHAK?! FROM FLAT TWELVE?
ALICE!
YOU'RE BACK!
I LIVE HERE. THAT'S MY BED.
I SLEEP IN IT... WITH MY BODY.
YOU GAVE ME AN *EMERGENCY KEY.* THIS IS AN EMERGENCY.
THEY ALL MOVED *IN,* YOU SEE.

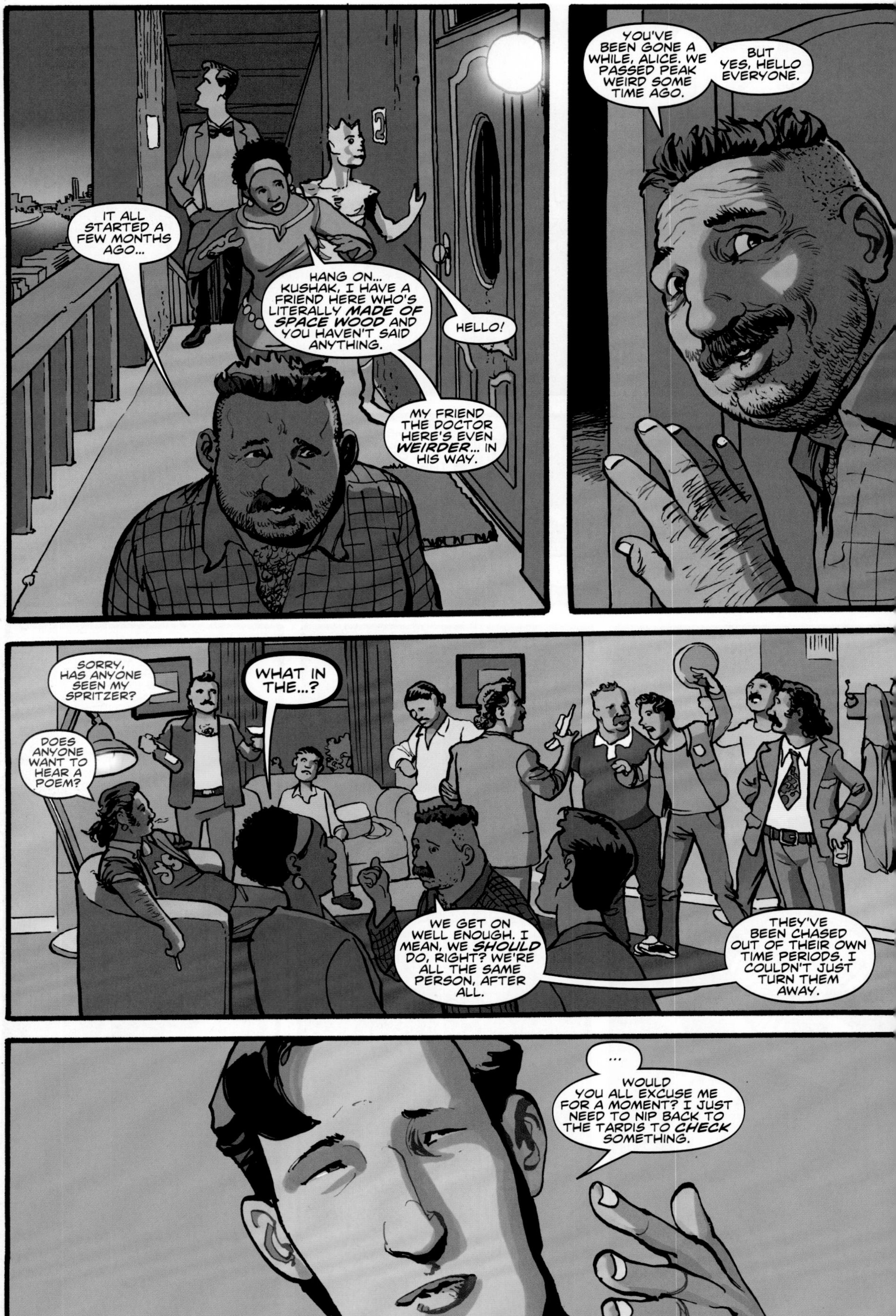
IT ALL STARTED A FEW MONTHS AGO...
HANG ON... KUSHAK, I HAVE A FRIEND HERE WHO'S LITERALLY MADE OF SPACE WOOD AND YOU HAVEN'T SAID ANYTHING.
HELLO!
MY FRIEND THE DOCTOR HERE'S EVEN WEIRDER... IN HIS WAY.
YOU'VE BEEN GONE A WHILE, ALICE. WE PASSED PEAK WEIRD SOME TIME AGO.
BUT YES, HELLO EVERYONE.
SORRY, HAS ANYONE SEEN MY SPRITZER?
WHAT IN THE...?
DOES ANYONE WANT TO HEAR A POEM?
WE GET ON WELL ENOUGH. I MEAN, WE SHOULD DO, RIGHT? WE'RE ALL THE SAME PERSON, AFTER ALL.
THEY'VE BEEN CHASED OUT OF THEIR OWN TIME PERIODS. I COULDN'T JUST TURN THEM AWAY.
...
WOULD YOU ALL EXCUSE ME FOR A MOMENT? I JUST NEED TO NIP BACK TO THE TARDIS TO CHECK SOMETHING.

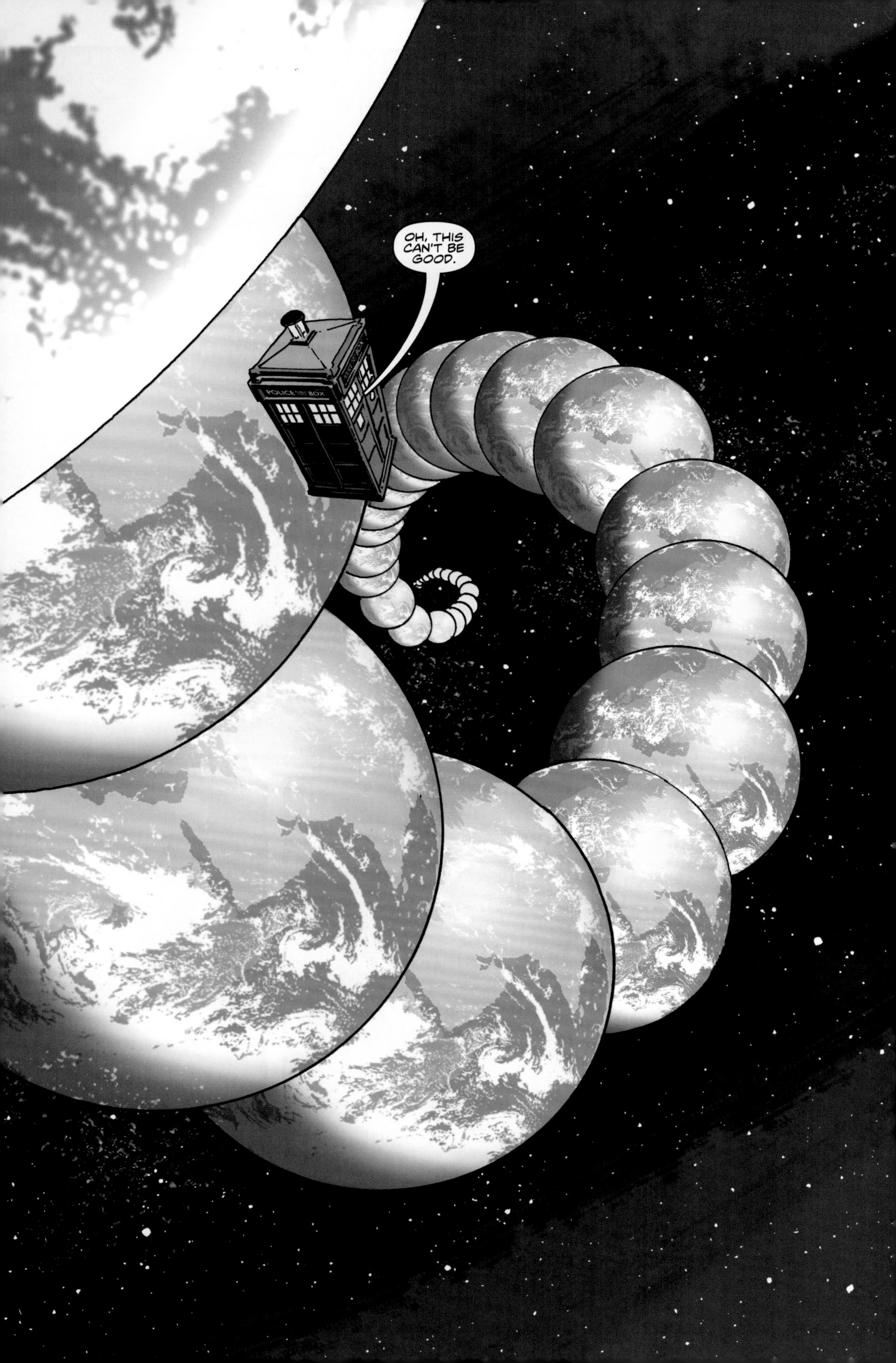
OH, THIS CAN'T BE GOOD.

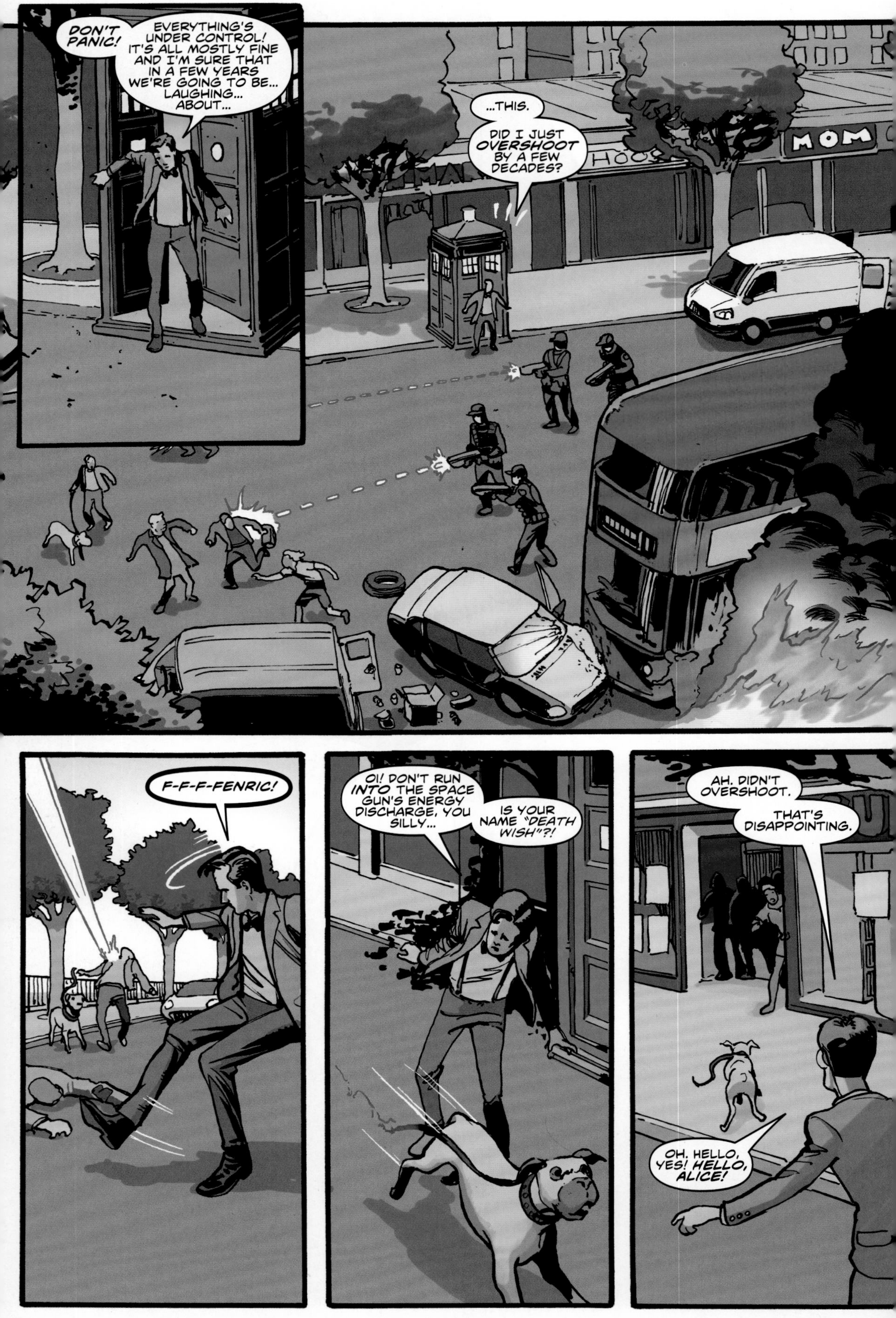
DON'T PANIC!
EVERYTHING'S UNDER CONTROL! IT'S ALL MOSTLY FINE AND I'M SURE THAT IN A FEW YEARS WE'RE GOING TO BE... LAUGHING... ABOUT...
...THIS.
DID I JUST OVERSHOOT BY A FEW DECADES?
MOM
F-F-F-FENRIC!
OI! DON'T RUN INTO THE SPACE GUN'S ENERGY DISCHARGE, YOU SILLY...
IS YOUR NAME "DEATH WISH"?!
AH. DIDN'T OVERSHOOT.
THAT'S DISAPPOINTING.
OH. HELLO, YES! HELLO, ALICE!

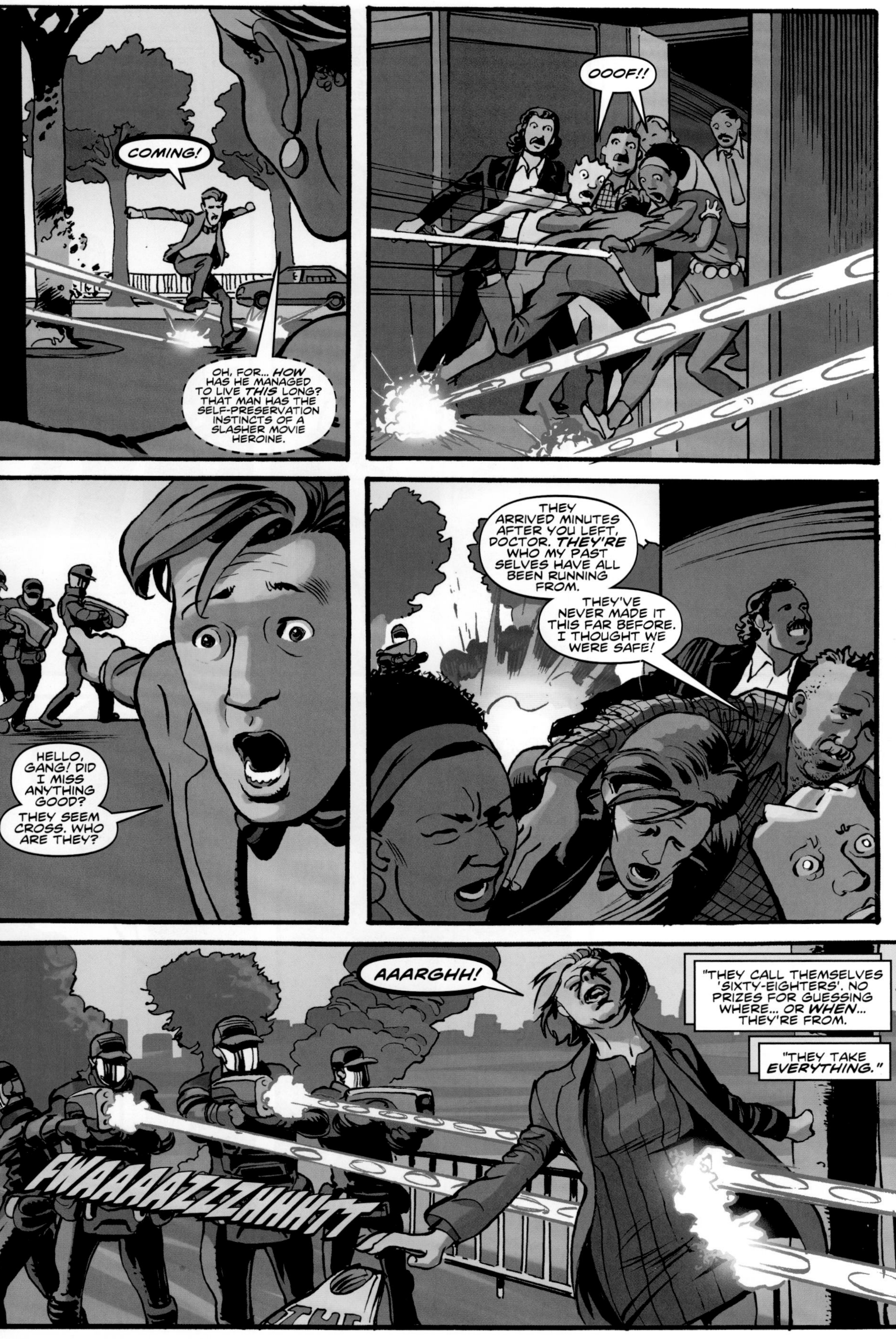
COMING!
OH, FOR... HOW HAS HE MANAGED TO LIVE THIS LONG? THAT MAN HAS THE SELF-PRESERVATION INSTINCTS OF A SLASHER MOVIE HEROINE.
OOOF!!
HELLO, GANG! DID I MISS ANYTHING GOOD?
THEY SEEM CROSS. WHO ARE THEY?
THEY ARRIVED MINUTES AFTER YOU LEFT, DOCTOR. THEY'RE WHO MY PAST SELVES HAVE ALL BEEN RUNNING FROM.
THEY'VE NEVER MADE IT THIS FAR BEFORE. I THOUGHT WE WERE SAFE!
AAARGHH!
"THEY CALL THEMSELVES 'SIXTY-EIGHTERS'. NO PRIZES FOR GUESSING WHERE... OR WHEN... THEY'RE FROM.
"THEY TAKE EVERYTHING."
FWAAAAZZZHHHTT

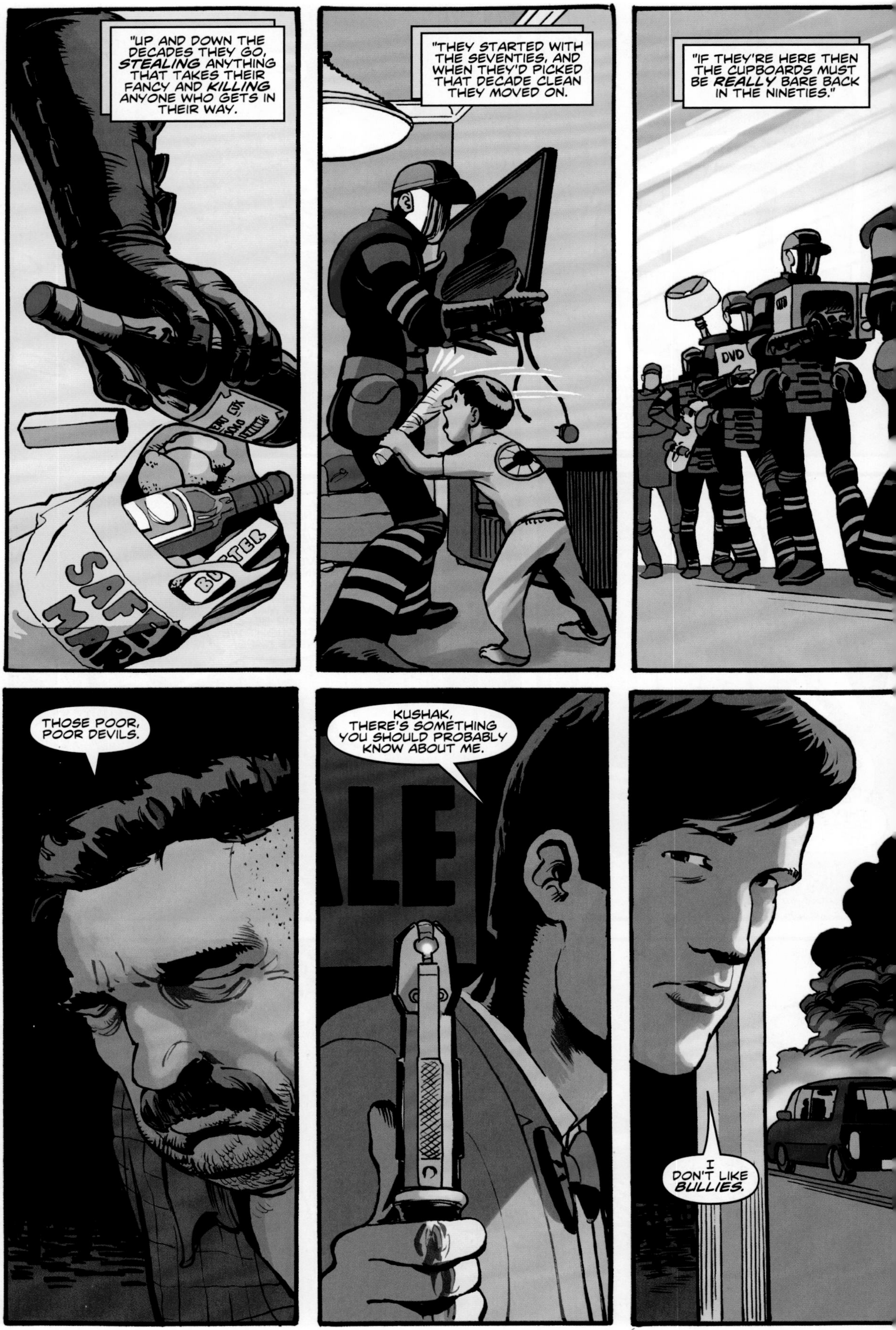
"UP AND DOWN THE DECADES THEY GO, *STEALING* ANYTHING THAT TAKES THEIR FANCY AND *KILLING* ANYONE WHO GETS IN THEIR WAY.
BUTTER
"THEY STARTED WITH THE SEVENTIES, AND WHEN THEY'D PICKED THAT DECADE CLEAN THEY MOVED ON.
"IF THEY'RE HERE THEN THE CUPBOARDS MUST BE *REALLY* BARE BACK IN THE NINETIES."
DVD
THOSE POOR, POOR DEVILS.
KUSHAK, THERE'S SOMETHING YOU SHOULD PROBABLY KNOW ABOUT ME.
I DON'T LIKE *BULLIES.*

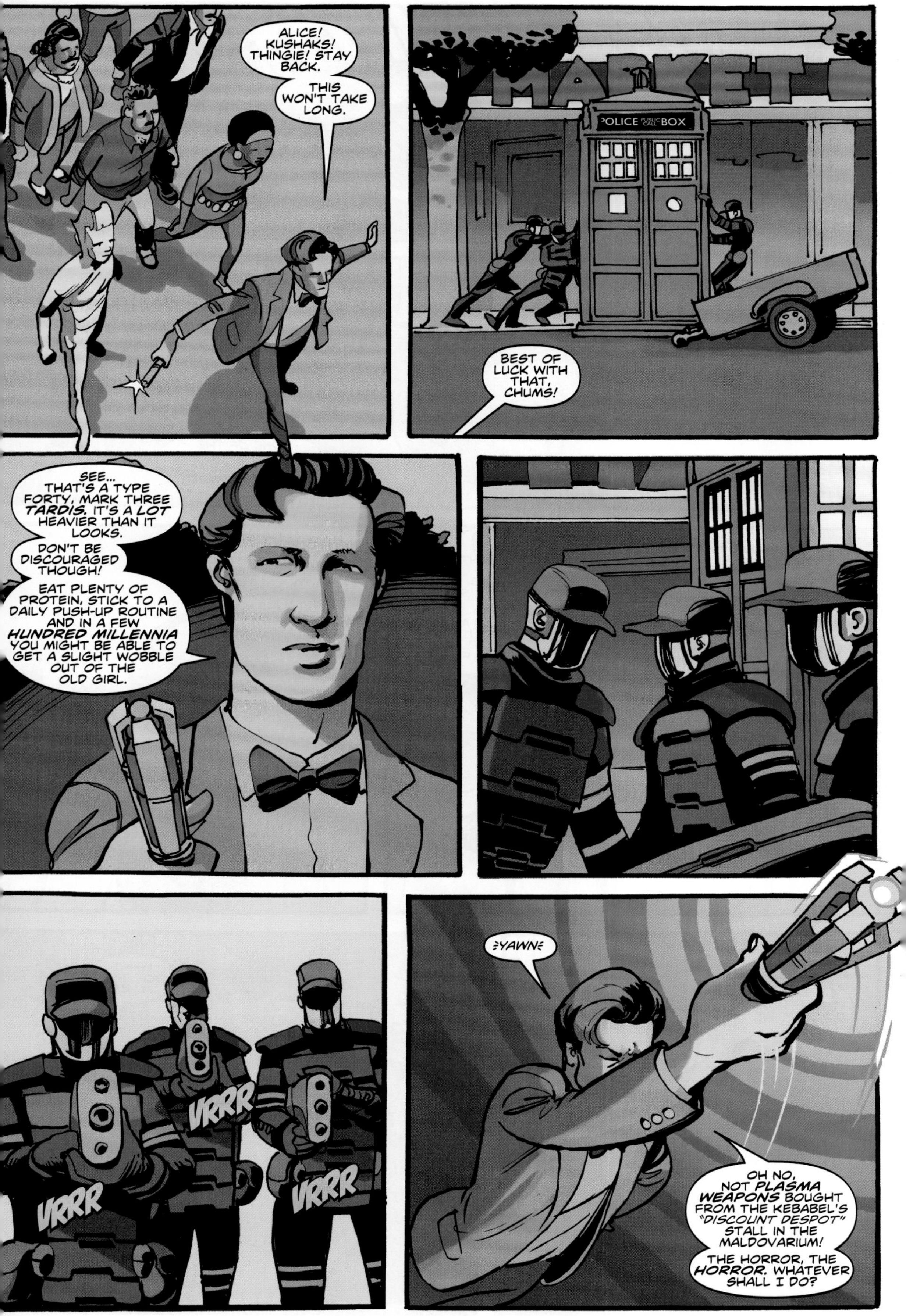
ALICE! KUSHAKS! THINGIE! STAY BACK.
THIS WON'T TAKE LONG.
MARKET
POLICE PUBLIC CALL BOX
BEST OF LUCK WITH THAT, CHUMS!
SEE... THAT'S A TYPE FORTY, MARK THREE TARDIS. IT'S A LOT HEAVIER THAN IT LOOKS.
DON'T BE DISCOURAGED THOUGH!
EAT PLENTY OF PROTEIN, STICK TO A DAILY PUSH-UP ROUTINE AND IN A FEW HUNDRED MILLENNIA YOU MIGHT BE ABLE TO GET A SLIGHT WOBBLE OUT OF THE OLD GIRL.
VRRR
VRRR
VRRR
YAWN
OH NO, NOT PLASMA WEAPONS BOUGHT FROM THE KEBABEL'S "DISCOUNT DESPOT" STALL IN THE MALDOVARIUM!
THE HORROR, THE HORROR. WHATEVER SHALL I DO?

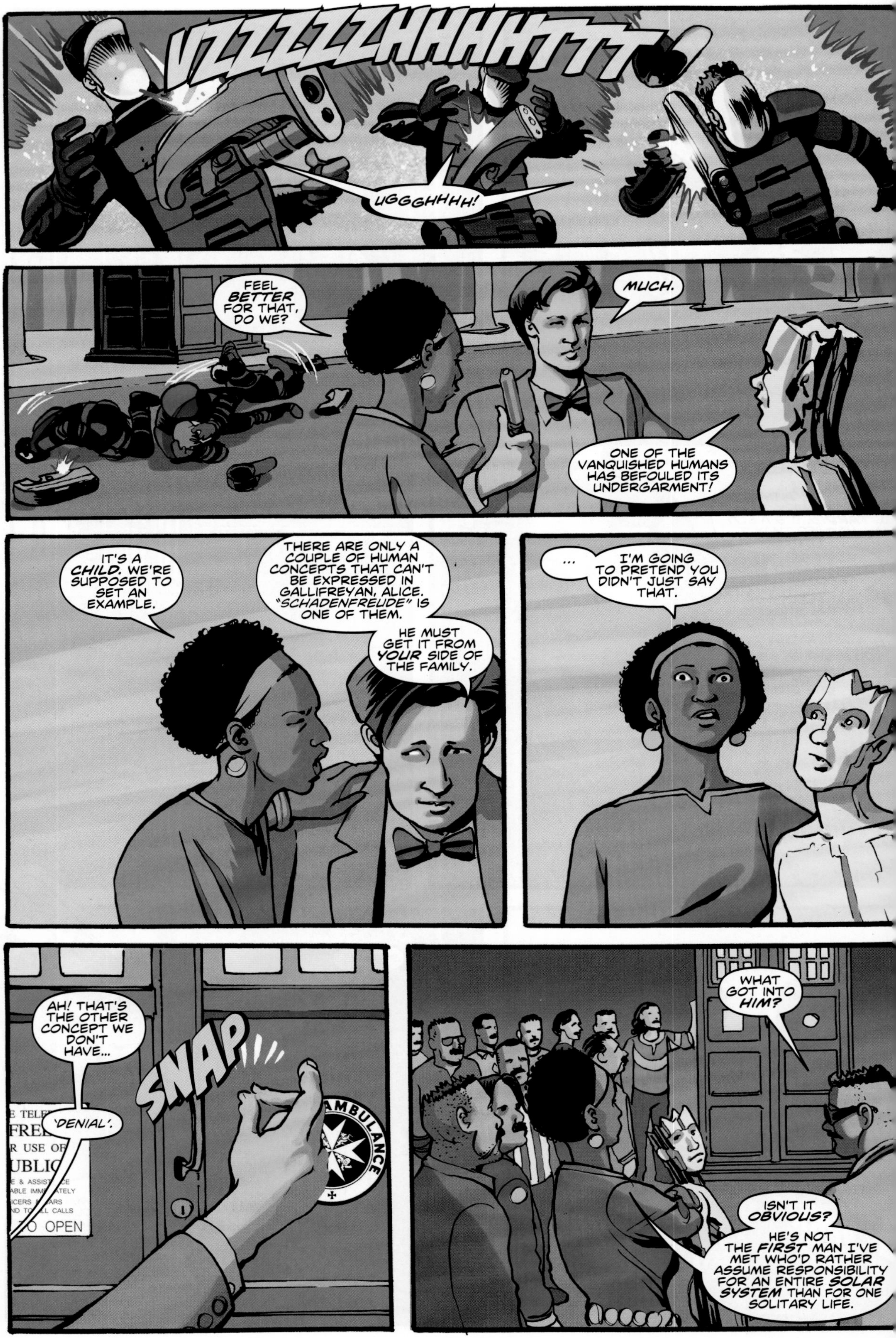
VZZZZZHHHHHTTTT
UGGGHHHH!
FEEL BETTER FOR THAT, DO WE?
MUCH.
ONE OF THE VANQUISHED HUMANS HAS BEFOULED ITS UNDERGARMENT!
IT'S A CHILD. WE'RE SUPPOSED TO SET AN EXAMPLE.
THERE ARE ONLY A COUPLE OF HUMAN CONCEPTS THAT CAN'T BE EXPRESSED IN GALLIFREYAN, ALICE. "SCHADENFREUDE" IS ONE OF THEM.
HE MUST GET IT FROM YOUR SIDE OF THE FAMILY.
...
I'M GOING TO PRETEND YOU DIDN'T JUST SAY THAT.
AH! THAT'S THE OTHER CONCEPT WE DON'T HAVE...
'DENIAL'.
SNAP
AMBULANCE
TO OPEN
WHAT GOT INTO HIM?
ISN'T IT OBVIOUS?
HE'S NOT THE FIRST MAN I'VE MET WHO'D RATHER ASSUME RESPONSIBILITY FOR AN ENTIRE SOLAR SYSTEM THAN FOR ONE SOLITARY LIFE.

ZZZZZHHHTTT

AIIEEEE!

AAARRGHH!

IT'S A *FRESH WAVE!* GET INSIDE, QUICKLY!

PERIL! HOW INVIGORATING!

HOW ARE WE ALL GOING TO FIT IN THERE?!

OH, DON'T START. *MOVE!*

DOCTOR! THEY NEED HELP!

OOP! RIGHT-O!

RRRLLLBBTTT

AAARGHH! WHY DOES *THAT* SETTING ALWAYS DRAIN THE *RUDDY* BATTERY!

POLICE PUBLIC CALL BOX

POLICE PUBLIC CALL BOX

WE'LL COME BACK FOR THEM!

AKKK!

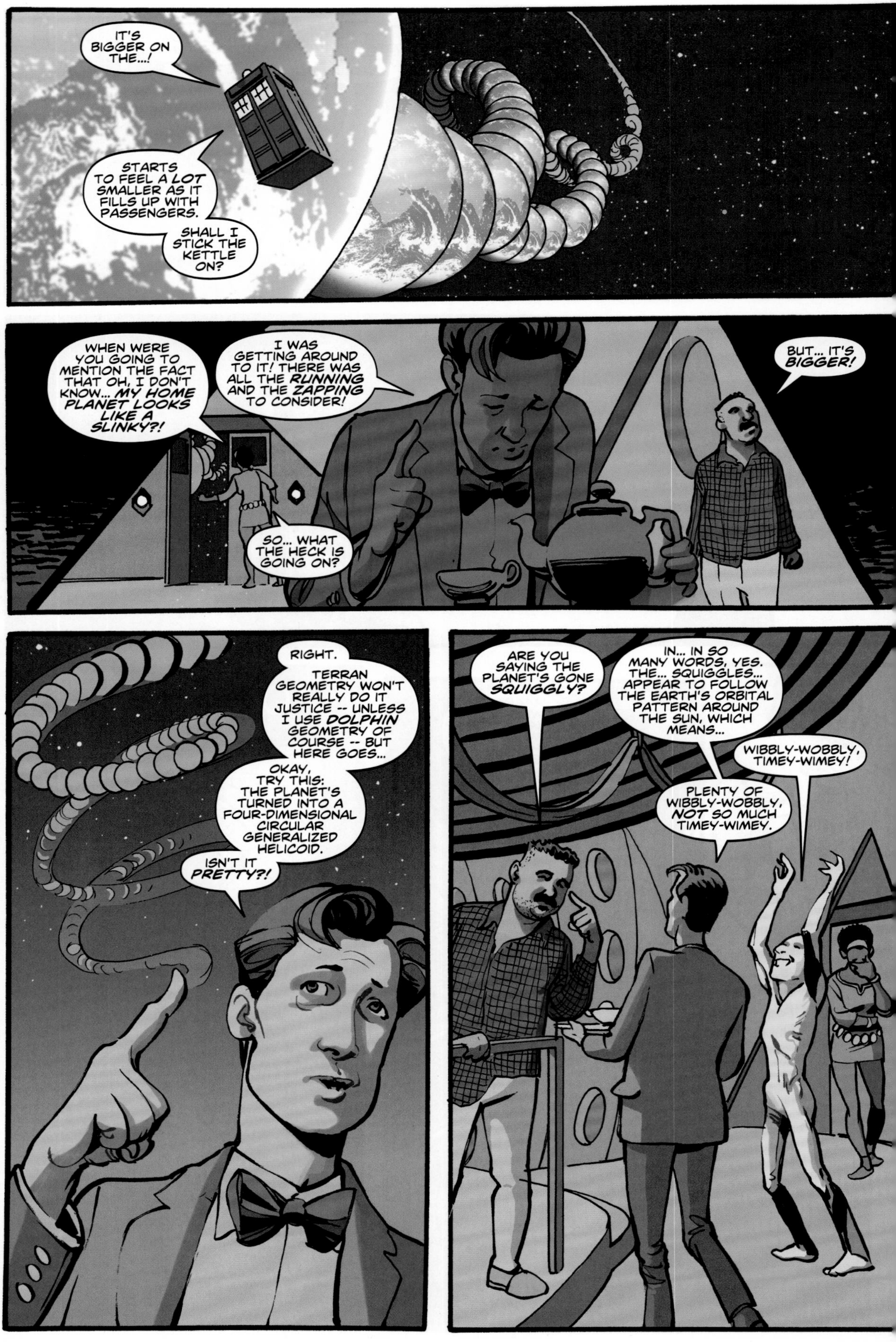
IT'S BIGGER ON THE...!
STARTS TO FEEL A *LOT* SMALLER AS IT FILLS UP WITH PASSENGERS.
SHALL I STICK THE KETTLE ON?
WHEN WERE YOU GOING TO MENTION THE FACT THAT OH, I DON'T KNOW... ***MY HOME PLANET LOOKS LIKE A SLINKY?!***
I WAS GETTING AROUND TO IT! THERE WAS ALL THE ***RUNNING*** AND THE ***ZAPPING*** TO CONSIDER!
BUT... IT'S ***BIGGER!***
SO... WHAT THE HECK IS GOING ON?
RIGHT.
TERRAN GEOMETRY WON'T REALLY DO IT JUSTICE -- UNLESS I USE ***DOLPHIN*** GEOMETRY OF COURSE -- BUT HERE GOES...
OKAY, TRY THIS: THE PLANET'S TURNED INTO A FOUR-DIMENSIONAL CIRCULAR GENERALIZED HELICOID.
ISN'T IT ***PRETTY?!***
ARE YOU SAYING THE PLANET'S GONE ***SQUIGGLY?***
IN... IN SO MANY WORDS, YES. THE... SQUIGGLES... APPEAR TO FOLLOW THE EARTH'S ORBITAL PATTERN AROUND THE SUN, WHICH MEANS...
PLENTY OF WIBBLY-WOBBLY, ***NOT*** SO MUCH TIMEY-WIMEY.
WIBBLY-WOBBLY, TIMEY-WIMEY!

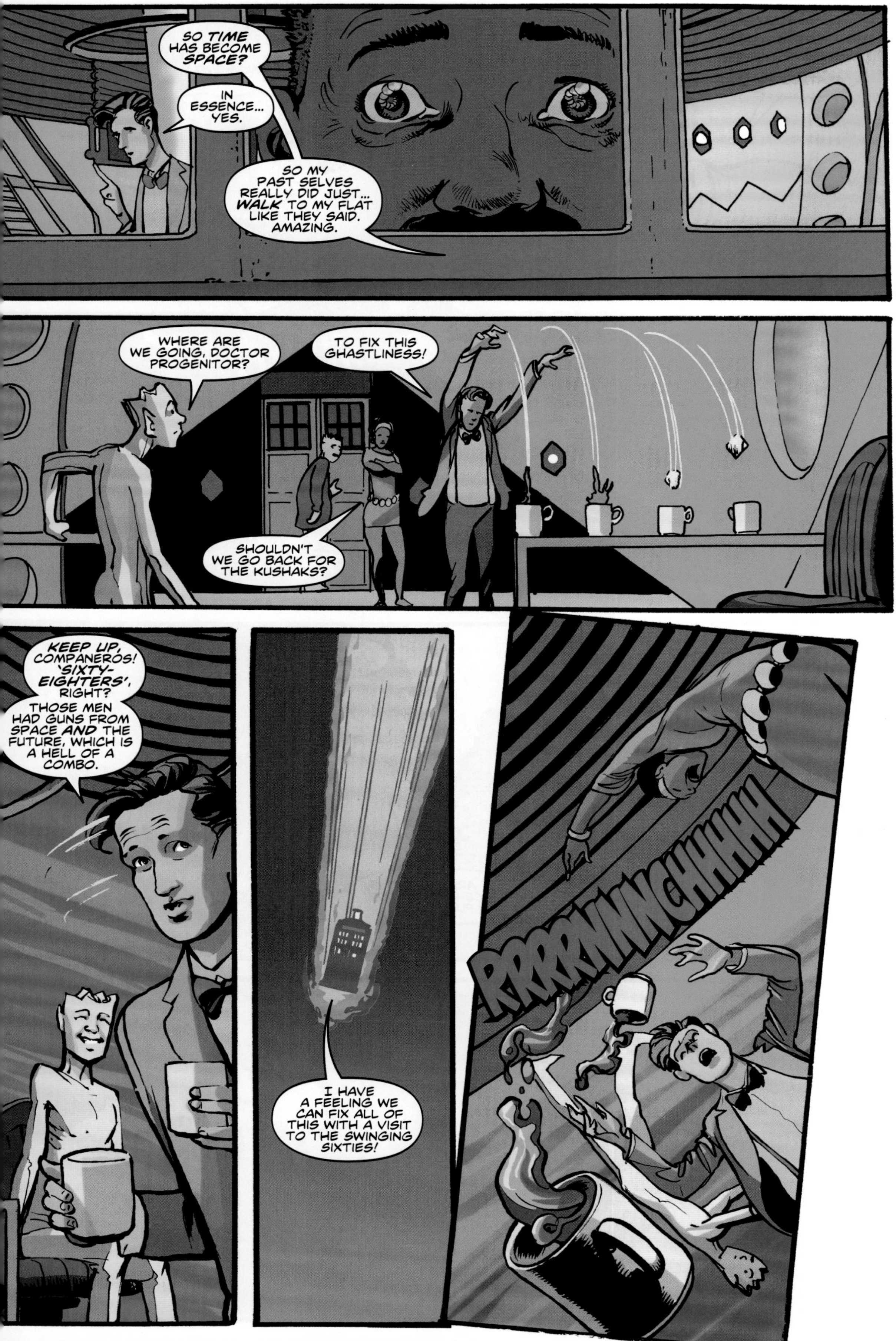
SO TIME HAS BECOME SPACE?
IN ESSENCE... YES.
SO MY PAST SELVES REALLY DID JUST... WALK TO MY FLAT LIKE THEY SAID. AMAZING.
WHERE ARE WE GOING, DOCTOR PROGENITOR?
TO FIX THIS GHASTLINESS!
SHOULDN'T WE GO BACK FOR THE KUSHAKS?
KEEP UP, COMPANEROS! 'SIXTY-EIGHTERS', RIGHT?
THOSE MEN HAD GUNS FROM SPACE AND THE FUTURE, WHICH IS A HELL OF A COMBO.
I HAVE A FEELING WE CAN FIX ALL OF THIS WITH A VISIT TO THE SWINGING SIXTIES!
RRRRNNNNCHHHHH

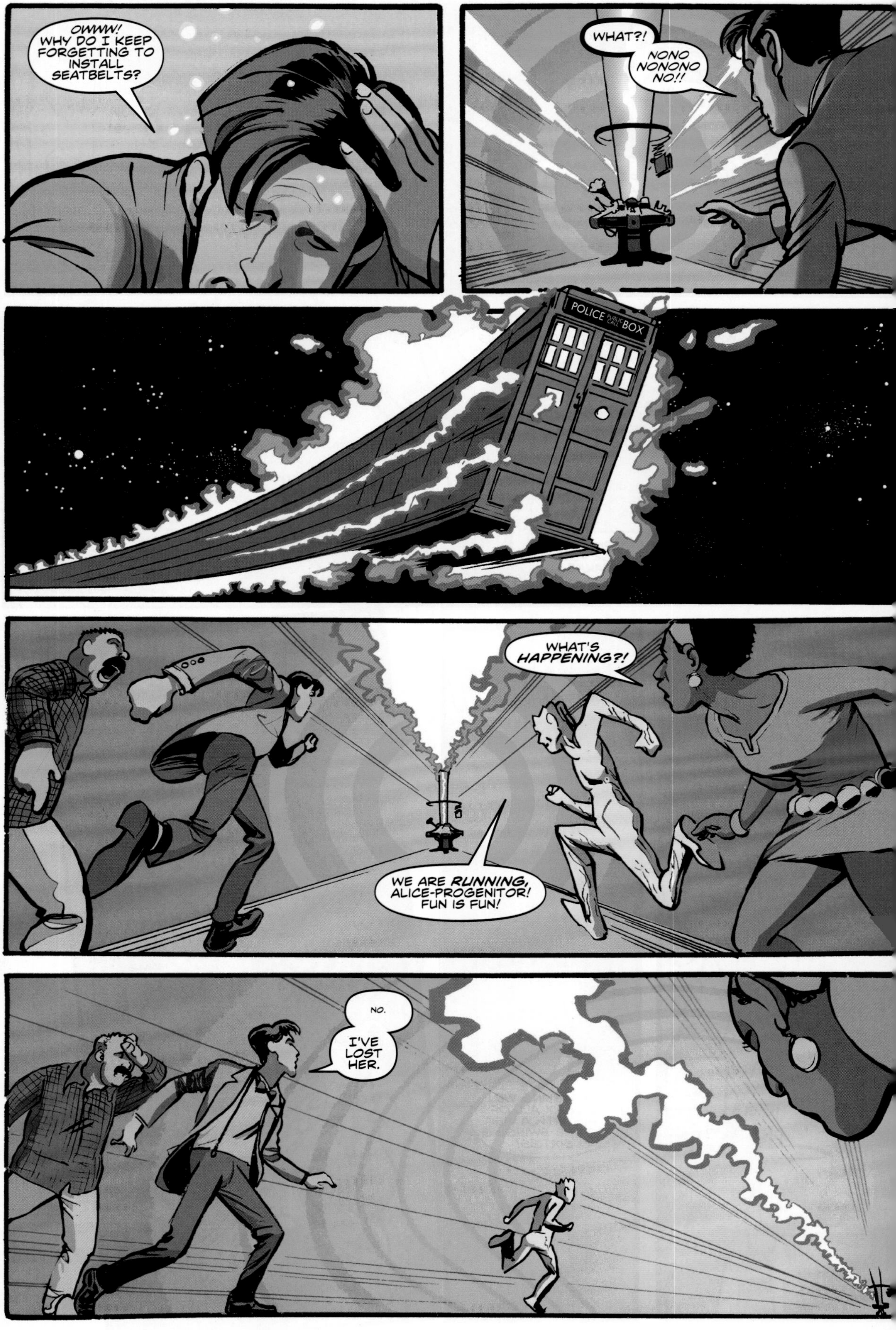
OWWW! WHY DO I KEEP FORGETTING TO INSTALL SEATBELTS?
WHAT?!
NONO NONONO NO!!
POLICE PUBLIC CALL BOX
WHAT'S HAPPENING?!
WE ARE RUNNING, ALICE-PROGENITOR! FUN IS FUN!
NO.
I'VE LOST HER.

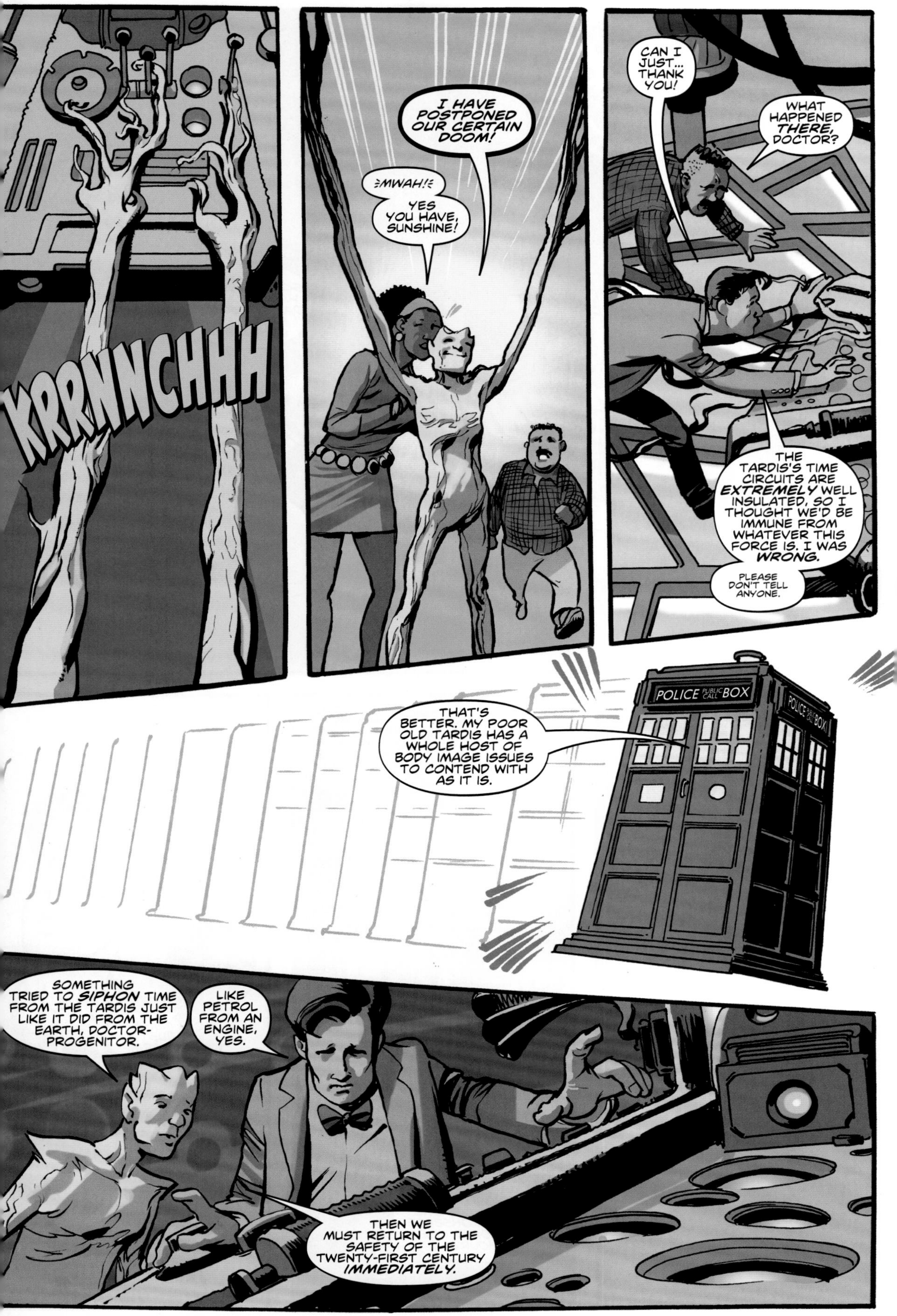

KRRNNCHHH
I HAVE POSTPONED OUR CERTAIN DOOM!
MWAH! YES YOU HAVE, SUNSHINE!
CAN I JUST... THANK YOU!
WHAT HAPPENED THERE, DOCTOR?
THE TARDIS'S TIME CIRCUITS ARE EXTREMELY WELL INSULATED, SO I THOUGHT WE'D BE IMMUNE FROM WHATEVER THIS FORCE IS. I WAS WRONG.
PLEASE DON'T TELL ANYONE.
POLICE PUBLIC CALL BOX
THAT'S BETTER. MY POOR OLD TARDIS HAS A WHOLE HOST OF BODY IMAGE ISSUES TO CONTEND WITH AS IT IS.
SOMETHING TRIED TO SIPHON TIME FROM THE TARDIS JUST LIKE IT DID FROM THE EARTH, DOCTOR-PROGENITOR.
LIKE PETROL FROM AN ENGINE, YES.
THEN WE MUST RETURN TO THE SAFETY OF THE TWENTY-FIRST CENTURY IMMEDIATELY.

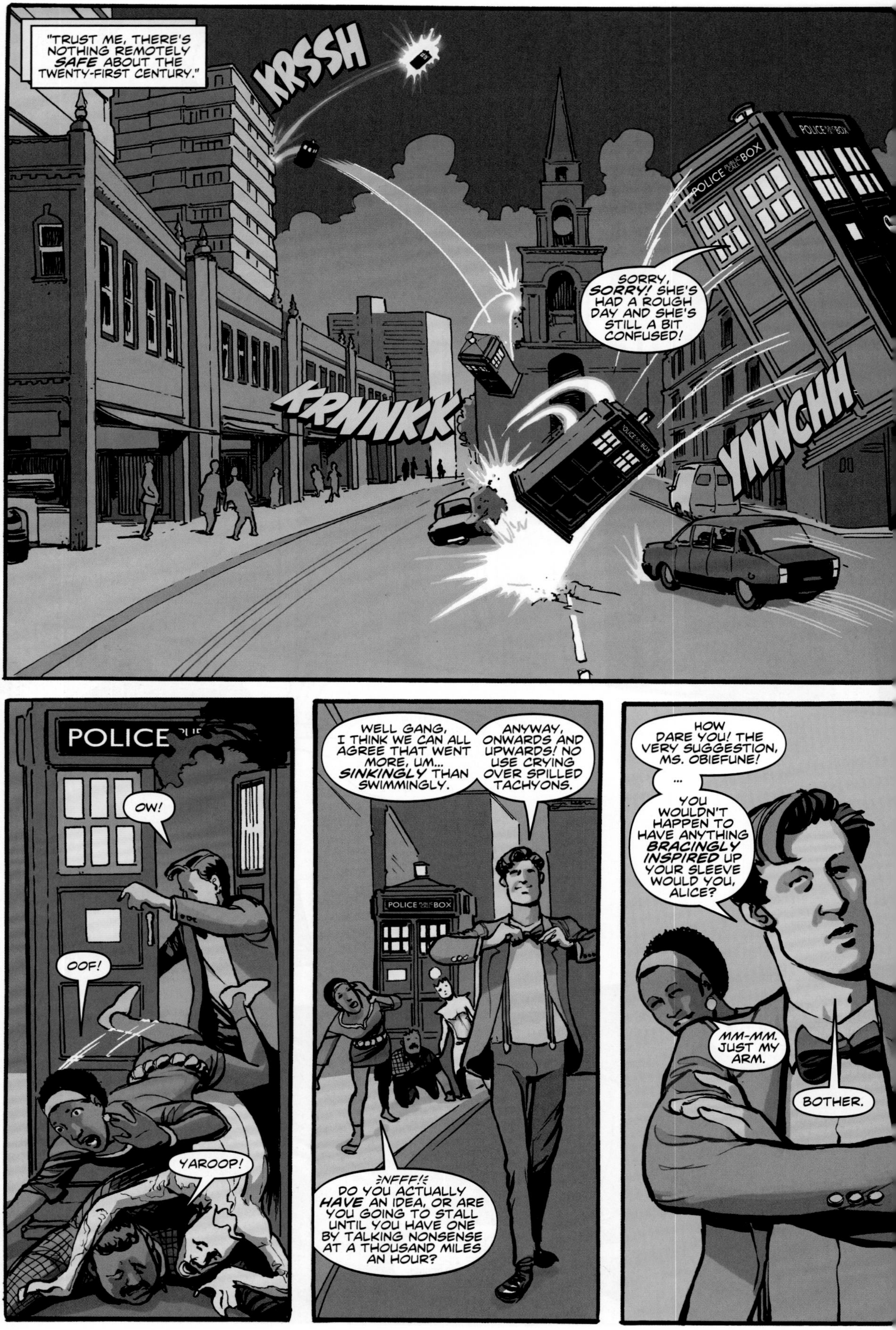
"TRUST ME, THERE'S NOTHING REMOTELY SAFE ABOUT THE TWENTY-FIRST CENTURY."
KRSSH
SORRY, SORRY! SHE'S HAD A ROUGH DAY AND SHE'S STILL A BIT CONFUSED!
KRNNKK
YNNCHH
POLICE
OW!
OOF!
YAROOP!
WELL GANG, I THINK WE CAN ALL AGREE THAT WENT MORE, UM... SINKINGLY THAN SWIMMINGLY.
ANYWAY, ONWARDS AND UPWARDS! NO USE CRYING OVER SPILLED TACHYONS.
POLICE BOX
NFFF! DO YOU ACTUALLY HAVE AN IDEA, OR ARE YOU GOING TO STALL UNTIL YOU HAVE ONE BY TALKING NONSENSE AT A THOUSAND MILES AN HOUR?
HOW DARE YOU! THE VERY SUGGESTION, MS. OBIEFUNE!
...
YOU WOULDN'T HAPPEN TO HAVE ANYTHING BRACINGLY INSPIRED UP YOUR SLEEVE WOULD YOU, ALICE?
MM-MM. JUST MY ARM.
BOTHER.

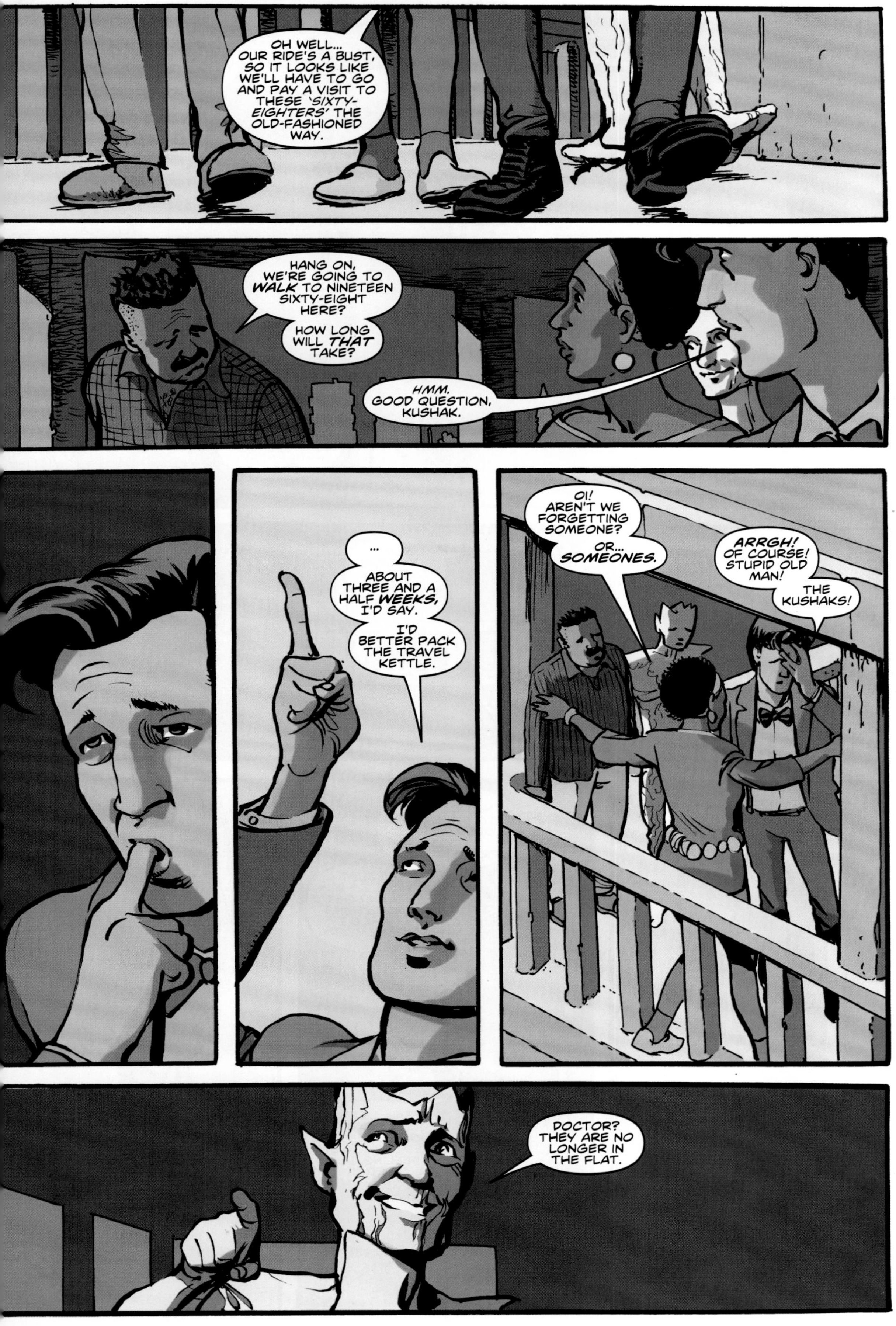
OH WELL... OUR RIDE'S A BUST, SO IT LOOKS LIKE WE'LL HAVE TO GO AND PAY A VISIT TO THESE 'SIXTY-EIGHTERS' THE OLD-FASHIONED WAY.
HANG ON, WE'RE GOING TO WALK TO NINETEEN SIXTY-EIGHT HERE?
HOW LONG WILL THAT TAKE?
HMM. GOOD QUESTION, KUSHAK.
...
ABOUT THREE AND A HALF WEEKS, I'D SAY.
I'D BETTER PACK THE TRAVEL KETTLE.
OI! AREN'T WE FORGETTING SOMEONE?
OR... SOMEONES.
ARRGH! OF COURSE! STUPID OLD MAN!
THE KUSHAKS!
DOCTOR? THEY ARE NO LONGER IN THE FLAT.

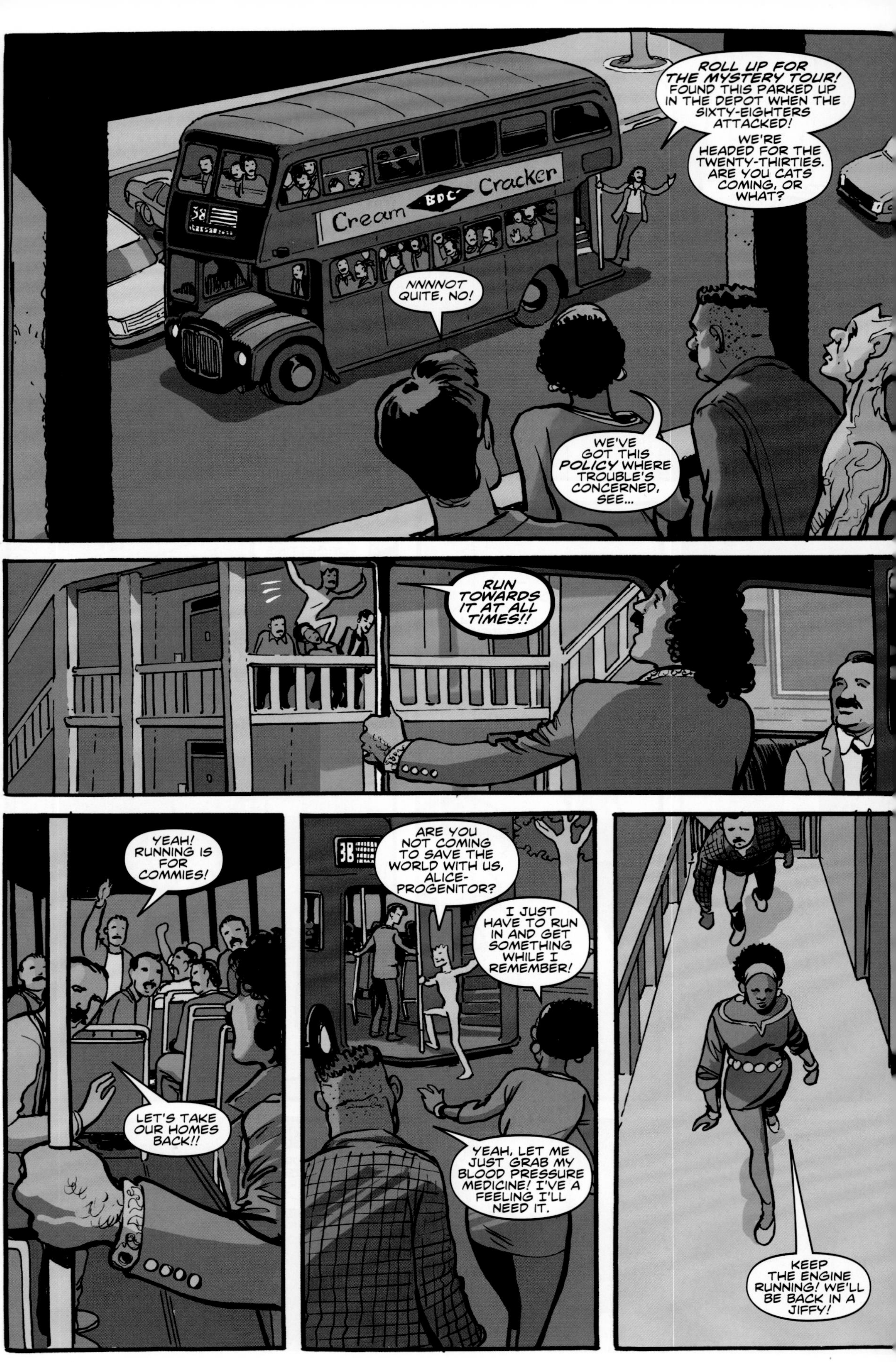
ROLL UP FOR THE MYSTERY TOUR! FOUND THIS PARKED UP IN THE DEPOT WHEN THE SIXTY-EIGHTERS ATTACKED!
WE'RE HEADED FOR THE TWENTY-THIRTIES. ARE YOU CATS COMING, OR WHAT?
Cream BDC Cracker
38
NNNNOT QUITE, NO!
WE'VE GOT THIS POLICY WHERE TROUBLE'S CONCERNED, SEE...
RUN TOWARDS IT AT ALL TIMES!!
YEAH! RUNNING IS FOR COMMIES!
LET'S TAKE OUR HOMES BACK!!
38
ARE YOU NOT COMING TO SAVE THE WORLD WITH US, ALICE-PROGENITOR?
I JUST HAVE TO RUN IN AND GET SOMETHING WHILE I REMEMBER!
YEAH, LET ME JUST GRAB MY BLOOD PRESSURE MEDICINE! I'VE A FEELING I'LL NEED IT.
KEEP THE ENGINE RUNNING! WE'LL BE BACK IN A JIFFY!

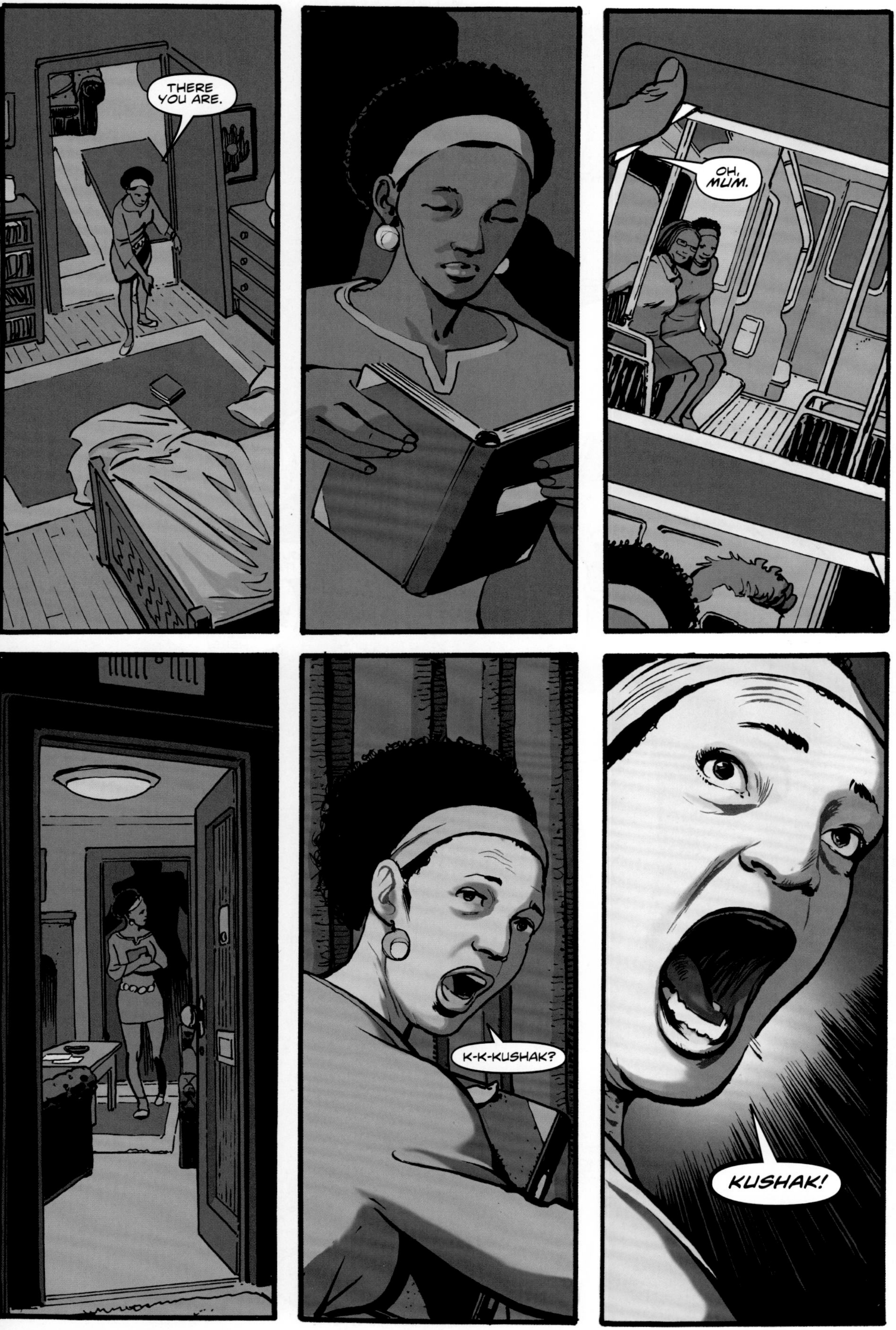
THERE YOU ARE.
OH, MUM.
K-K-KUSHAK?
KUSHAK!

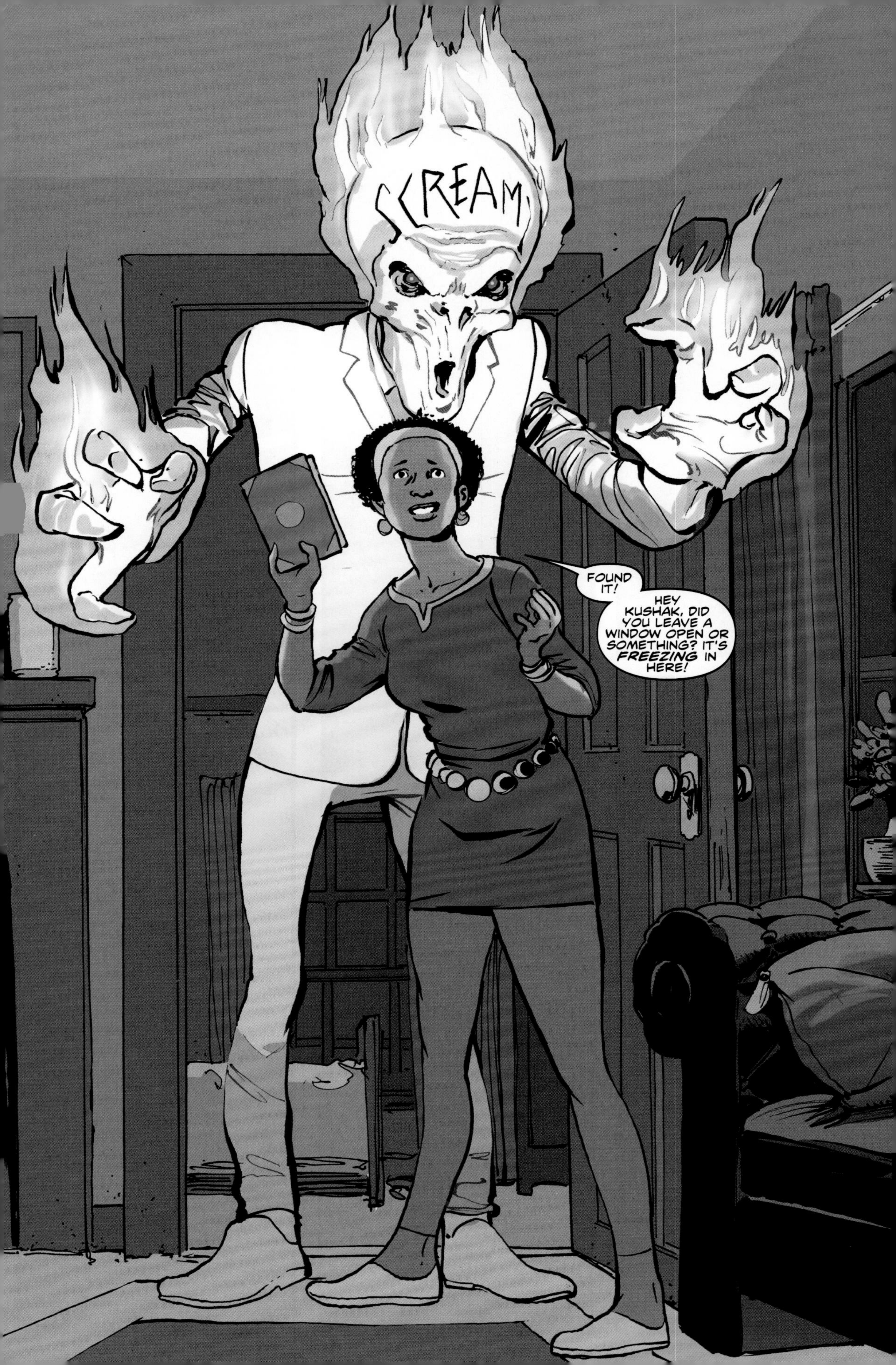
SCREAM
FOUND IT!
HEY KUSHAK, DID YOU LEAVE A WINDOW OPEN OR SOMETHING? IT'S *FREEZING* IN HERE!

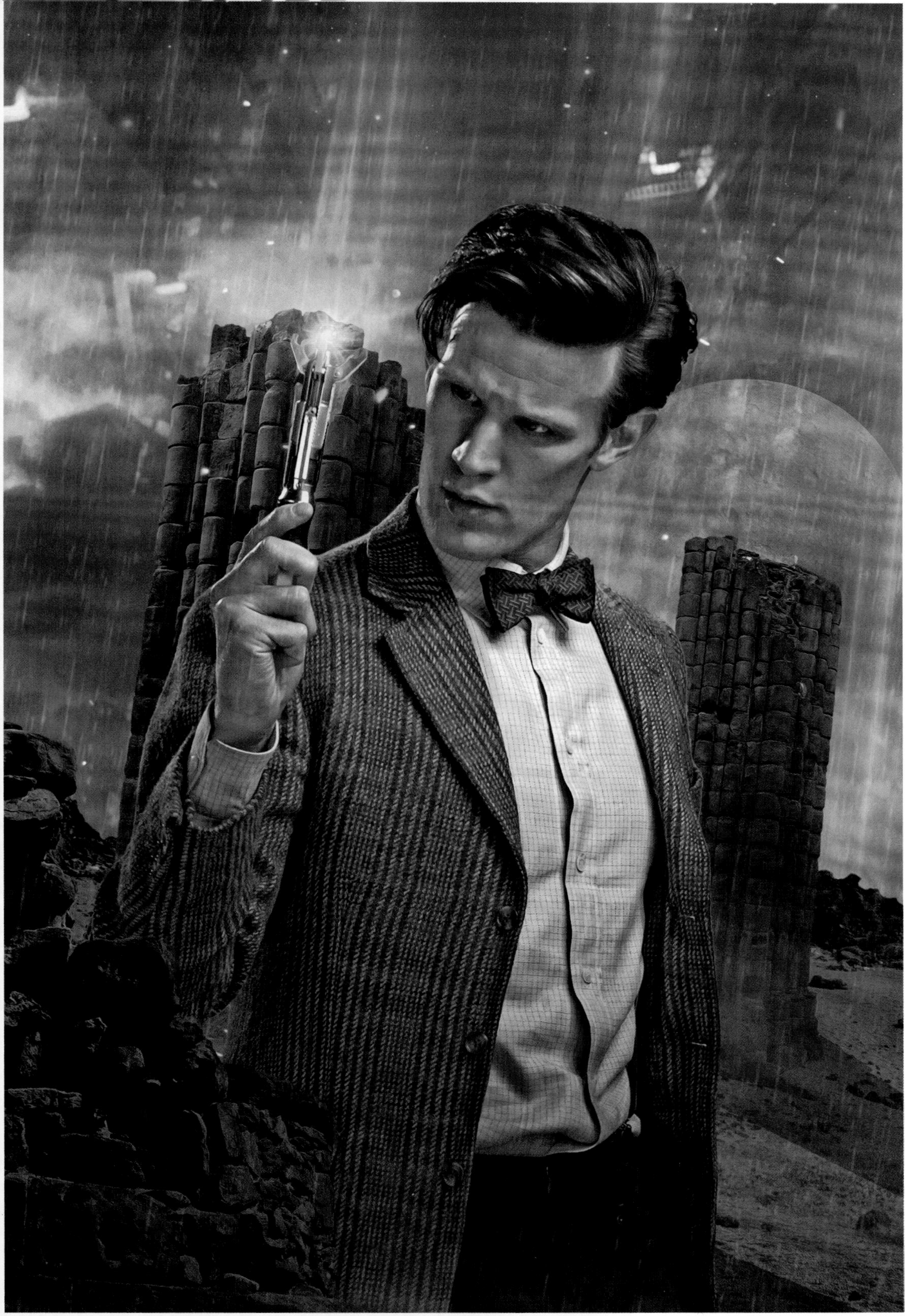

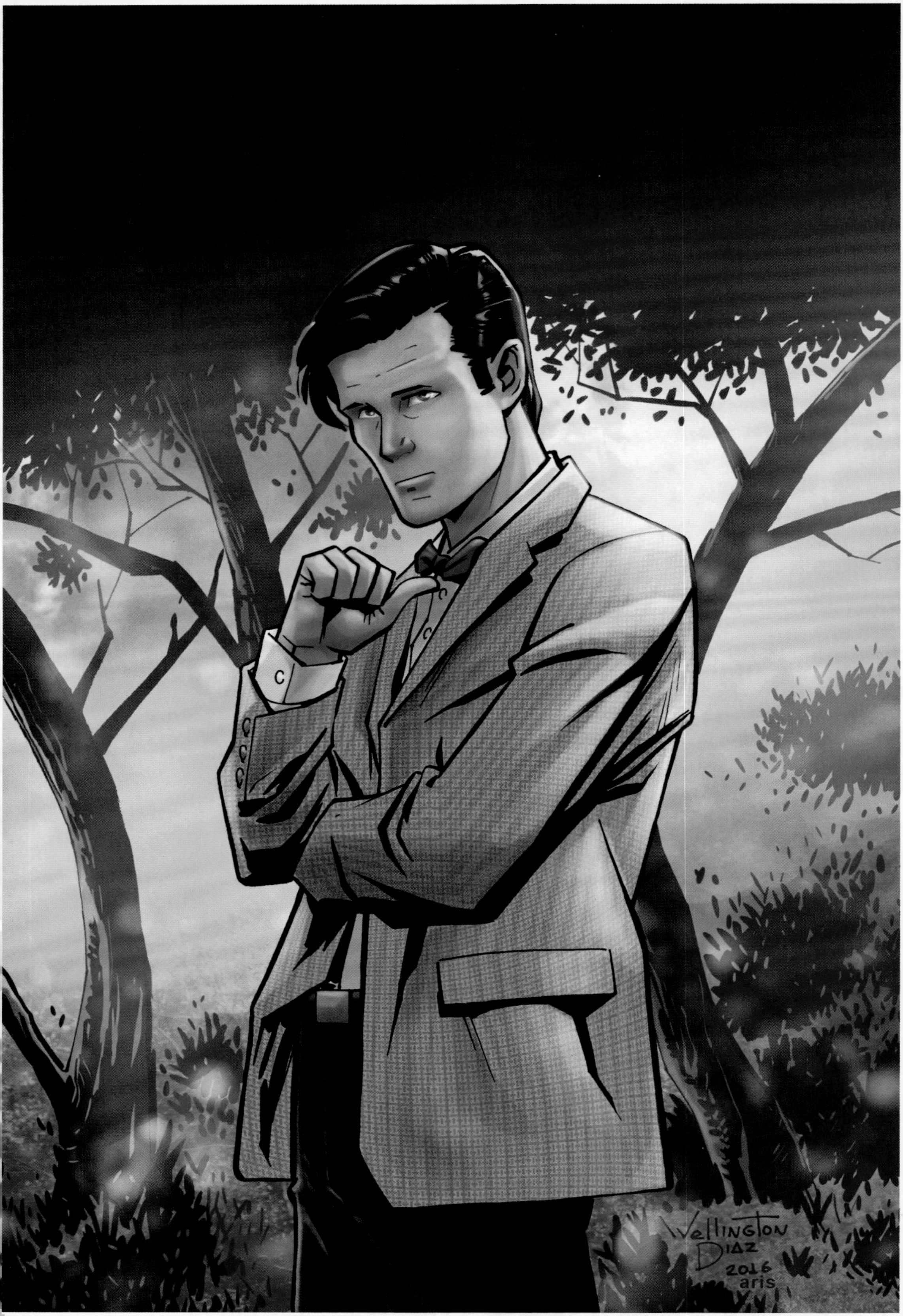
WELLINGTON
DIAZ
2016
aris

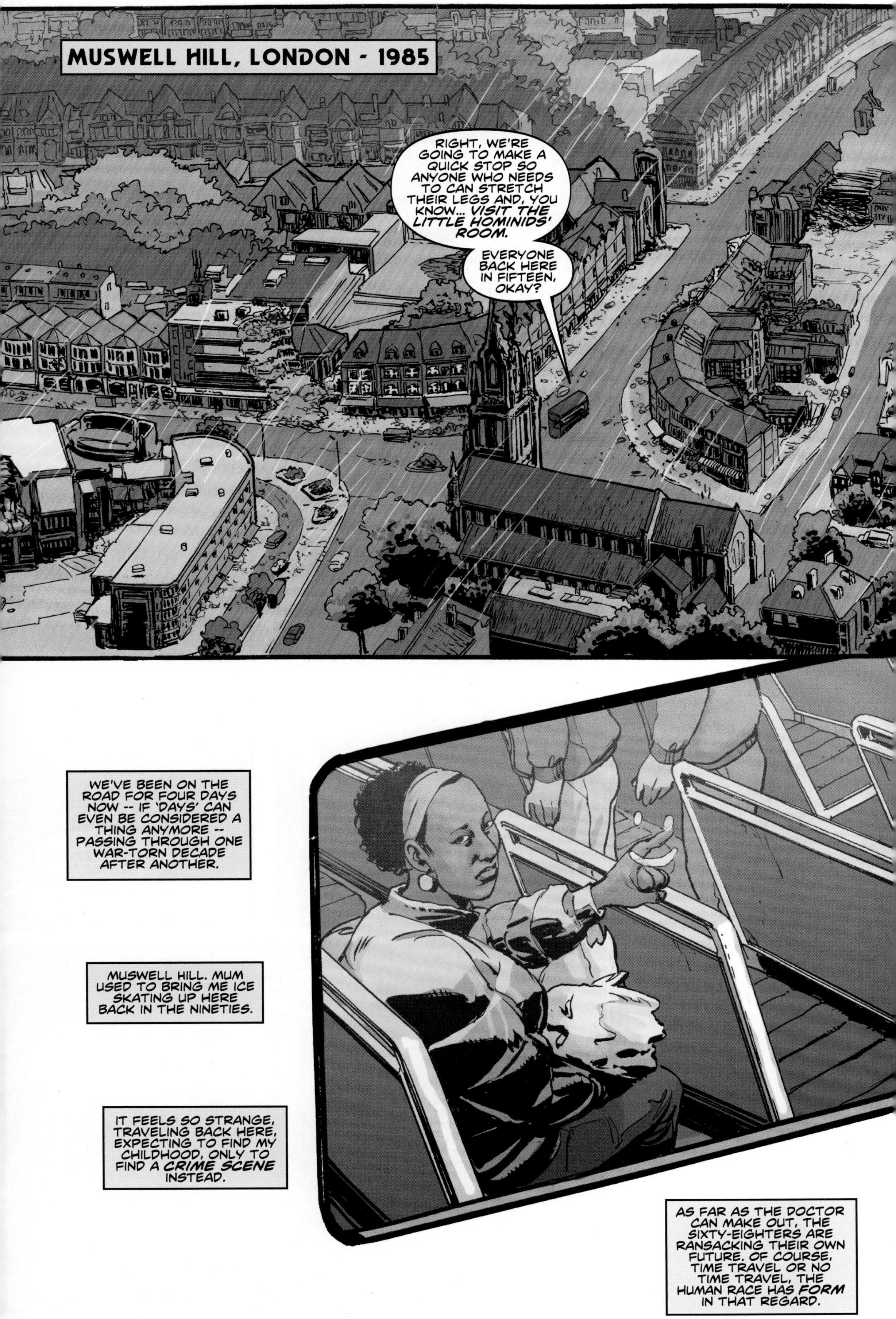
MUSWELL HILL, LONDON - 1985
RIGHT, WE'RE GOING TO MAKE A QUICK STOP SO ANYONE WHO NEEDS TO CAN STRETCH THEIR LEGS AND, YOU KNOW... *VISIT THE LITTLE HOMINIDS' ROOM.*
EVERYONE BACK HERE IN FIFTEEN, OKAY?
WE'VE BEEN ON THE ROAD FOR FOUR DAYS NOW -- IF 'DAYS' CAN EVEN BE CONSIDERED A THING ANYMORE -- PASSING THROUGH ONE WAR-TORN DECADE AFTER ANOTHER.
MUSWELL HILL. MUM USED TO BRING ME ICE SKATING UP HERE BACK IN THE NINETIES.
IT FEELS SO STRANGE, TRAVELING BACK HERE, EXPECTING TO FIND MY CHILDHOOD, ONLY TO FIND A *CRIME SCENE* INSTEAD.
AS FAR AS THE DOCTOR CAN MAKE OUT, THE SIXTY-EIGHTERS ARE RANSACKING THEIR OWN FUTURE. OF COURSE, TIME TRAVEL OR NO TIME TRAVEL, THE HUMAN RACE HAS *FORM* IN THAT REGARD.

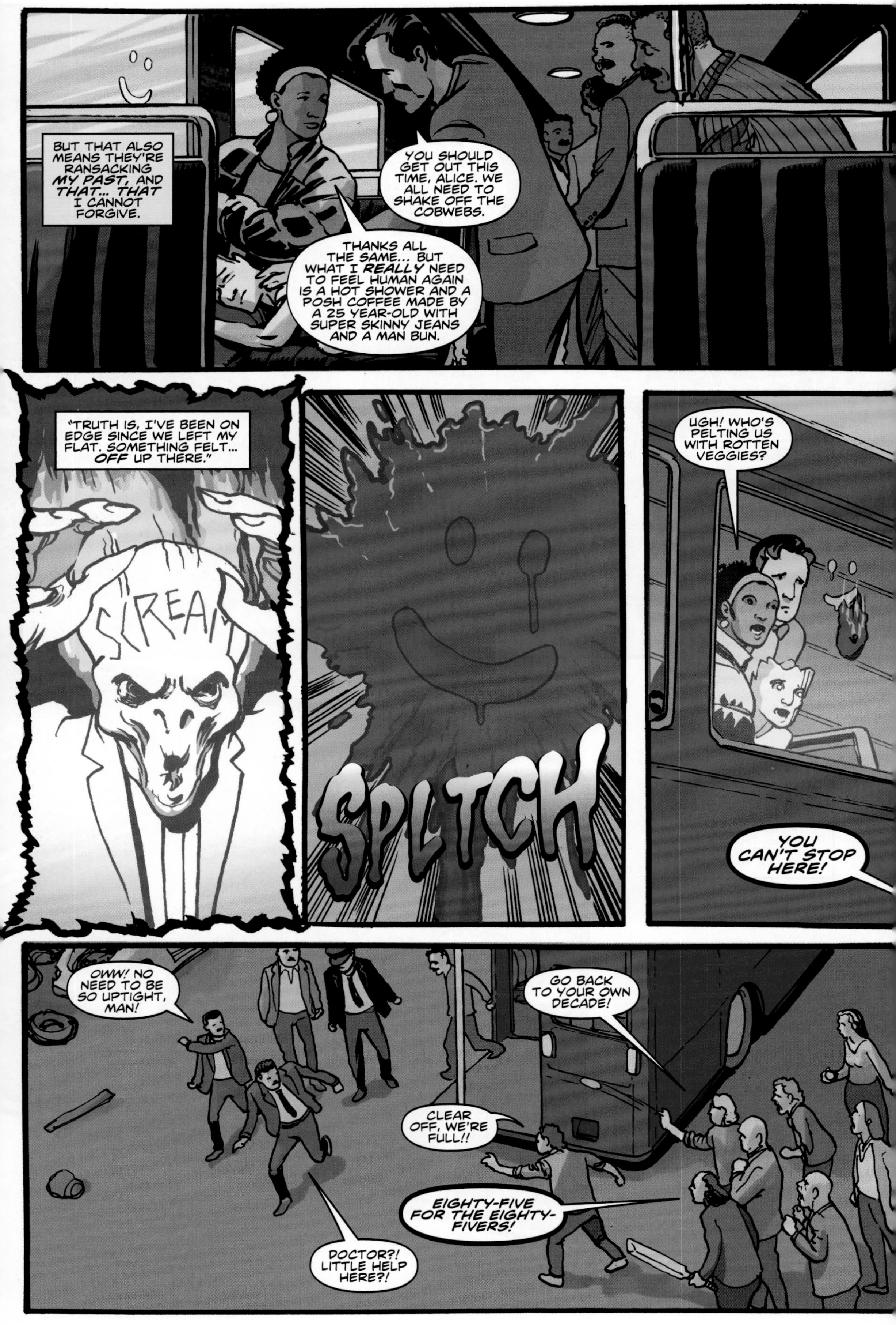
BUT THAT ALSO MEANS THEY'RE RANSACKING *MY PAST*, AND *THAT... THAT* I CANNOT FORGIVE.
YOU SHOULD GET OUT THIS TIME, ALICE. WE ALL NEED TO SHAKE OFF THE COBWEBS.
THANKS ALL THE SAME... BUT WHAT I *REALLY* NEED TO FEEL HUMAN AGAIN IS A HOT SHOWER AND A POSH COFFEE MADE BY A 25 YEAR-OLD WITH SUPER SKINNY JEANS AND A MAN BUN.
"TRUTH IS, I'VE BEEN ON EDGE SINCE WE LEFT MY FLAT. SOMETHING FELT... *OFF* UP THERE."
SCREAM
SPLTCH
UGH! WHO'S PELTING US WITH ROTTEN VEGGIES?
YOU CAN'T STOP HERE!
OWW! NO NEED TO BE SO UPTIGHT, MAN!
GO BACK TO YOUR OWN DECADE!
CLEAR OFF, WE'RE FULL!!
EIGHTY-FIVE FOR THE EIGHTY-FIVERS!
DOCTOR?! LITTLE HELP HERE?!

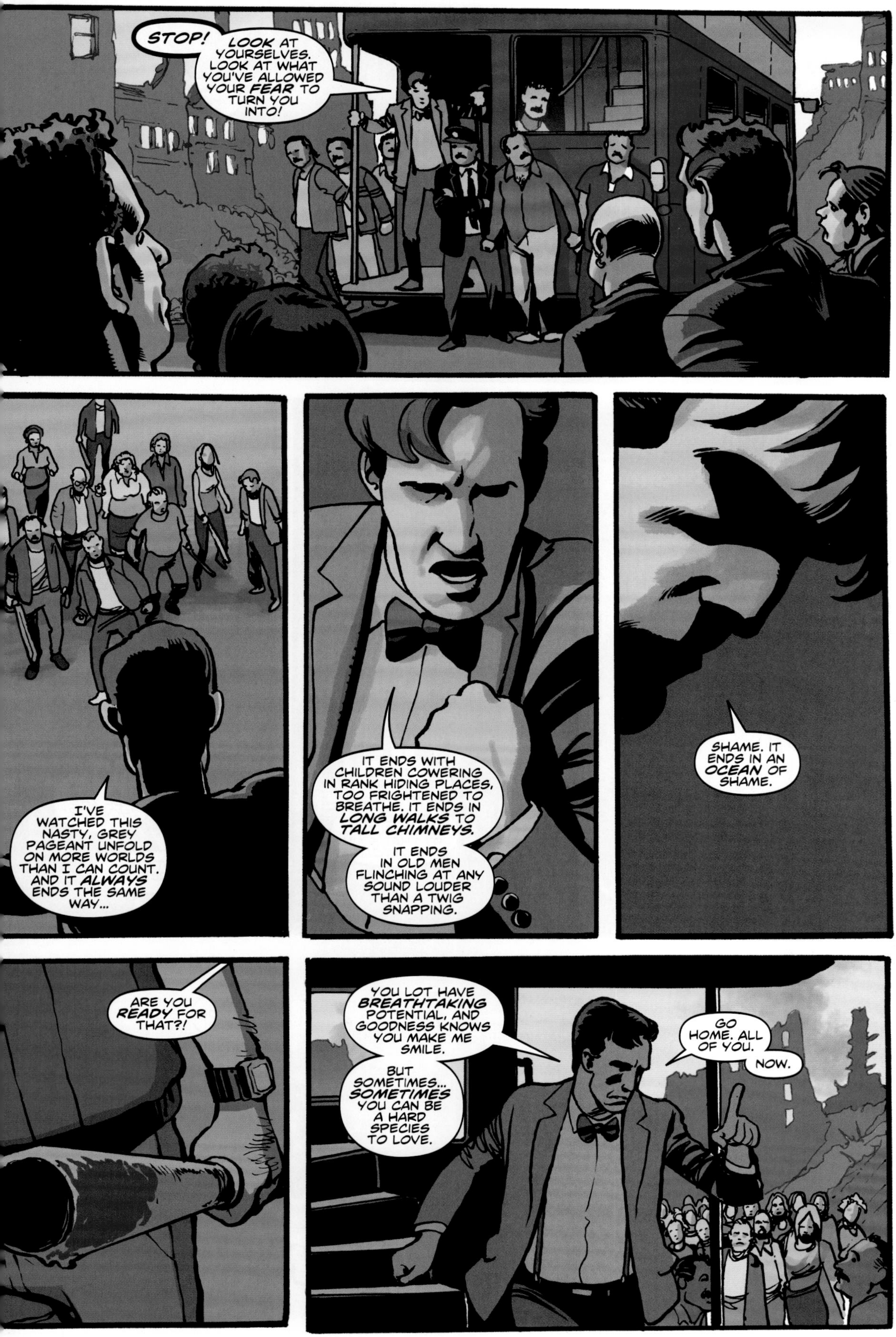
STOP!
LOOK AT YOURSELVES. LOOK AT WHAT YOU'VE ALLOWED YOUR FEAR TO TURN YOU INTO!
I'VE WATCHED THIS NASTY, GREY PAGEANT UNFOLD ON MORE WORLDS THAN I CAN COUNT. AND IT ALWAYS ENDS THE SAME WAY...
IT ENDS WITH CHILDREN COWERING IN RANK HIDING PLACES, TOO FRIGHTENED TO BREATHE. IT ENDS IN LONG WALKS TO TALL CHIMNEYS.
IT ENDS IN OLD MEN FLINCHING AT ANY SOUND LOUDER THAN A TWIG SNAPPING.
SHAME. IT ENDS IN AN OCEAN OF SHAME.
ARE YOU READY FOR THAT?!
YOU LOT HAVE BREATHTAKING POTENTIAL, AND GOODNESS KNOWS YOU MAKE ME SMILE.
BUT SOMETIMES... SOMETIMES YOU CAN BE A HARD SPECIES TO LOVE.
GO HOME. ALL OF YOU.
NOW.

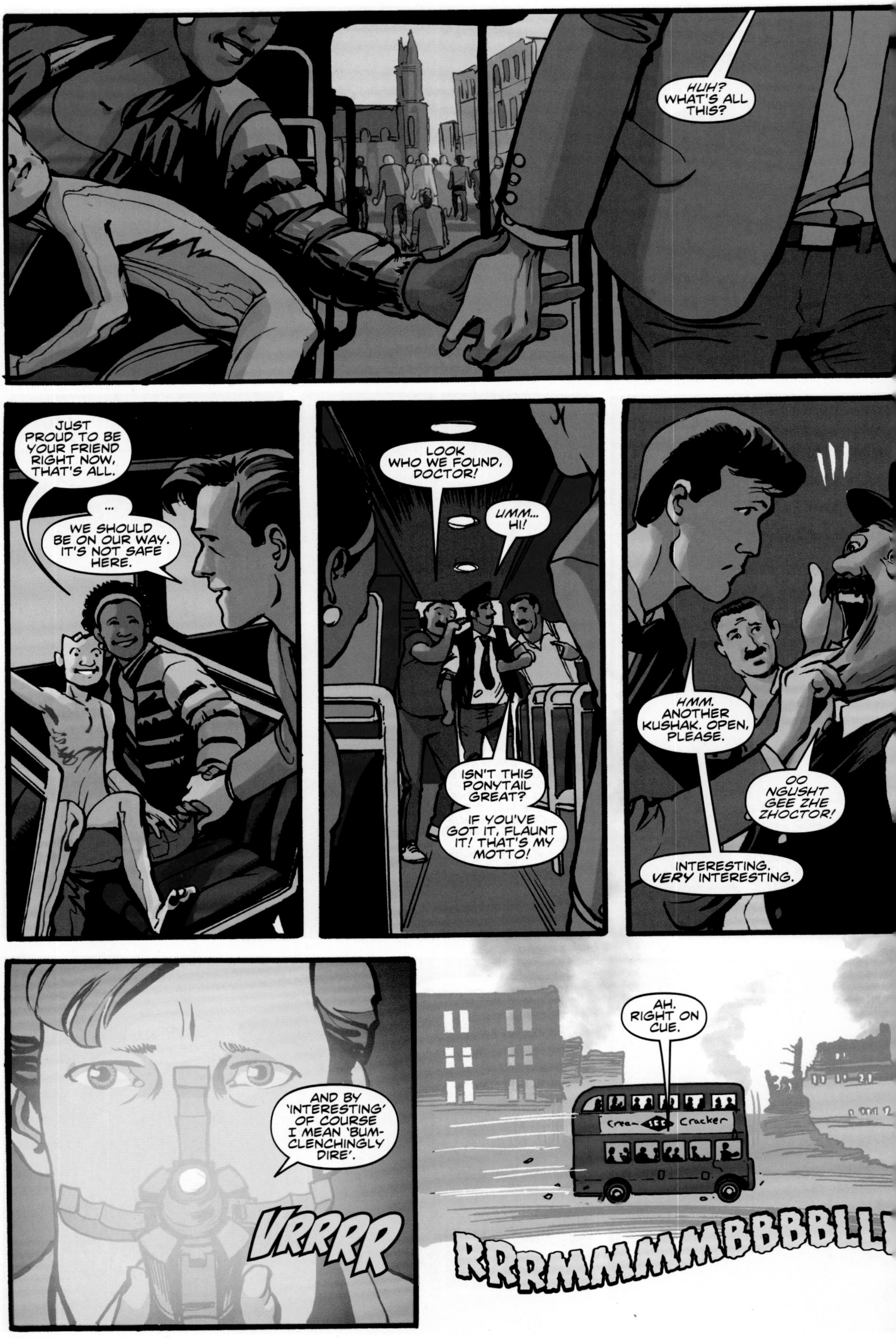
HUH? WHAT'S ALL THIS?
JUST PROUD TO BE YOUR FRIEND RIGHT NOW, THAT'S ALL.
...
WE SHOULD BE ON OUR WAY. IT'S NOT SAFE HERE.
LOOK WHO WE FOUND, DOCTOR!
UMM... HI!
ISN'T THIS PONYTAIL GREAT?
IF YOU'VE GOT IT, FLAUNT IT! THAT'S MY MOTTO!
HMM. ANOTHER KUSHAK. OPEN, PLEASE.
OO NGUSHT GEE ZHE ZHOCTOR!
INTERESTING. VERY INTERESTING.
AND BY 'INTERESTING' OF COURSE I MEAN 'BUM-CLENCHINGLY DIRE'.
VRRRR
AH. RIGHT ON CUE.
Cream Cracker
RRRMMMMMBBBBLLL

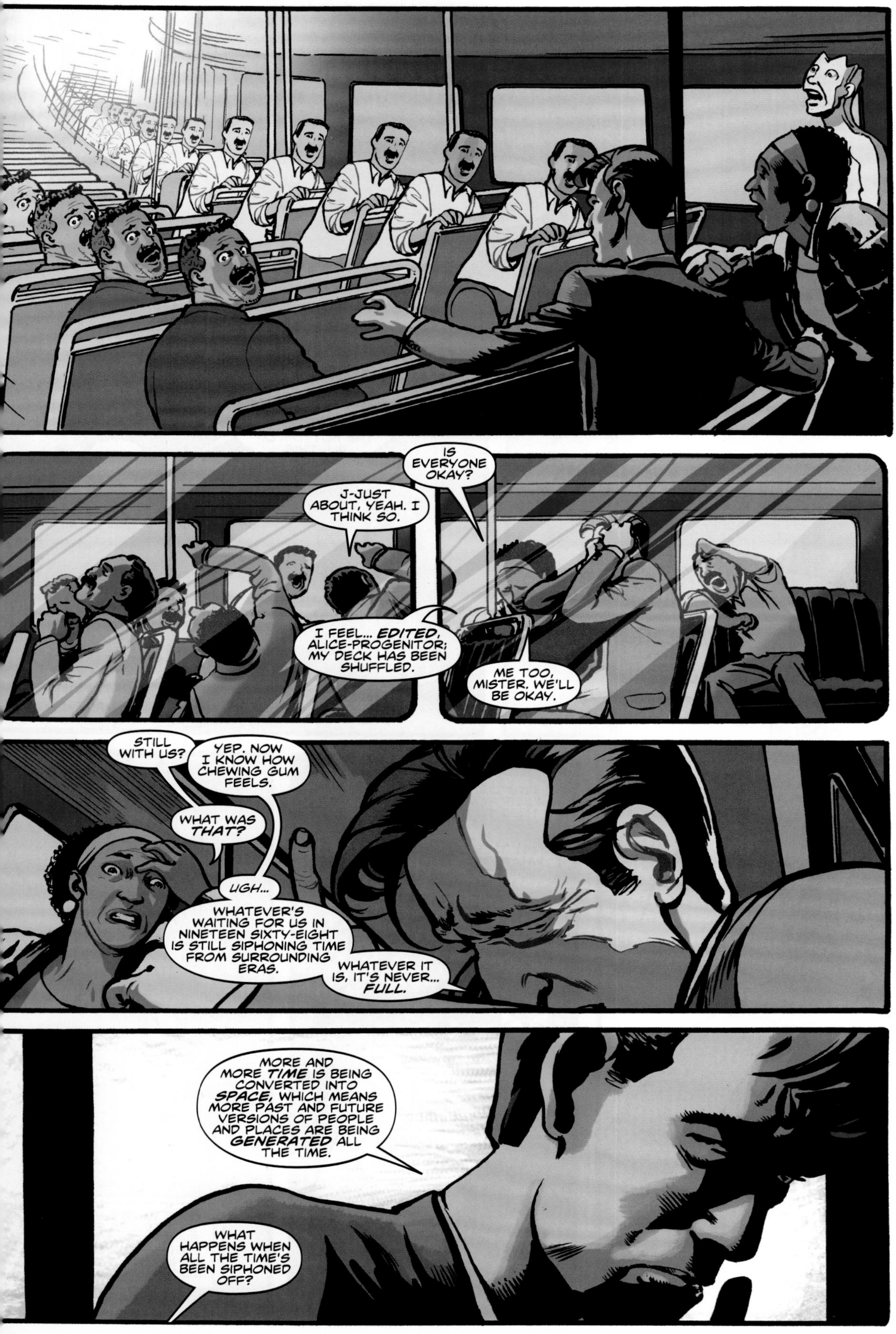

IS EVERYONE OKAY?
J-JUST ABOUT, YEAH. I THINK SO.
I FEEL... EDITED, ALICE-PROGENITOR; MY DECK HAS BEEN SHUFFLED.
ME TOO, MISTER. WE'LL BE OKAY.
STILL WITH US?
YEP. NOW I KNOW HOW CHEWING GUM FEELS.
WHAT WAS THAT?
UGH...
WHATEVER'S WAITING FOR US IN NINETEEN SIXTY-EIGHT IS STILL SIPHONING TIME FROM SURROUNDING ERAS.
WHATEVER IT IS, IT'S NEVER... FULL.
MORE AND MORE TIME IS BEING CONVERTED INTO SPACE, WHICH MEANS MORE PAST AND FUTURE VERSIONS OF PEOPLE AND PLACES ARE BEING GENERATED ALL THE TIME.
WHAT HAPPENS WHEN ALL THE TIME'S BEEN SIPHONED OFF?

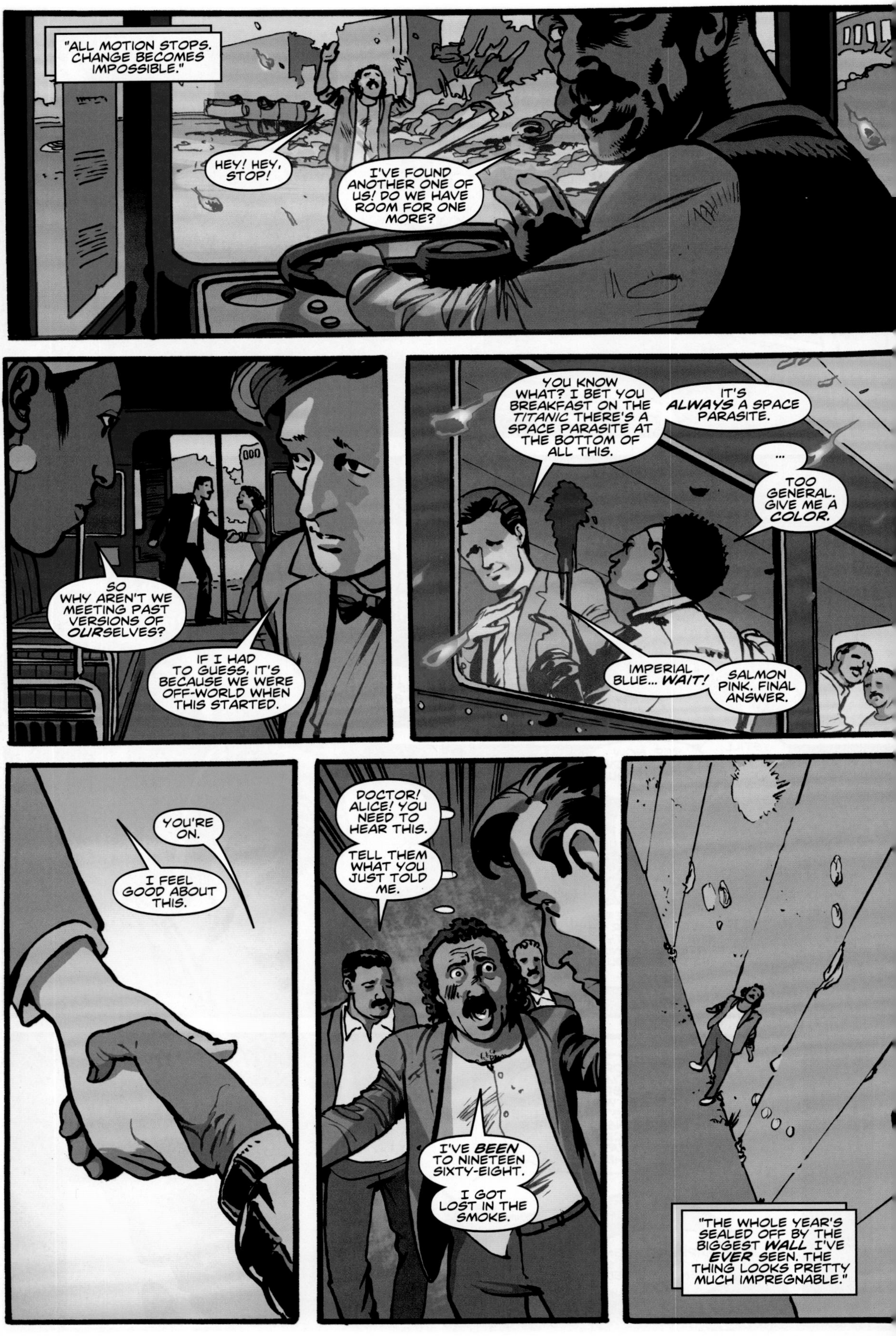
"ALL MOTION STOPS. CHANGE BECOMES IMPOSSIBLE."
HEY! HEY, STOP!
I'VE FOUND ANOTHER ONE OF US! DO WE HAVE ROOM FOR ONE MORE?
SO WHY AREN'T WE MEETING PAST VERSIONS OF *OURSELVES*?
IF I HAD TO GUESS, IT'S BECAUSE WE WERE OFF-WORLD WHEN THIS STARTED.
YOU KNOW WHAT? I BET YOU BREAKFAST ON THE *TITANIC* THERE'S A SPACE PARASITE AT THE BOTTOM OF ALL THIS.
IT'S *ALWAYS* A SPACE PARASITE.
...
TOO GENERAL. GIVE ME A *COLOR*.
IMPERIAL BLUE... *WAIT!*
SALMON PINK. FINAL ANSWER.
YOU'RE ON.
I FEEL GOOD ABOUT THIS.
DOCTOR! ALICE! YOU NEED TO HEAR THIS.
TELL THEM WHAT YOU JUST TOLD ME.
I'VE *BEEN* TO NINETEEN SIXTY-EIGHT.
I GOT LOST IN THE SMOKE.
"THE WHOLE YEAR'S SEALED OFF BY THE BIGGEST *WALL* I'VE *EVER* SEEN. THE THING LOOKS PRETTY MUCH IMPREGNABLE."

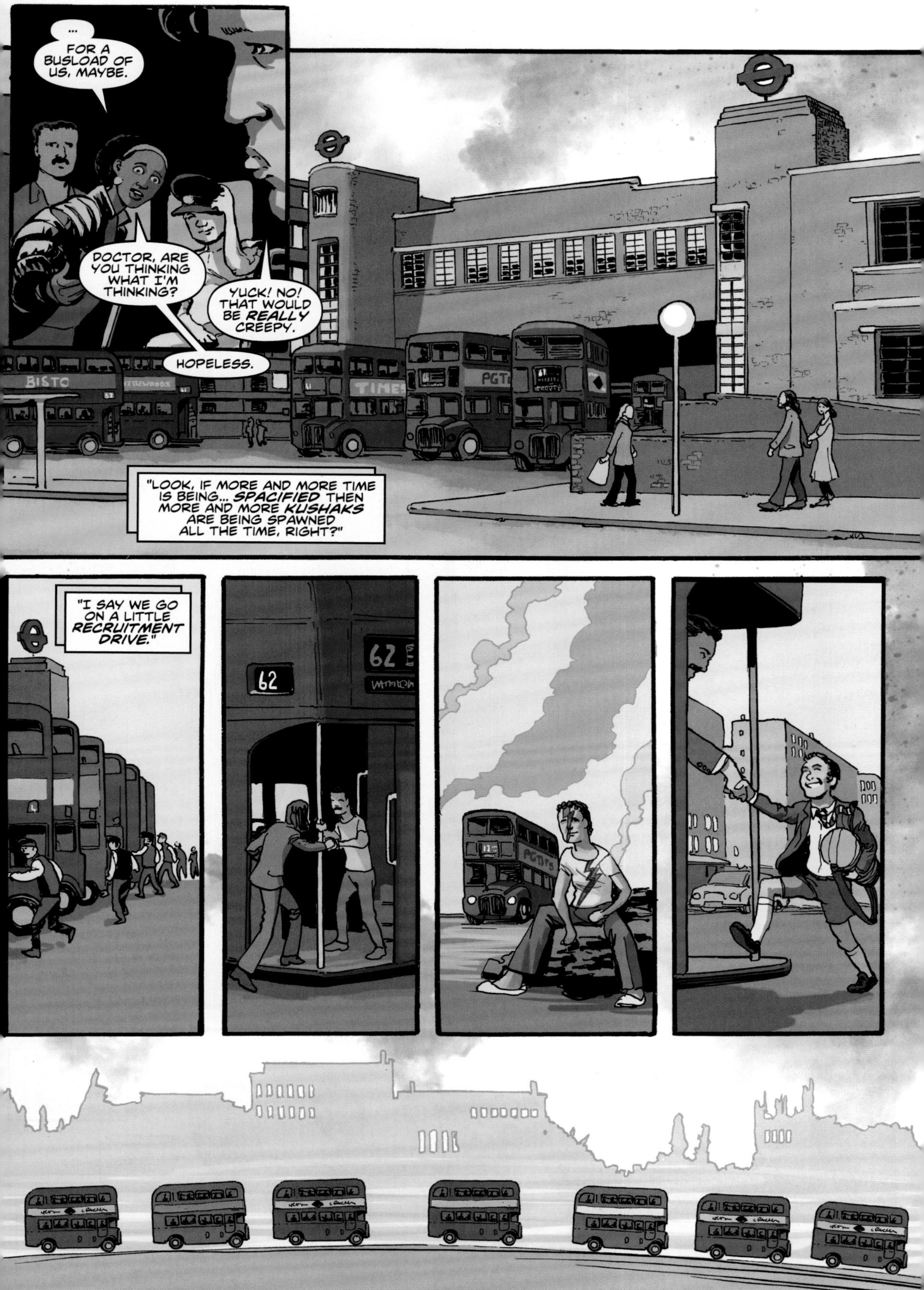
... FOR A BUSLOAD OF US, MAYBE.
DOCTOR, ARE YOU THINKING WHAT I'M THINKING?
YUCK! NO! THAT WOULD BE REALLY CREEPY.
HOPELESS.
BISTO
TIMES
"LOOK, IF MORE AND MORE TIME IS BEING... SPACIFIED THEN MORE AND MORE KUSHAKS ARE BEING SPAWNED ALL THE TIME, RIGHT?"
"I SAY WE GO ON A LITTLE RECRUITMENT DRIVE."
62
62

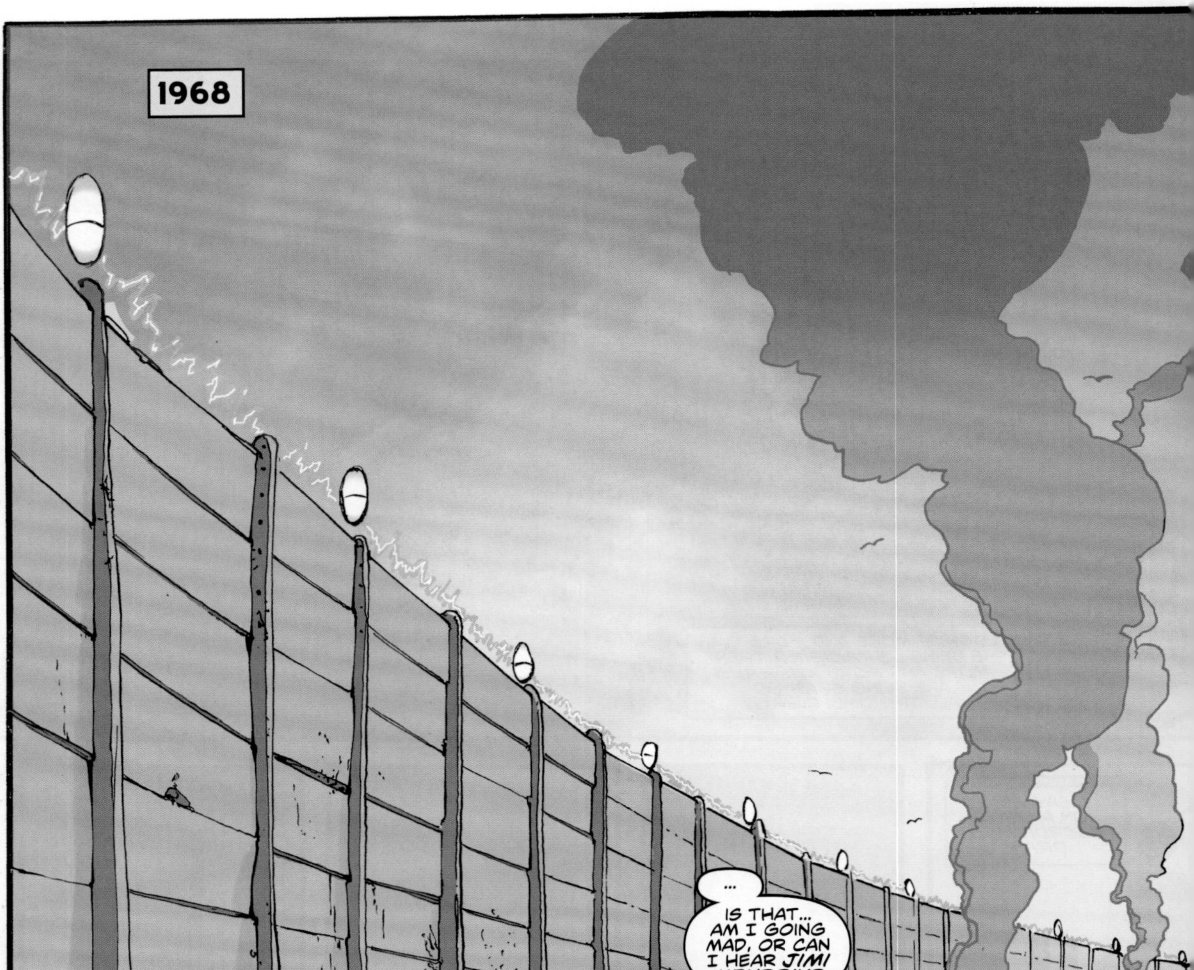
1968
...
IS THAT... AM I GOING MAD, OR CAN I HEAR *JIMI HENDRIX*?

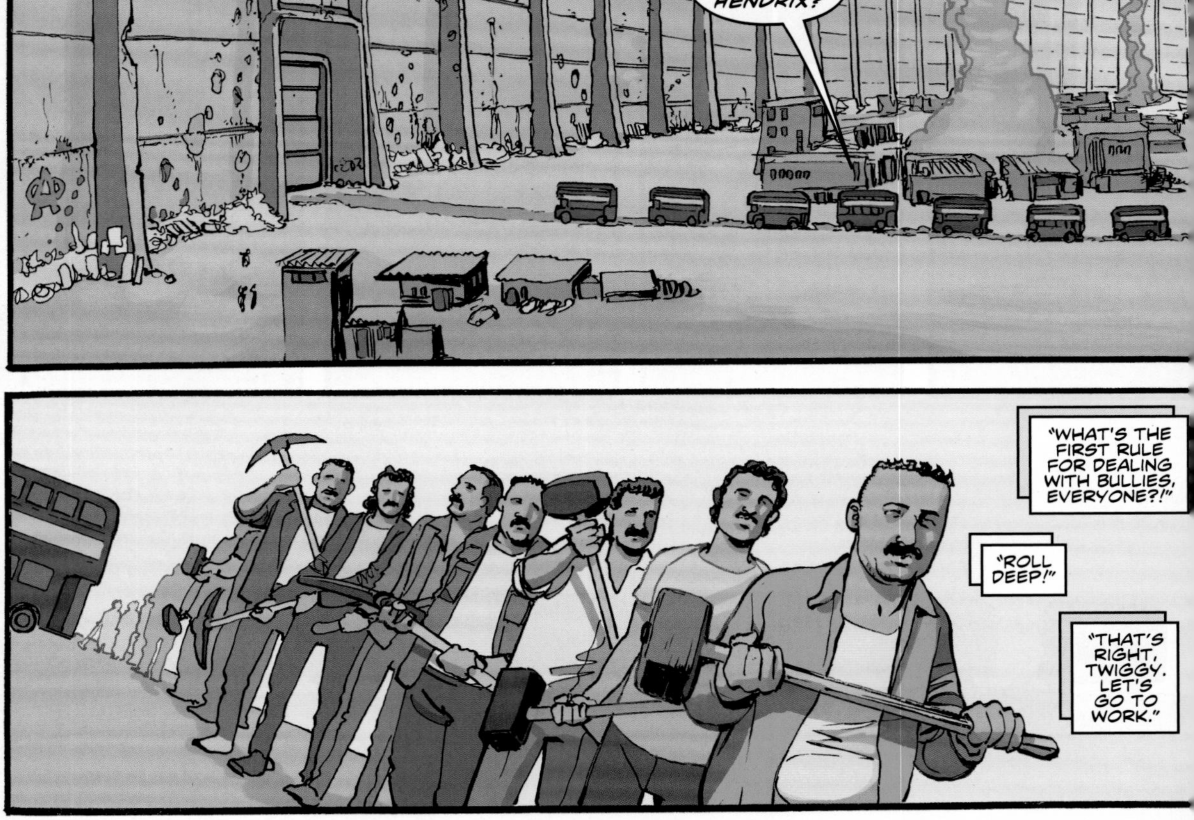
"WHAT'S THE FIRST RULE FOR DEALING WITH BULLIES, EVERYONE?!"
"ROLL DEEP!"
"THAT'S RIGHT, TWIGGY. LET'S GO TO WORK."

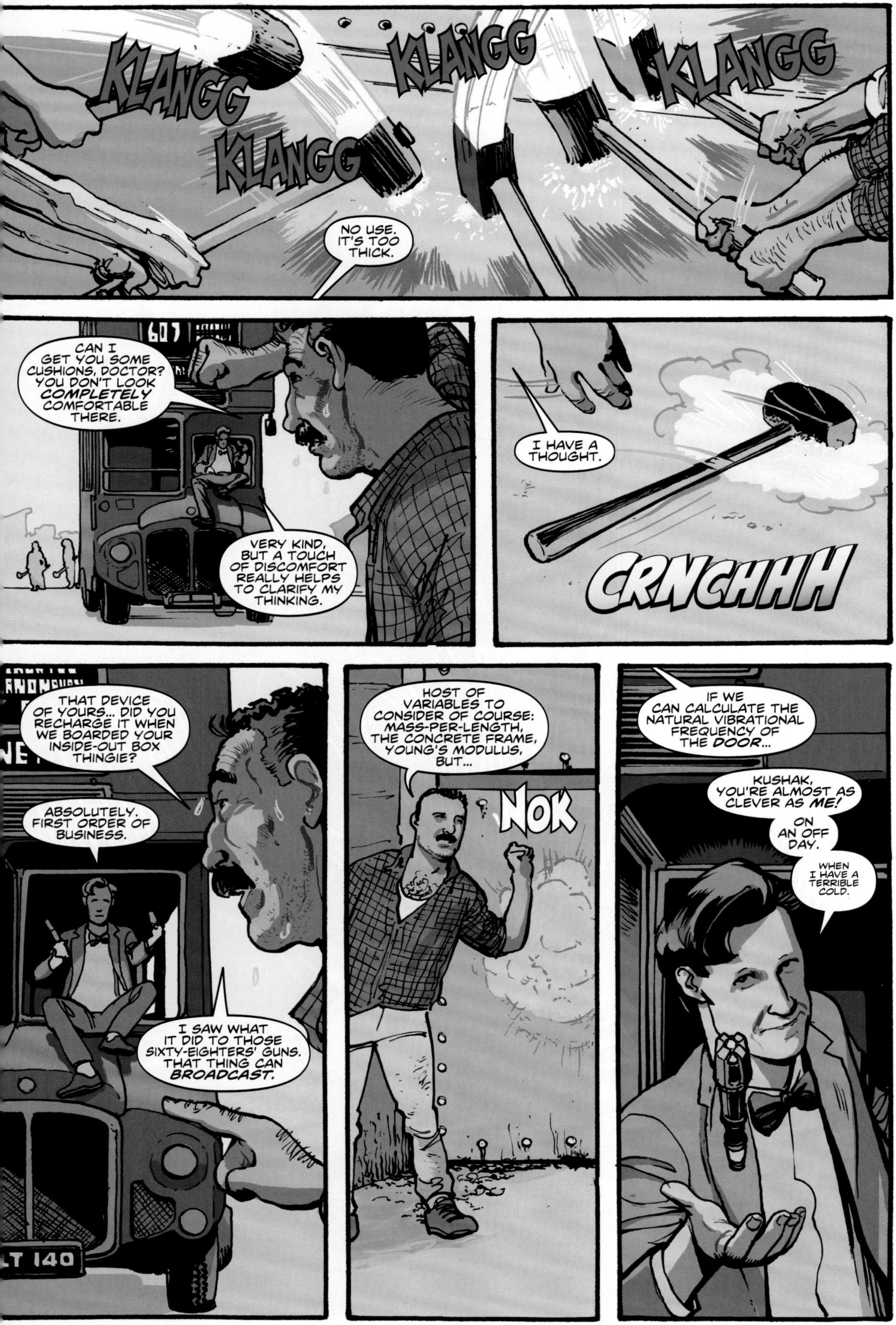
KLANGG
KLANGG
KLANGG
KLANGG
NO USE. IT'S TOO THICK.
607
CAN I GET YOU SOME CUSHIONS, DOCTOR? YOU DON'T LOOK *COMPLETELY* COMFORTABLE THERE.
VERY KIND, BUT A TOUCH OF DISCOMFORT REALLY HELPS TO CLARIFY MY THINKING.
I HAVE A THOUGHT.
CRNCHHH
THAT DEVICE OF YOURS... DID YOU RECHARGE IT WHEN WE BOARDED YOUR INSIDE-OUT BOX THINGIE?
ABSOLUTELY. FIRST ORDER OF BUSINESS.
I SAW WHAT IT DID TO THOSE SIXTY-EIGHTERS' GUNS. THAT THING CAN *BROADCAST.*
LT 140
HOST OF VARIABLES TO CONSIDER OF COURSE: MASS-PER-LENGTH, THE CONCRETE FRAME, YOUNG'S MODULUS, BUT...
NOK
IF WE CAN CALCULATE THE NATURAL VIBRATIONAL FREQUENCY OF THE *DOOR*...
KUSHAK, YOU'RE ALMOST AS CLEVER AS *ME!*
ON AN OFF DAY.
WHEN I HAVE A TERRIBLE COLD.

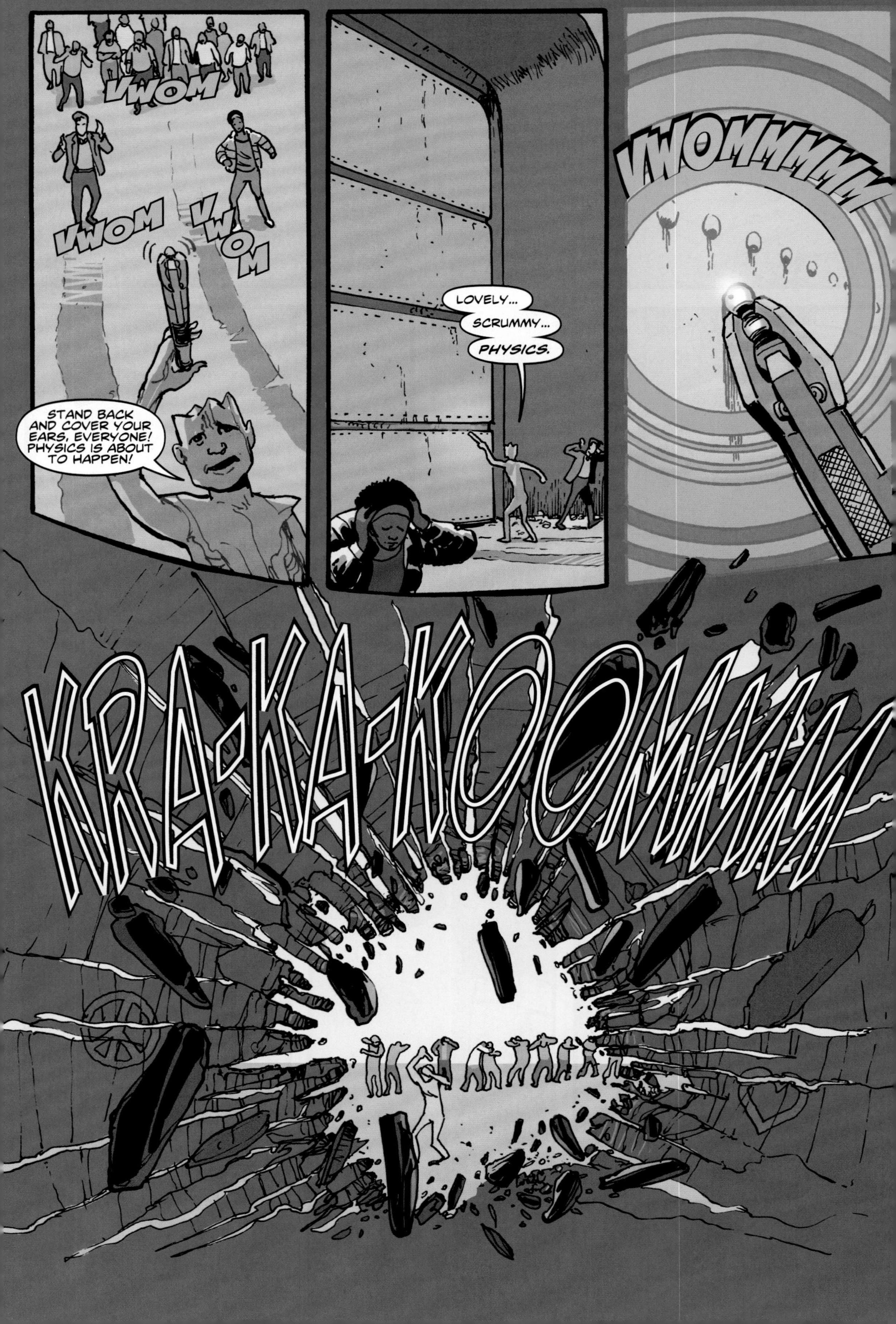
VWOM
VWOM
VWOM
STAND BACK AND COVER YOUR EARS, EVERYONE! PHYSICS IS ABOUT TO HAPPEN!
LOVELY...
SCRUMMY...
PHYSICS.
VWOMMMMM
KRA-KA-KOOMMMM

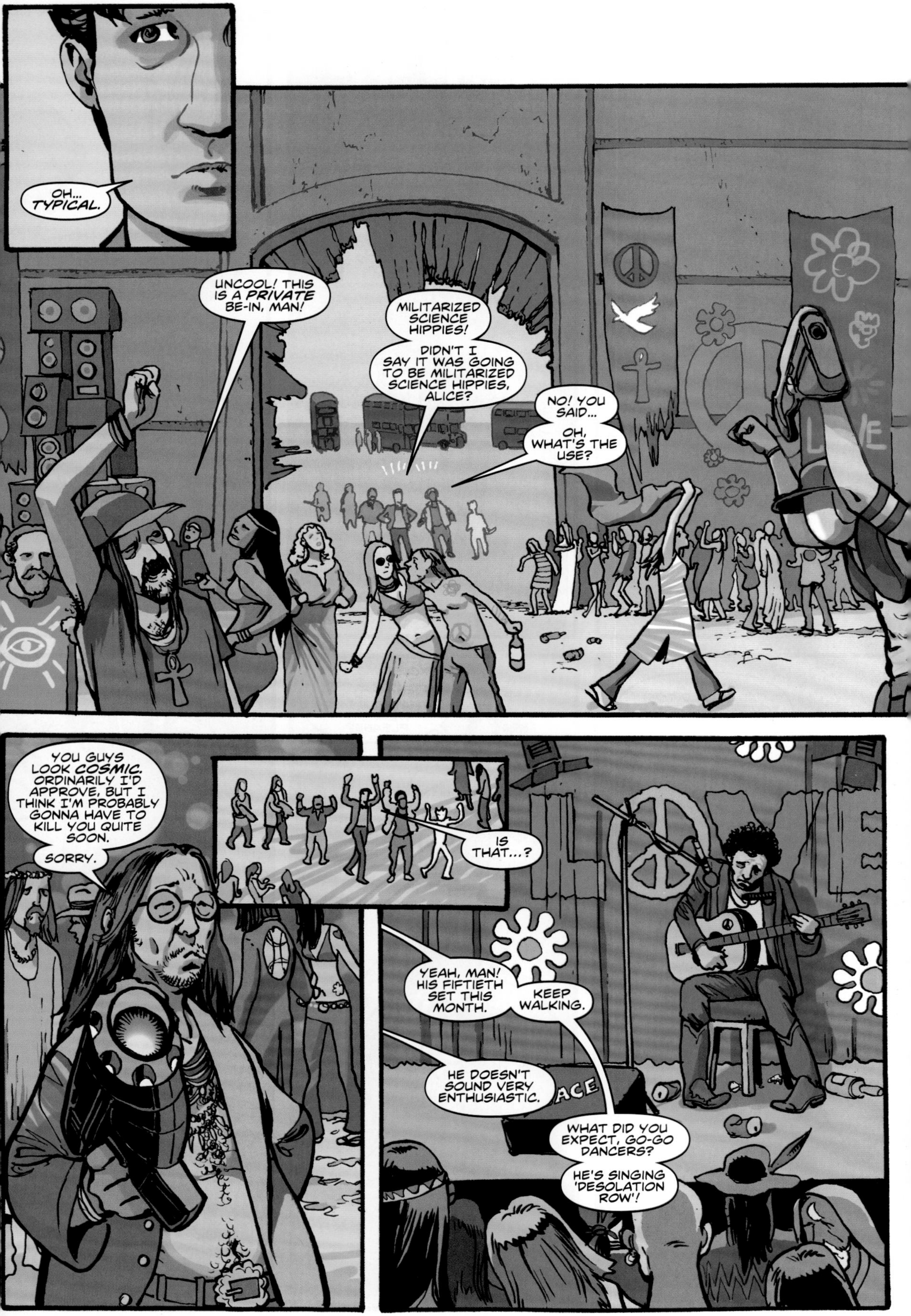
OH... TYPICAL.
UNCOOL! THIS IS A PRIVATE BE-IN, MAN!
MILITARIZED SCIENCE HIPPIES!
DIDN'T I SAY IT WAS GOING TO BE MILITARIZED SCIENCE HIPPIES, ALICE?
NO! YOU SAID...
OH, WHAT'S THE USE?
LOVE
YOU GUYS LOOK COSMIC. ORDINARILY I'D APPROVE, BUT I THINK I'M PROBABLY GONNA HAVE TO KILL YOU QUITE SOON.
SORRY.
IS THAT...?
YEAH, MAN! HIS FIFTIETH SET THIS MONTH.
KEEP WALKING.
HE DOESN'T SOUND VERY ENTHUSIASTIC.
ACE
WHAT DID YOU EXPECT, GO-GO DANCERS?
HE'S SINGING 'DESOLATION ROW'!

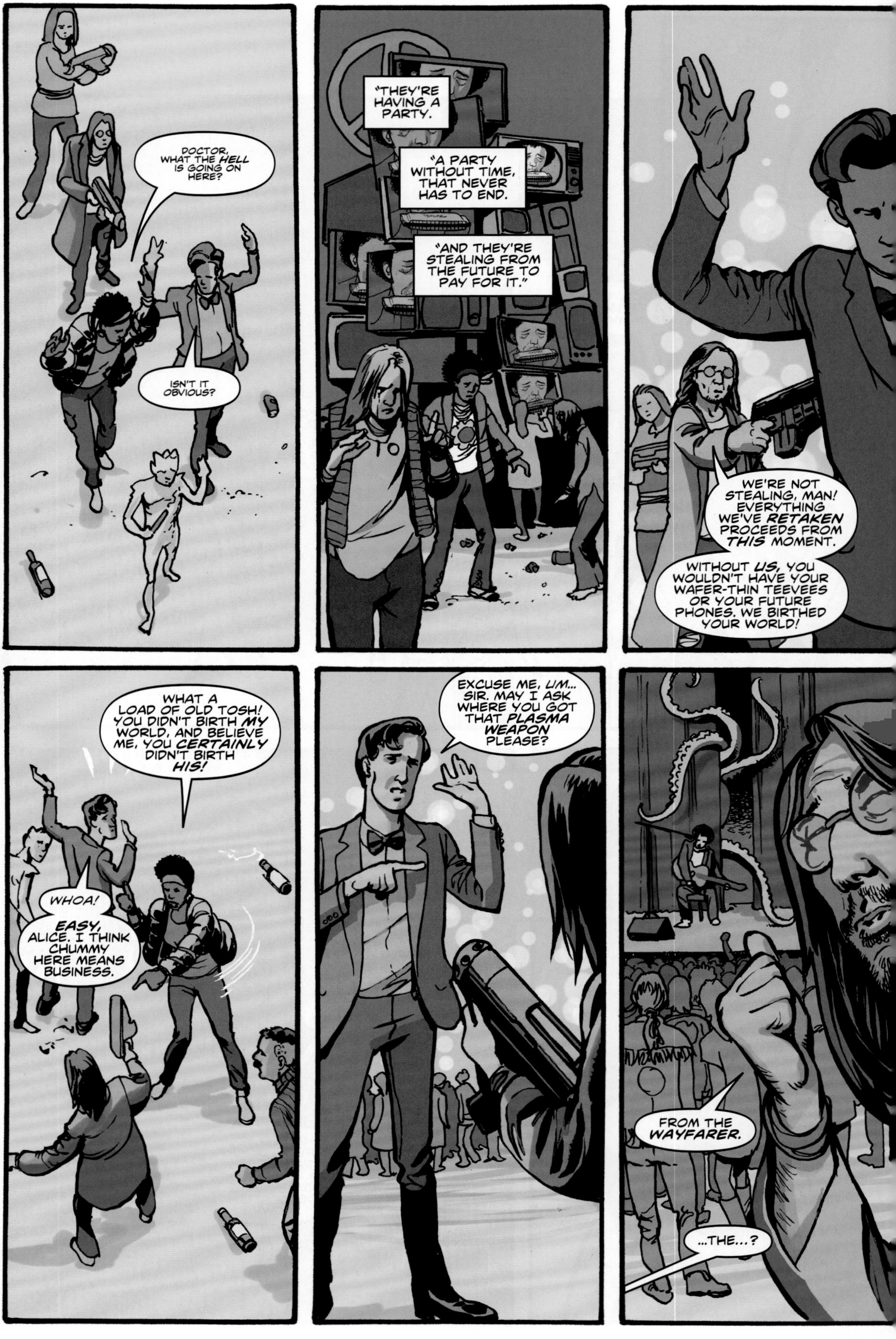
DOCTOR, WHAT THE *HELL* IS GOING ON HERE?
ISN'T IT OBVIOUS?
"THEY'RE HAVING A PARTY.
"A PARTY WITHOUT TIME, THAT NEVER HAS TO END.
"AND THEY'RE STEALING FROM THE FUTURE TO PAY FOR IT."
WE'RE NOT STEALING, MAN! EVERYTHING WE'VE ***RETAKEN*** PROCEEDS FROM ***THIS*** MOMENT.
WITHOUT ***US***, YOU WOULDN'T HAVE YOUR WAFER-THIN TEEVEES OR YOUR FUTURE PHONES. WE BIRTHED YOUR WORLD!
WHAT A LOAD OF OLD TOSH! YOU DIDN'T BIRTH ***MY*** WORLD, AND BELIEVE ME, YOU ***CERTAINLY*** DIDN'T BIRTH ***HIS***!
WHOA!
EASY, ALICE. I THINK CHUMMY HERE MEANS BUSINESS.
EXCUSE ME, *UM*... SIR. MAY I ASK WHERE YOU GOT THAT ***PLASMA WEAPON*** PLEASE?
FROM THE ***WAYFARER***.
...THE...?

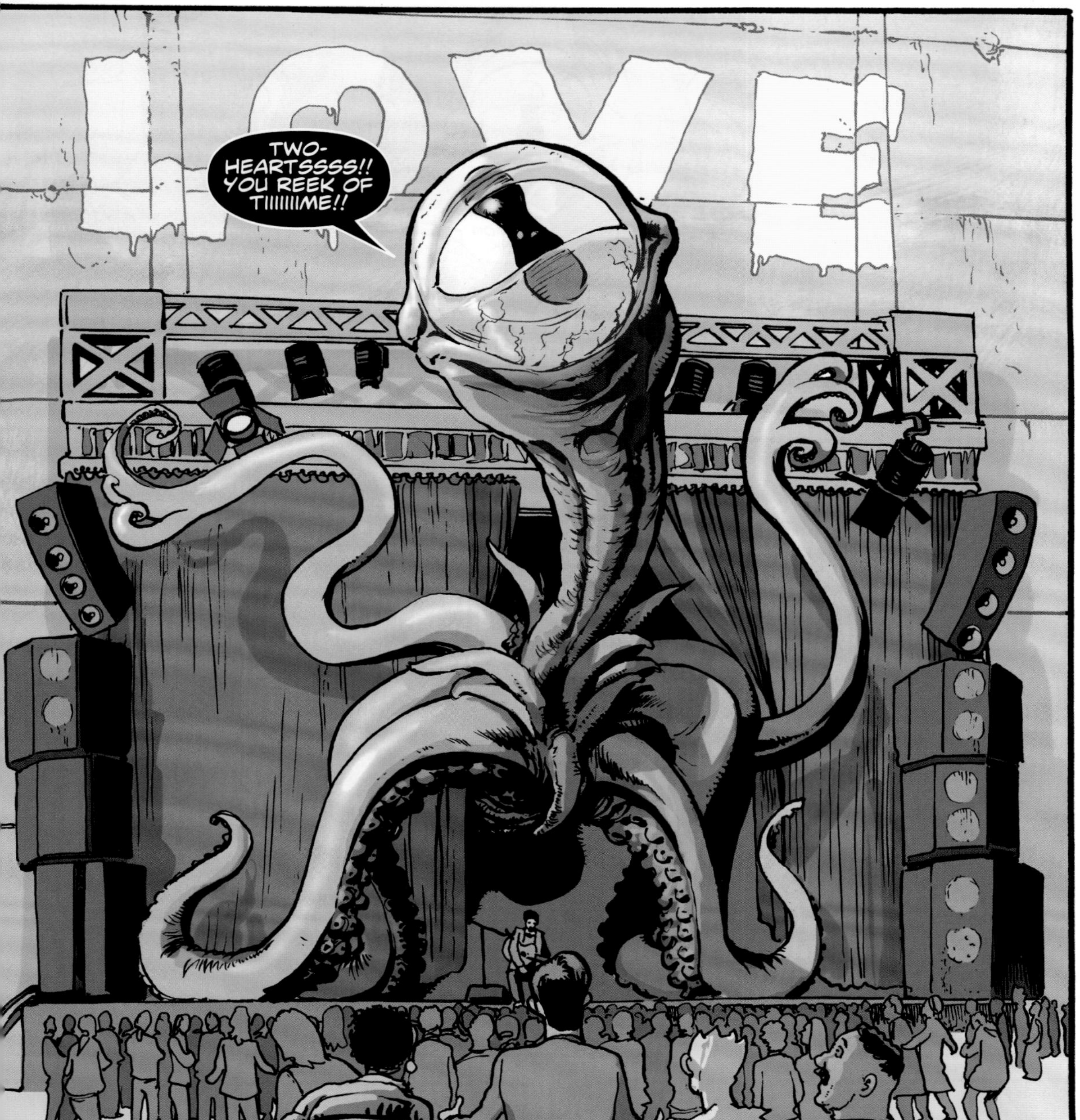
TWO-HEARTSSSS!! YOU REEK OF TIIIIIIME!!

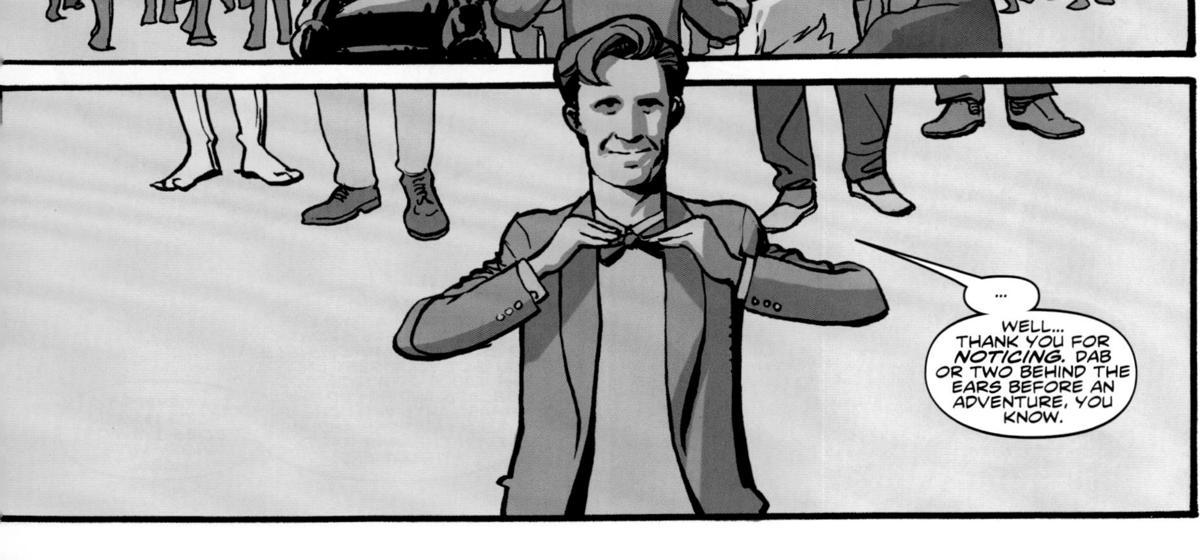
...
WELL... THANK YOU FOR *NOTICING.* DAB OR TWO BEHIND THE EARS BEFORE AN ADVENTURE, YOU KNOW.

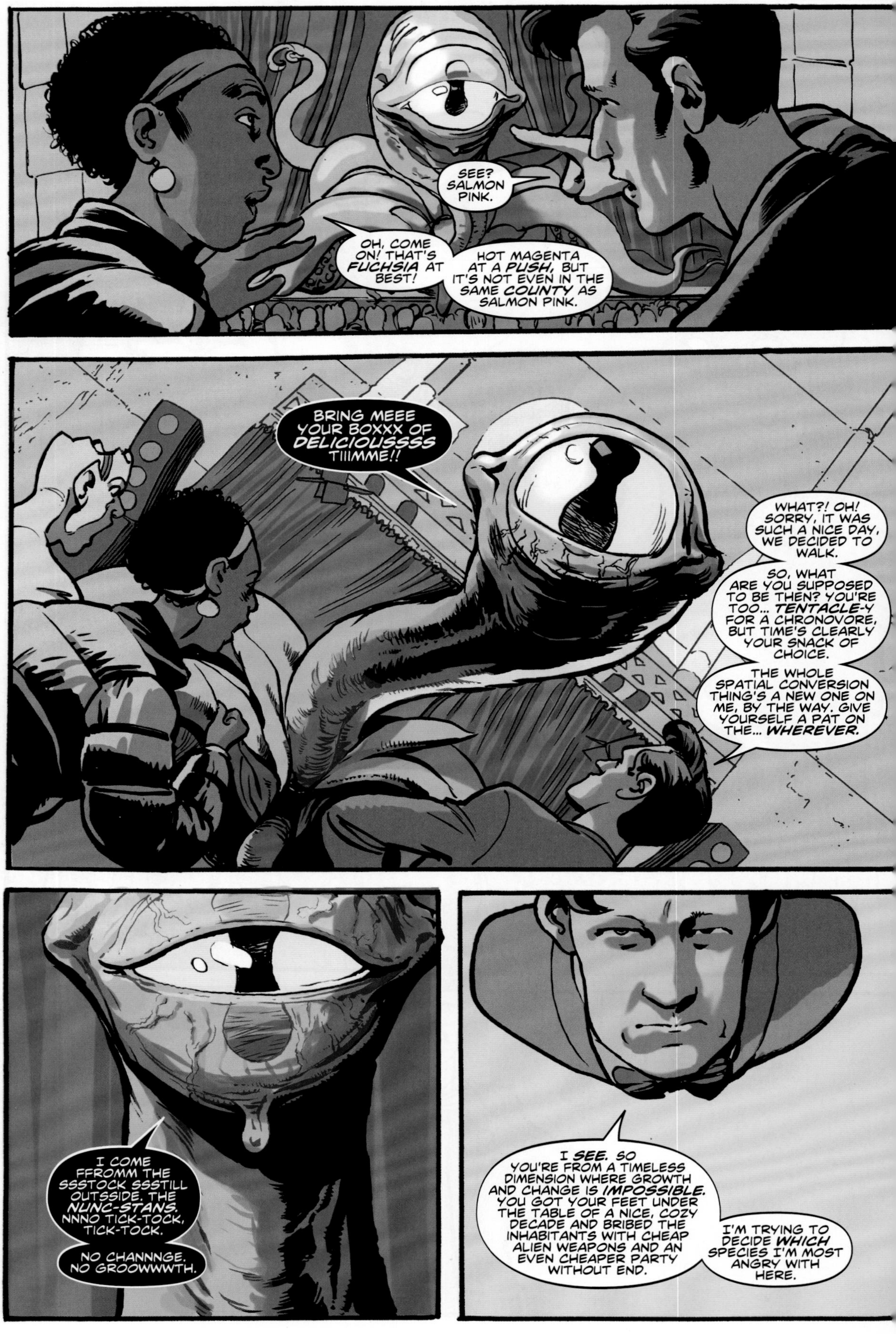
SEE? SALMON PINK.
OH, COME ON! THAT'S FUCHSIA AT BEST!
HOT MAGENTA AT A PUSH, BUT IT'S NOT EVEN IN THE SAME COUNTY AS SALMON PINK.
BRING MEEE YOUR BOXXX OF DELICIOUSSSS TIIIMME!!
WHAT?! OH! SORRY, IT WAS SUCH A NICE DAY, WE DECIDED TO WALK.
SO, WHAT ARE YOU SUPPOSED TO BE THEN? YOU'RE TOO... TENTACLE-Y FOR A CHRONOVORE, BUT TIME'S CLEARLY YOUR SNACK OF CHOICE.
THE WHOLE SPATIAL CONVERSION THING'S A NEW ONE ON ME, BY THE WAY. GIVE YOURSELF A PAT ON THE... WHEREVER.
I COME FFROMM THE SSSTOCK SSSTILL OUTSSIDE. THE NUNC-STANS. NNNO TICK-TOCK, TICK-TOCK.
NO CHANNNGE. NO GROOWWWTH.
I SEE. SO YOU'RE FROM A TIMELESS DIMENSION WHERE GROWTH AND CHANGE IS IMPOSSIBLE. YOU GOT YOUR FEET UNDER THE TABLE OF A NICE, COZY DECADE AND BRIBED THE INHABITANTS WITH CHEAP ALIEN WEAPONS AND AN EVEN CHEAPER PARTY WITHOUT END.
I'M TRYING TO DECIDE WHICH SPECIES I'M MOST ANGRY WITH HERE.

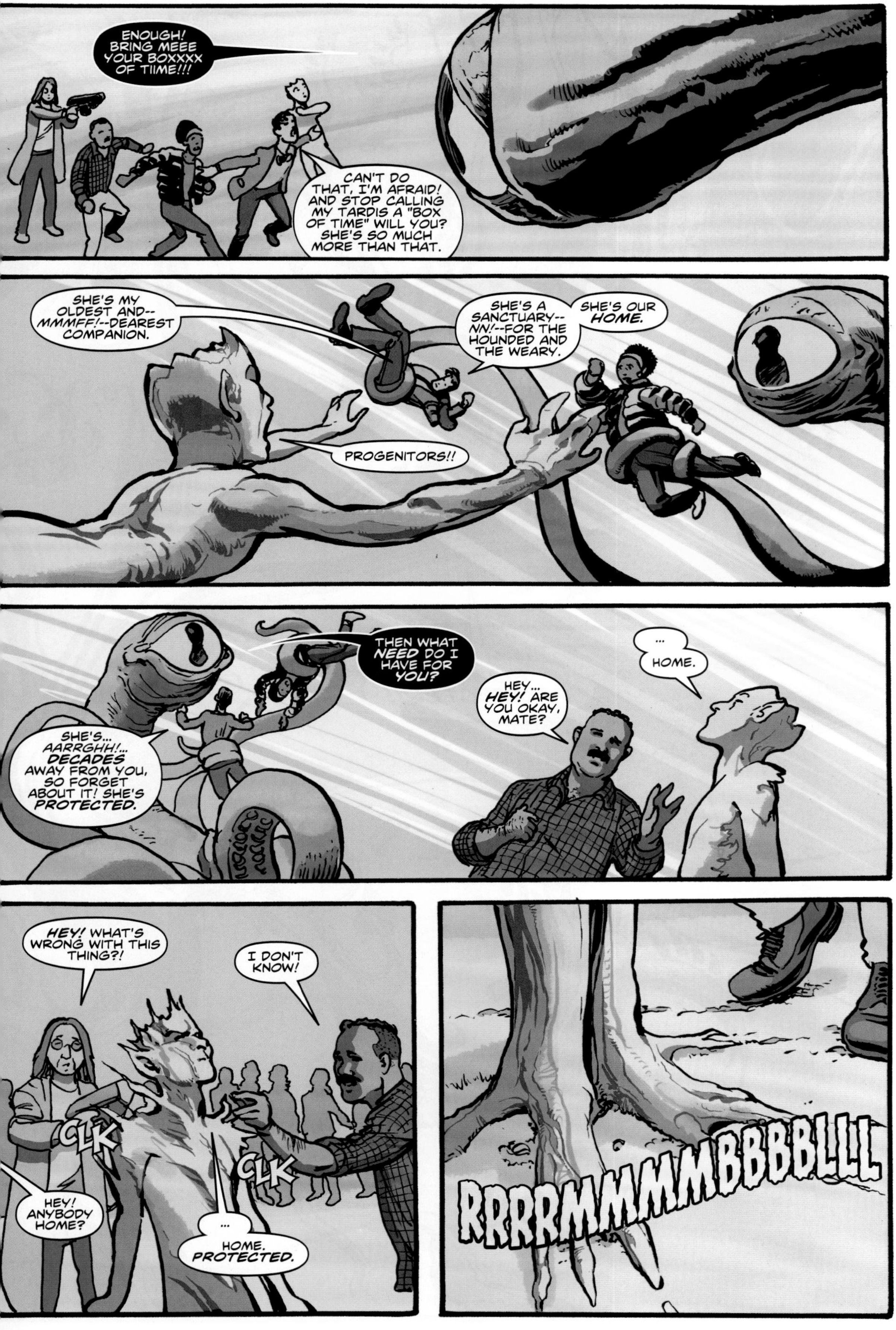

ENOUGH! BRING MEEE YOUR BOXXXX OF TIIME!!!
CAN'T DO THAT, I'M AFRAID! AND STOP CALLING MY TARDIS A "BOX OF TIME" WILL YOU? SHE'S SO MUCH MORE THAN THAT.
SHE'S MY OLDEST AND-- MMMFF!--DEAREST COMPANION.
SHE'S A SANCTUARY-- NN!--FOR THE HOUNDED AND THE WEARY.
SHE'S OUR HOME.
PROGENITORS!!
THEN WHAT NEED DO I HAVE FOR YOU?
SHE'S... AARRGHH!... DECADES AWAY FROM YOU, SO FORGET ABOUT IT! SHE'S PROTECTED.
HEY... HEY! ARE YOU OKAY, MATE?
... HOME.
HEY! WHAT'S WRONG WITH THIS THING?!
I DON'T KNOW!
CLK
CLK
HEY! ANYBODY HOME?
... HOME. PROTECTED.
RRRRMMMMMBBBBLLL

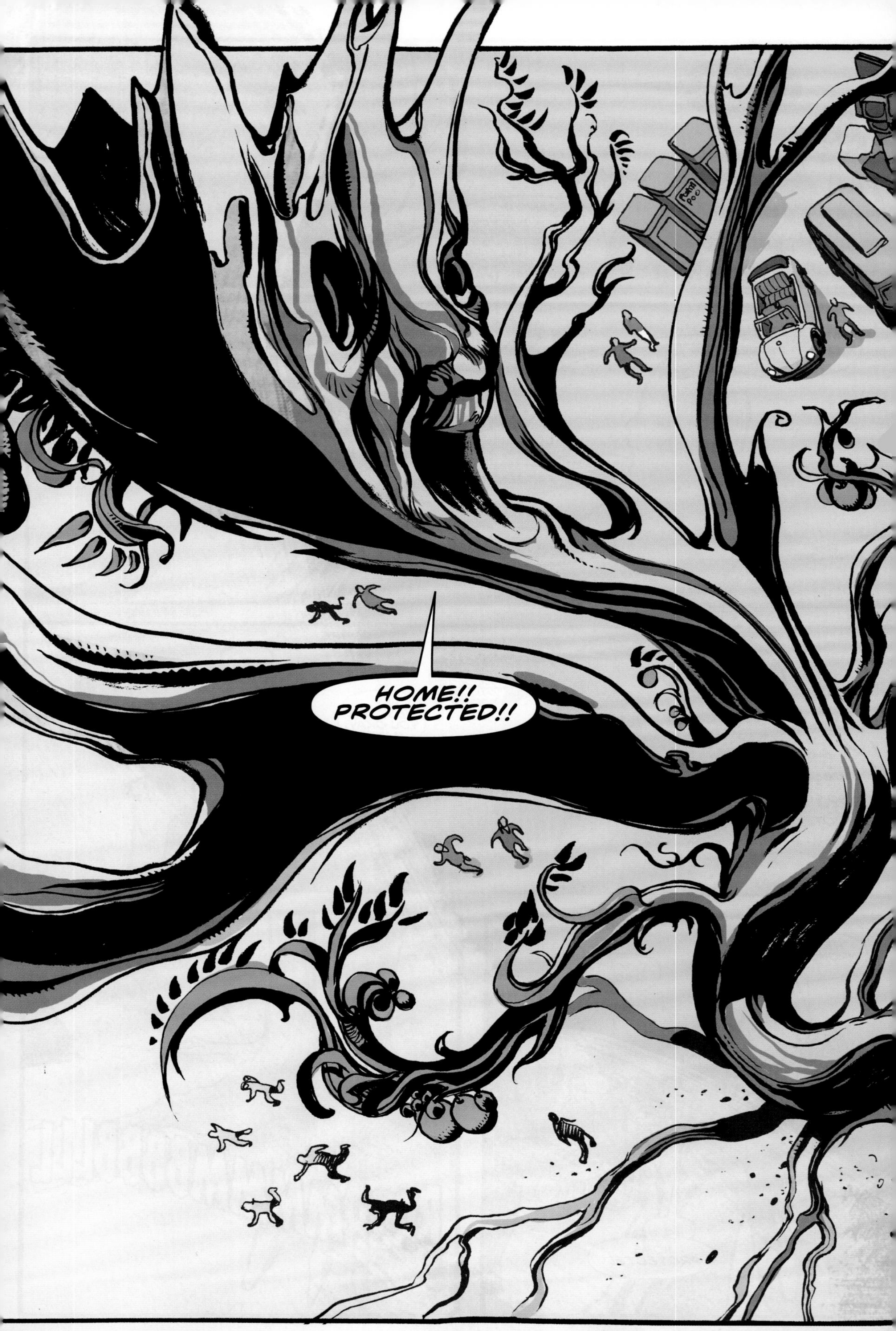
HOME!! PROTECTED!!

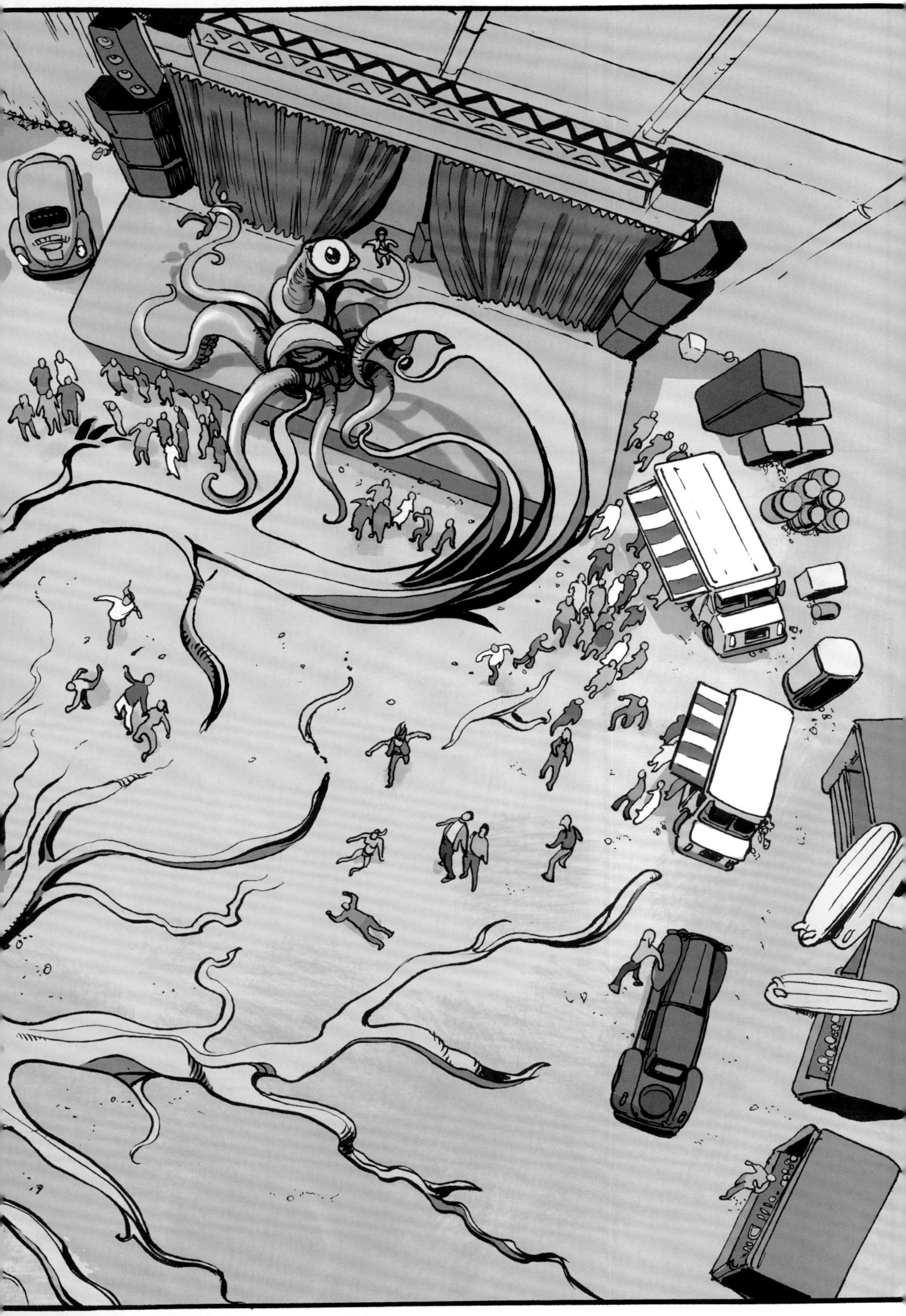

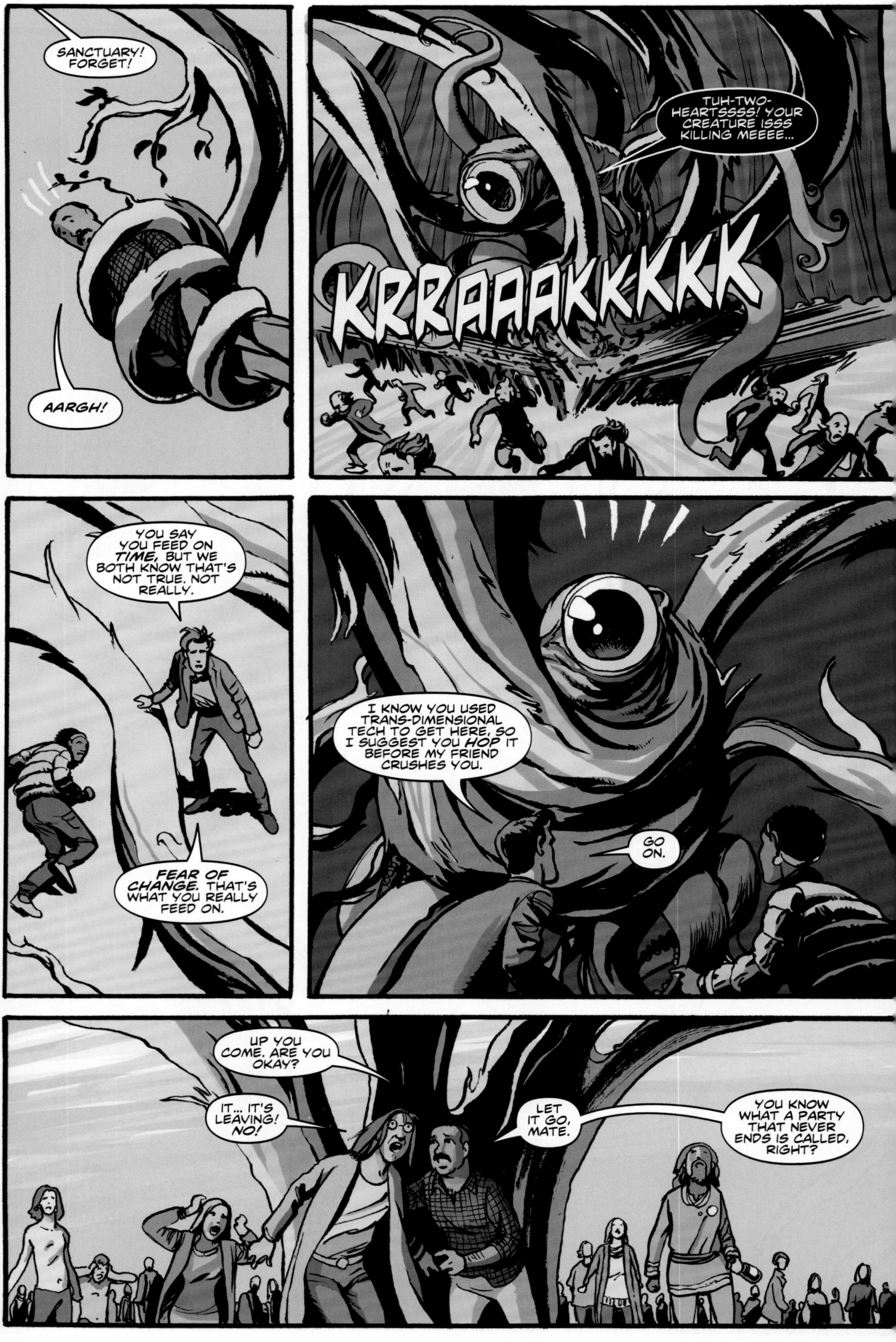
SANCTUARY! FORGET!
AARGH!
TUH-TWO-HEARTSSSS! YOUR CREATURE ISSS KILLING MEEEE...
KRRAAAKKKKK
YOU SAY YOU FEED ON TIME, BUT WE BOTH KNOW THAT'S NOT TRUE. NOT REALLY.
FEAR OF CHANGE. THAT'S WHAT YOU REALLY FEED ON.
I KNOW YOU USED TRANS-DIMENSIONAL TECH TO GET HERE, SO I SUGGEST YOU HOP IT BEFORE MY FRIEND CRUSHES YOU.
GO ON.
UP YOU COME. ARE YOU OKAY?
IT... IT'S LEAVING! NO!
LET IT GO, MATE.
YOU KNOW WHAT A PARTY THAT NEVER ENDS IS CALLED, RIGHT?

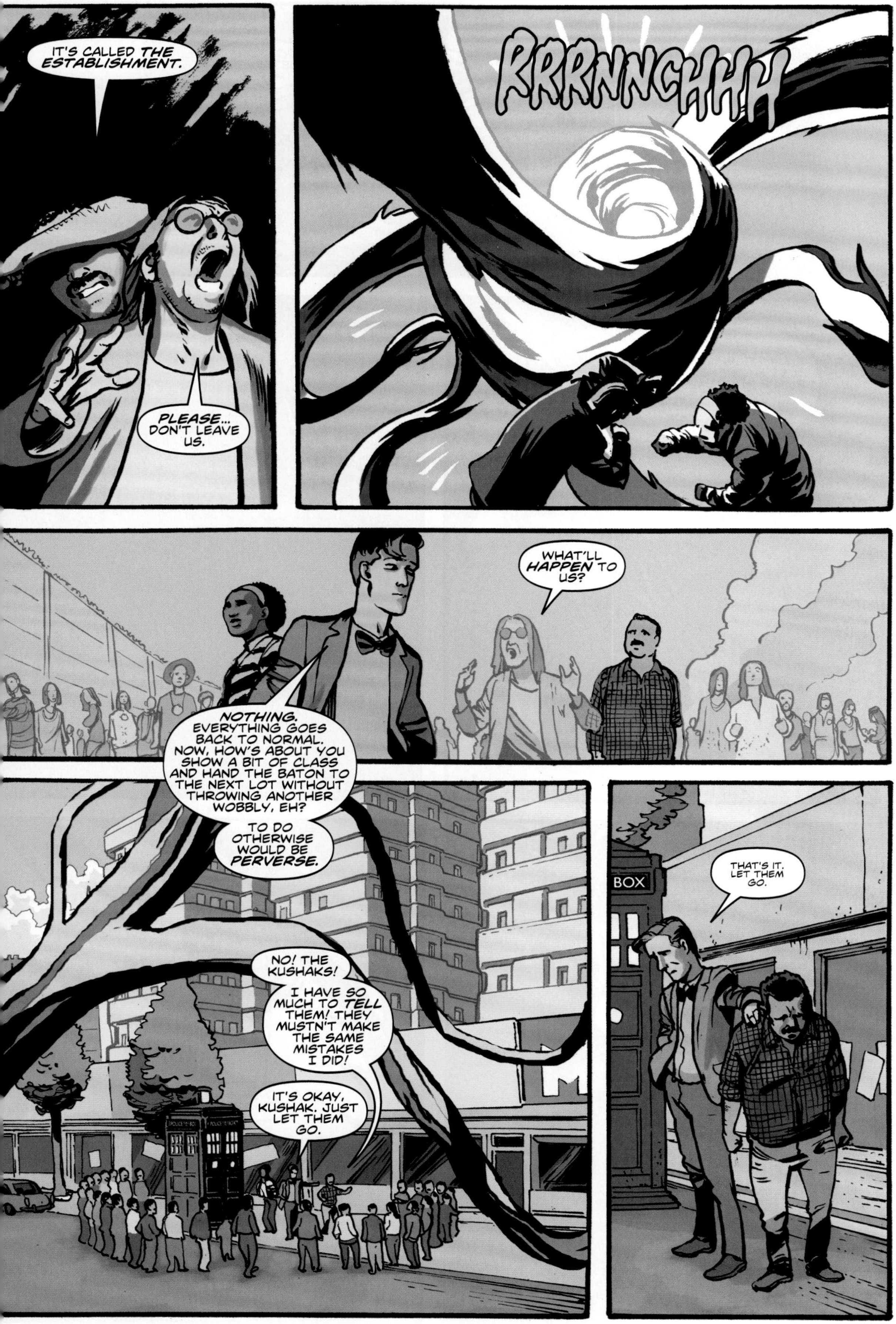
IT'S CALLED *THE ESTABLISHMENT.*
PLEASE... DON'T LEAVE US.
RRRNNCHHH
WHAT'LL *HAPPEN* TO US?
NOTHING. EVERYTHING GOES BACK TO NORMAL. NOW, HOW'S ABOUT YOU SHOW A BIT OF CLASS AND HAND THE BATON TO THE NEXT LOT WITHOUT THROWING ANOTHER WOBBLY, EH?
TO DO OTHERWISE WOULD BE *PERVERSE.*
NO! THE KUSHAKS!
I HAVE SO MUCH TO *TELL* THEM! THEY MUSTN'T MAKE THE SAME MISTAKES I DID!
IT'S OKAY, KUSHAK. JUST LET THEM GO.
BOX
THAT'S IT. LET THEM GO.

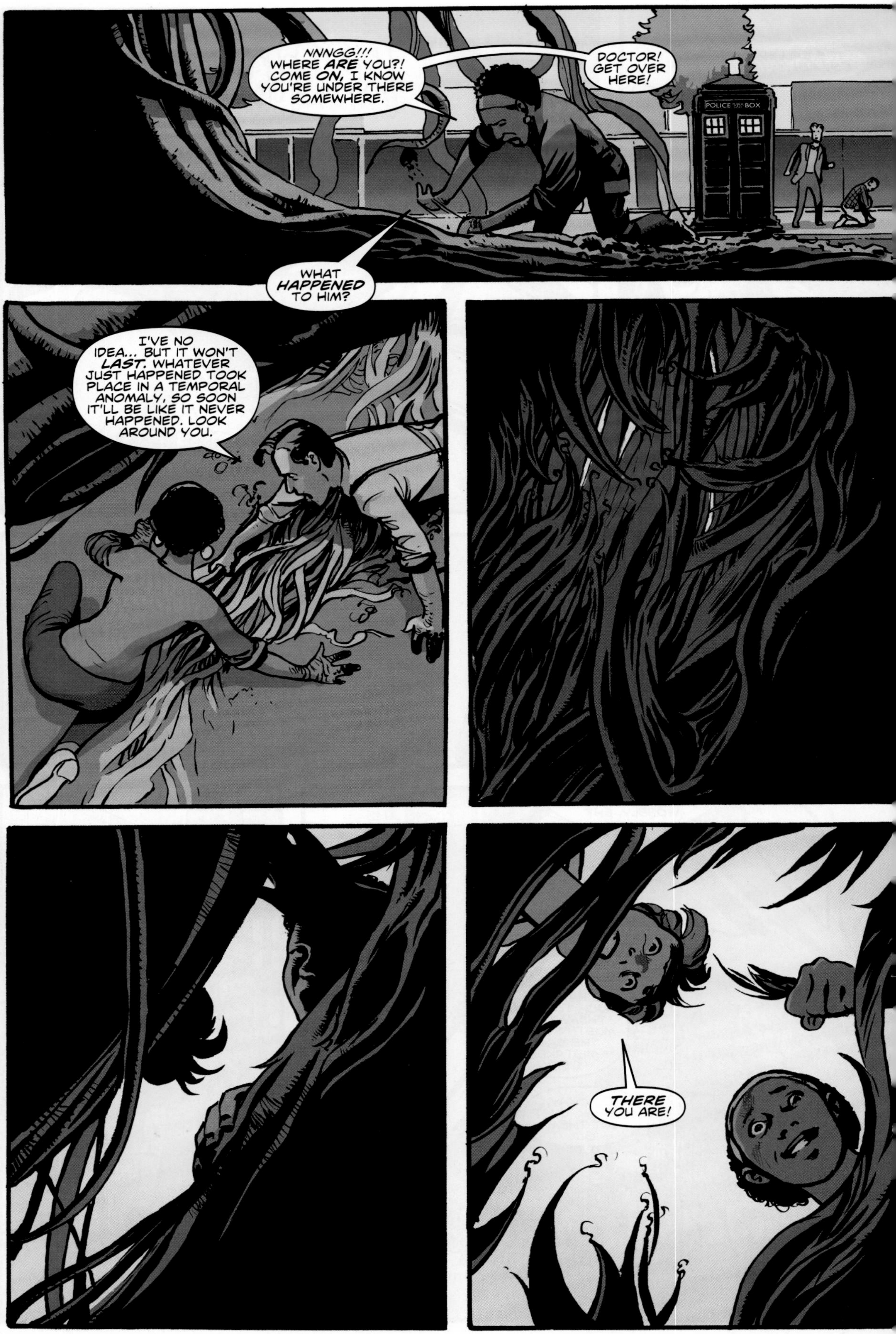
NNNGG!!! WHERE ARE YOU?! COME ON, I KNOW YOU'RE UNDER THERE SOMEWHERE.
DOCTOR! GET OVER HERE!
POLICE BOX
WHAT HAPPENED TO HIM?
I'VE NO IDEA... BUT IT WON'T LAST. WHATEVER JUST HAPPENED TOOK PLACE IN A TEMPORAL ANOMALY, SO SOON IT'LL BE LIKE IT NEVER HAPPENED. LOOK AROUND YOU.
THERE YOU ARE!

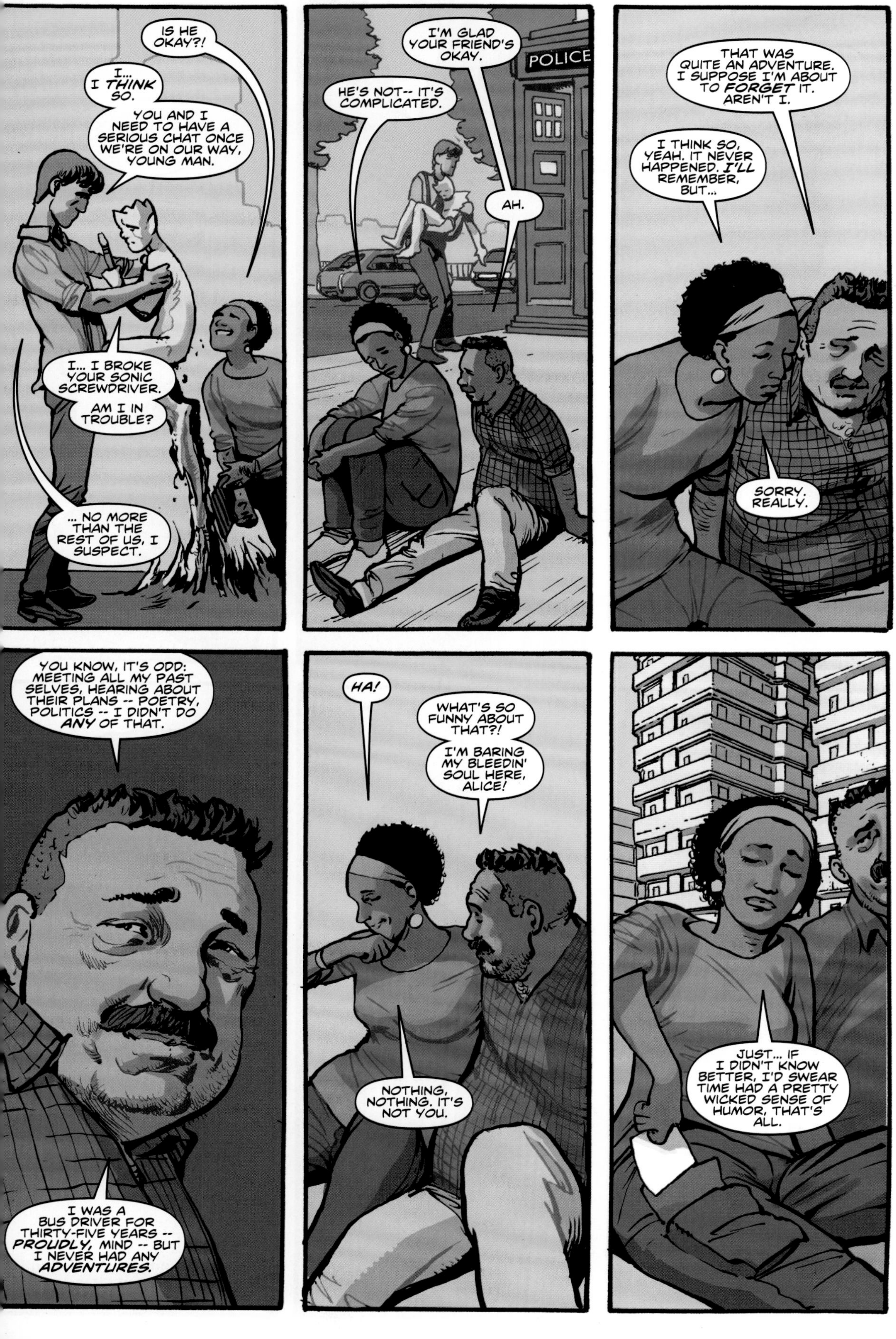
IS HE OKAY?!
I... I THINK SO.
YOU AND I NEED TO HAVE A SERIOUS CHAT ONCE WE'RE ON OUR WAY, YOUNG MAN.
I... I BROKE YOUR SONIC SCREWDRIVER.
AM I IN TROUBLE?
... NO MORE THAN THE REST OF US, I SUSPECT.
I'M GLAD YOUR FRIEND'S OKAY.
HE'S NOT-- IT'S COMPLICATED.
AH.
POLICE
THAT WAS QUITE AN ADVENTURE. I SUPPOSE I'M ABOUT TO FORGET IT. AREN'T I.
I THINK SO, YEAH. IT NEVER HAPPENED. I'LL REMEMBER, BUT...
SORRY. REALLY.
YOU KNOW, IT'S ODD: MEETING ALL MY PAST SELVES, HEARING ABOUT THEIR PLANS -- POETRY, POLITICS -- I DIDN'T DO ANY OF THAT.
I WAS A BUS DRIVER FOR THIRTY-FIVE YEARS -- PROUDLY, MIND -- BUT I NEVER HAD ANY ADVENTURES.
HA!
WHAT'S SO FUNNY ABOUT THAT?!
I'M BARING MY BLEEDIN' SOUL HERE, ALICE!
NOTHING, NOTHING. IT'S NOT YOU.
JUST... IF I DIDN'T KNOW BETTER, I'D SWEAR TIME HAD A PRETTY WICKED SENSE OF HUMOR, THAT'S ALL.

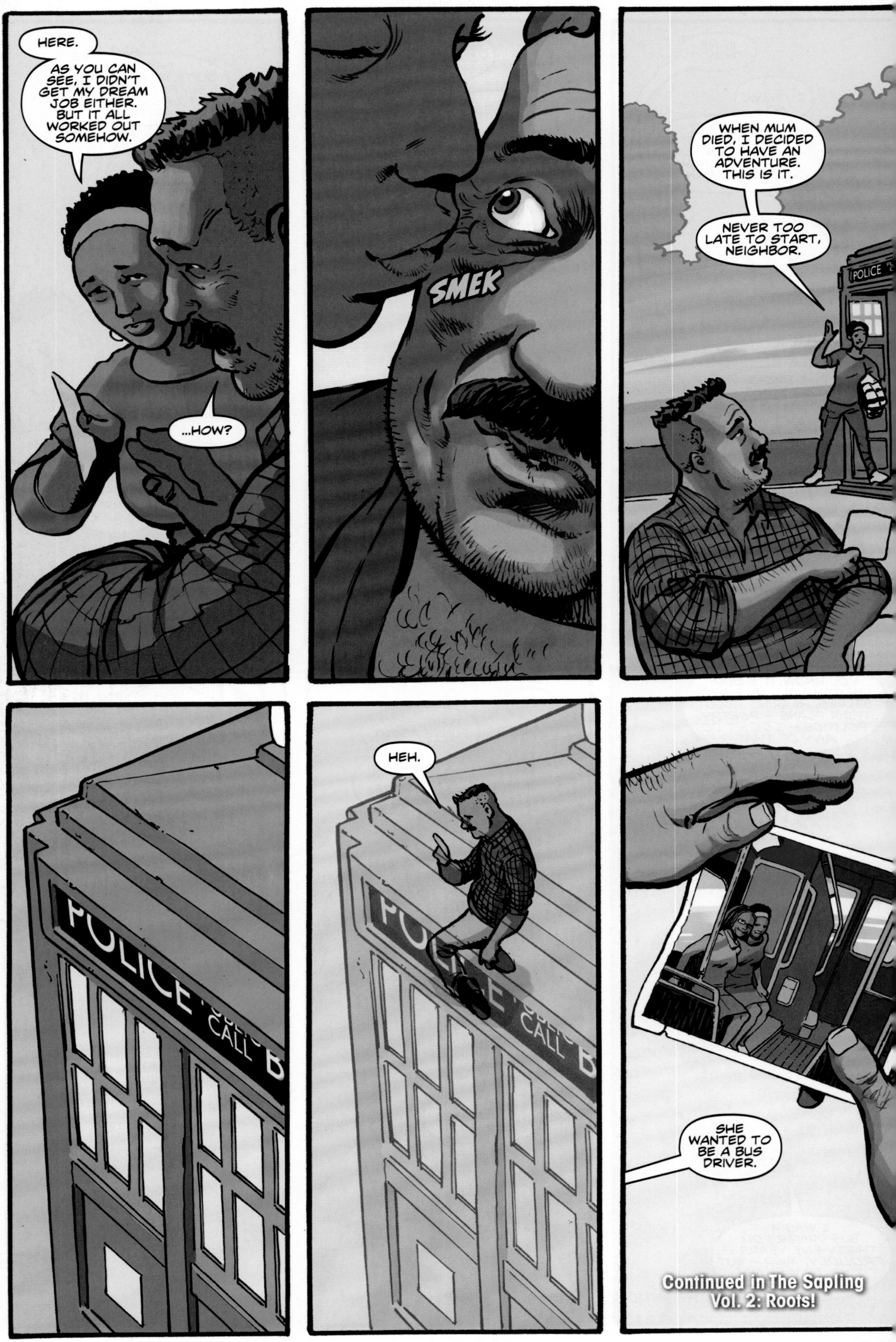
HERE.
AS YOU CAN SEE, I DIDN'T GET MY DREAM JOB EITHER. BUT IT ALL WORKED OUT SOMEHOW.
...HOW?
SMEK
WHEN MUM DIED, I DECIDED TO HAVE AN ADVENTURE. THIS IS IT.
NEVER TOO LATE TO START, NEIGHBOR.
POLICE
POLICE
CALL
HEH.
CALL
SHE WANTED TO BE A BUS DRIVER.
Continued in The Sapling Vol. 2: Roots!

ISSUE #3.1

BBC THE ELEVENTH DOCTOR ADVENTURES YEAR THREE
DOCTOR WHO
ELEVEN #01
DOCTOR WHO
ROB WILLIAMS
I.N.J. CULBARD
TRIONA FARRELL
POLICE PUBLIC CALL BOX
3.1 2017 $3.99
TITAN COMICS
COVER B
WILL BROOKS

Cover B
Will Brooks

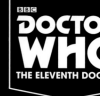

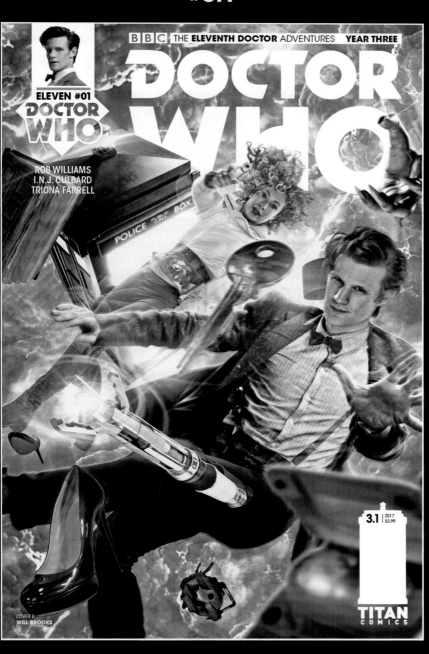

COVER GALLERY

BBC THE ELEVENTH DOCTOR ADVENTURES YEAR THREE
DOCTOR WHO
ELEVEN #01
DOCTOR WHO
ROB WILLIAMS
I.N.J. CULBARD
TRIONA FARRELL
3.1 2017 $3.99
TITAN COMICS
COVER C
QUESTION NO.6

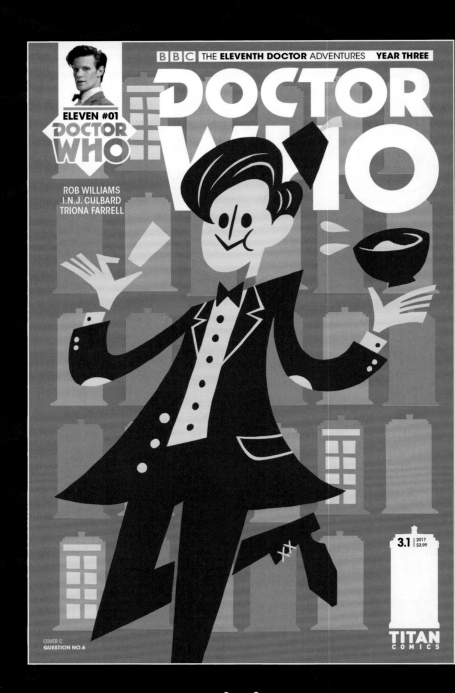

Cover C
Question No. 6

BBC DOCTOR WHO THE ELEVENTH DOCTOR

COVER GALLERY

BBC THE ELEVENTH DOCTOR ADVENTURES YEAR THREE
DOCTOR WHO
ELEVEN #01
DOCTOR WHO
ROB WILLIAMS
I.N.J. CULBARD
TRIONA FARRELL
3.1 2017 $3.99
TITAN COMICS
COVER D
SIMON FRASER

Cover D
Simon Fraser

BBC THE ELEVENTH DOCTOR ADVENTURES YEAR THREE
DOCTOR WHO
ELEVEN #01
DOCTOR WHO
3.1 2017 $3.99
ROB WILLIAMS
I.N.J. CULBARD
TRIONA FARRELL
TITAN COMICS
COVER E
SIMONE DI MEO

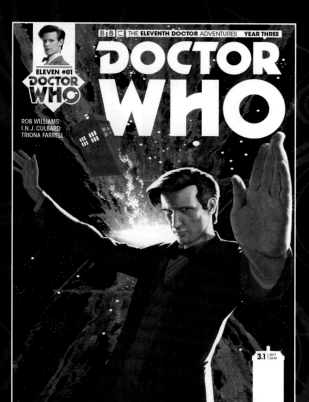

Cover E
Simone di Meo

COVER GALLERY

BBC THE ELEVENTH DOCTOR ADVENTURES YEAR THREE
DOCTOR WHO
ELEVEN #02
DOCTOR WHO
ROB WILLIAMS
I.N.J CULBARD
TRIONA FARRELL
THE SCREAM
3.2 2017 $3.99
TITAN COMICS
COVER C
MATT BAXTER

ISSUE #3.2

Cover C
Matt Baxter

BBC THE ELEVENTH DOCTOR ADVENTURES YEAR THREE
DOCTOR WHO
ELEVEN #02
DOCTOR WHO
THE SCREAM
POLICE
PULL TO OPEN
ADVICE & ASSISTANCE OBTAINABLE IMMEDIATELY
OFFICER & CARS RESPOND TO ALL CALLS
3.2 2017 $3.99
TITAN COMICS
ROB WILLIAMS
I.N.J CULBARD
TRIONA FARRELL
COVER D
SIMONE DI MEO

Cover D
Simone di Meo

COVER GALLERY

ISSUE #3.3

Cover C
Marc Ellerby

BBC THE ELEVENTH DOCTOR ADVENTURES YEAR THREE
DOCTOR WHO
ELEVEN #03
DOCTOR WHO
ALEX PAKNADEL
SIMON FRASER
GARY CALDWELL
BANG!
3.3 2017 $3.99
TITAN COMICS
COVER C
MARC ELLERBY

BBC THE ELEVENTH DOCTOR ADVENTURES YEAR THREE
DOCTOR WHO
ELEVEN #03
THE TRAGICAL HISTORY TOUR
PART 1
3.3 2017 $3.99
TITAN COMICS
ALEX PAKNADEL
SIMON FRASER
GARY CALDWELL
COVER D
SIMON FRASER

Cover D
Simon Fraser

COVER GALLERY

BBC THE ELEVENTH DOCTOR ADVENTURES YEAR THREE
DOCTOR WHO
ELEVEN #04
DOCTOR WHO
ALEX PAKNADEL
SIMON FRASER
GARY CALDWELL
3.4 MAY '17 $3.99
TITAN COMICS
COVER B
WILL BROOKS

ISSUE #3.4

Cover B
Will Brooks

BBC THE ELEVENTH DOCTOR ADVENTURES YEAR THREE
DOCTOR WHO
ELEVEN #04
DOCTOR WHO
ALEX PAKNADEL
SIMON FRASER
GARY CALDWELL
POLICE PUBLIC CALL BOX
3.4 MAY '17 $3.99
TITAN COMICS

Cover C
Rachael Smith

SEE HOW SIMON FRASER'S
FANTASTIC PAGES ARE BROUGHT
TO LIFE WITH COLORS BY
GARY CALDWELL!

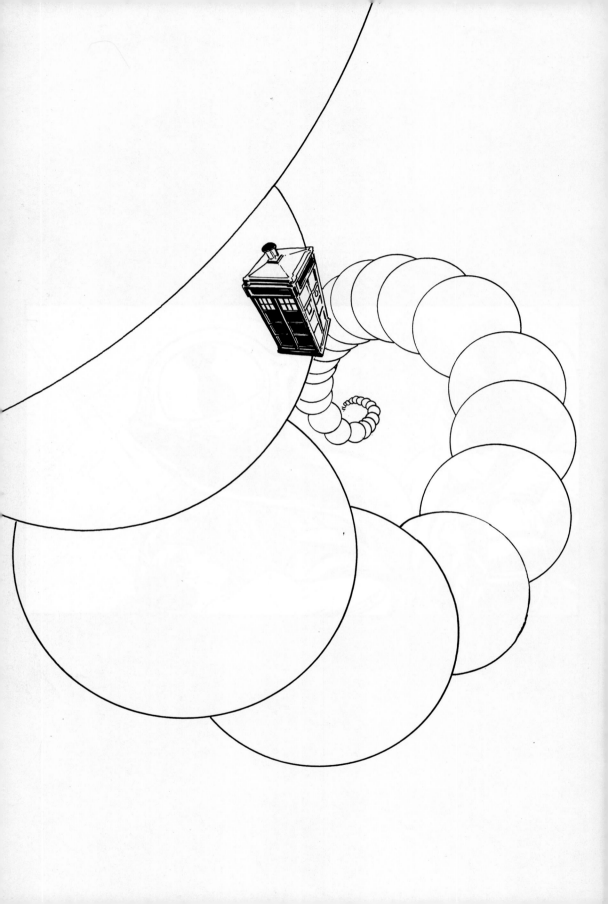

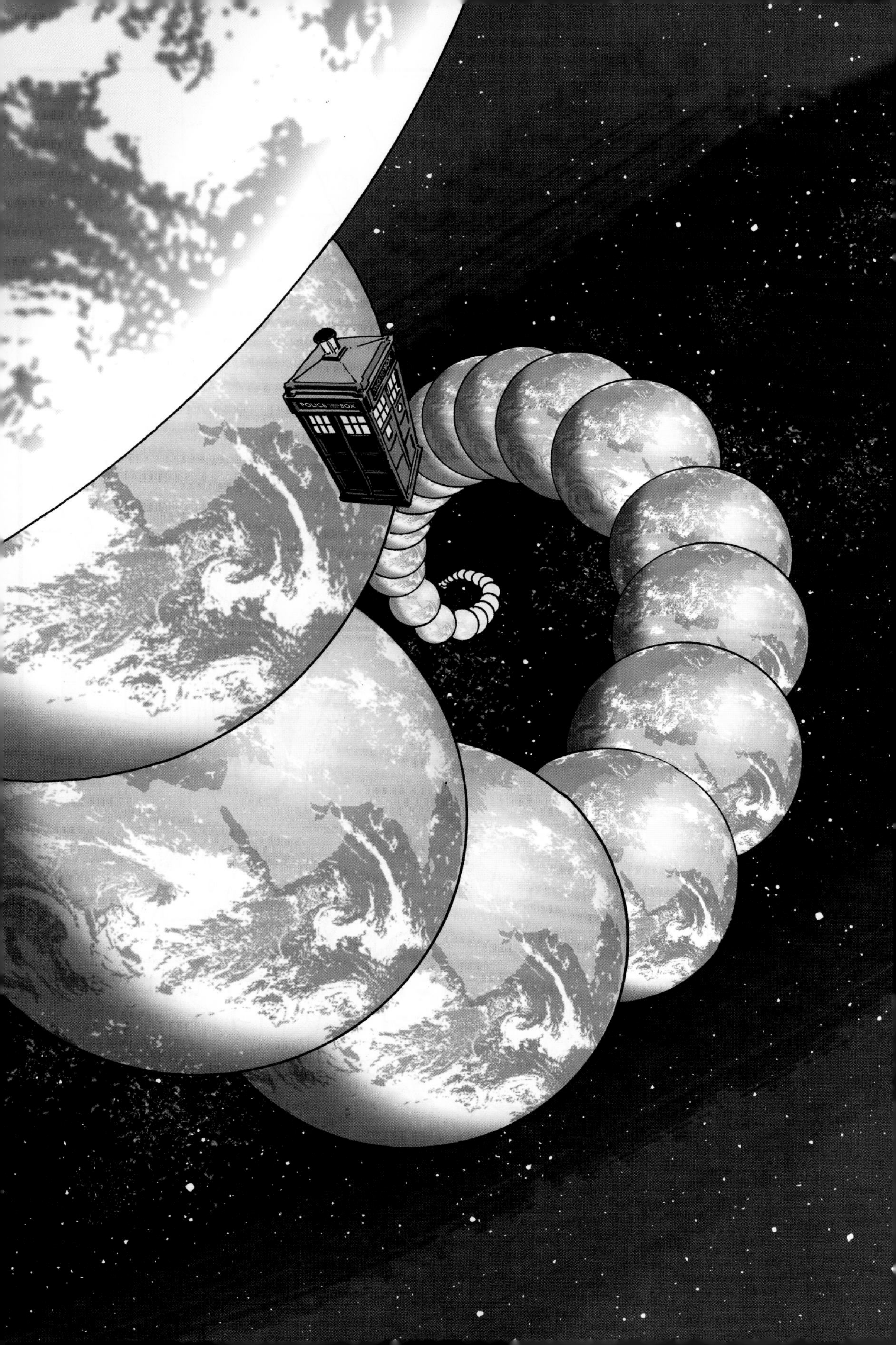
POLICE BOX

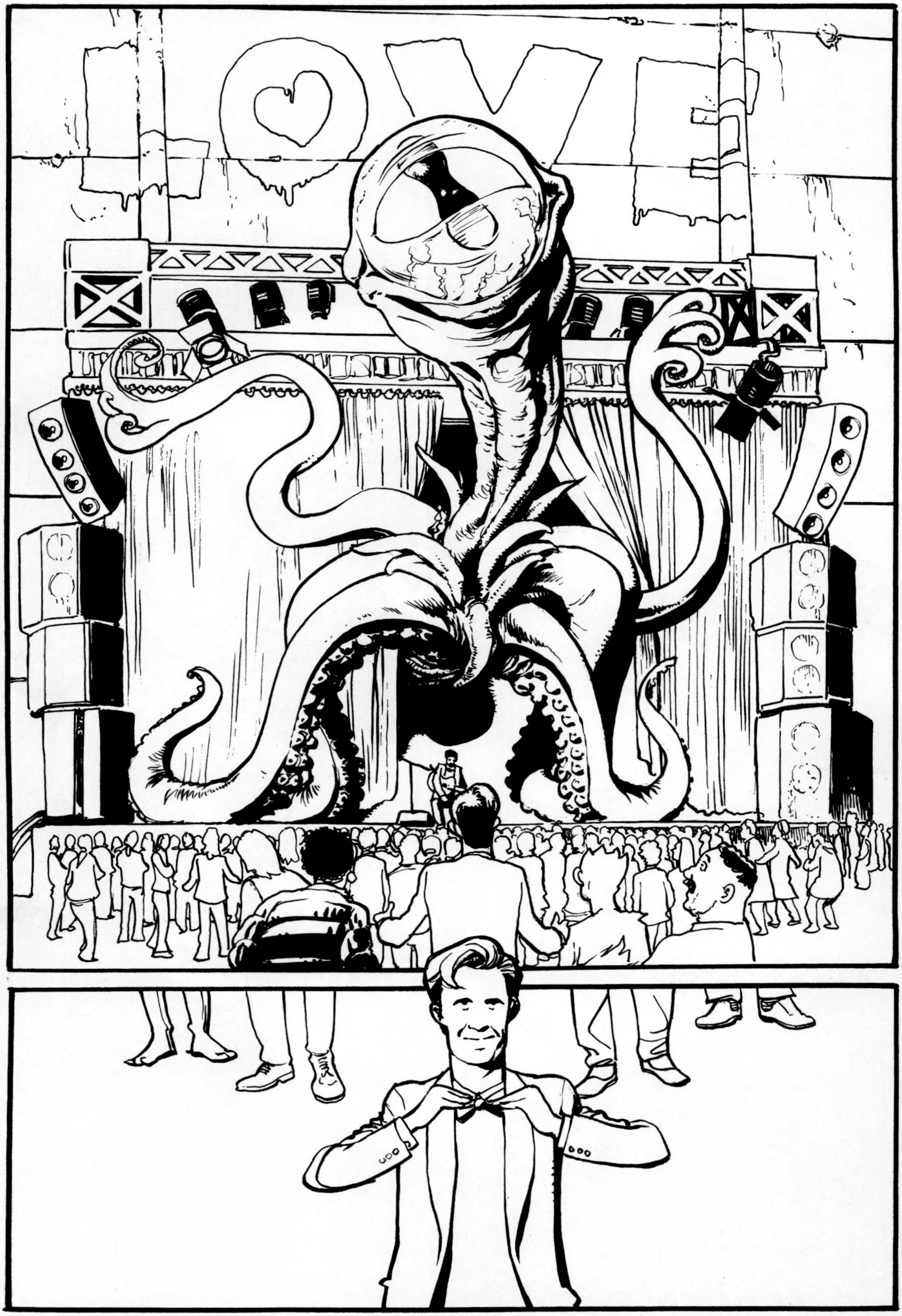
LOVE

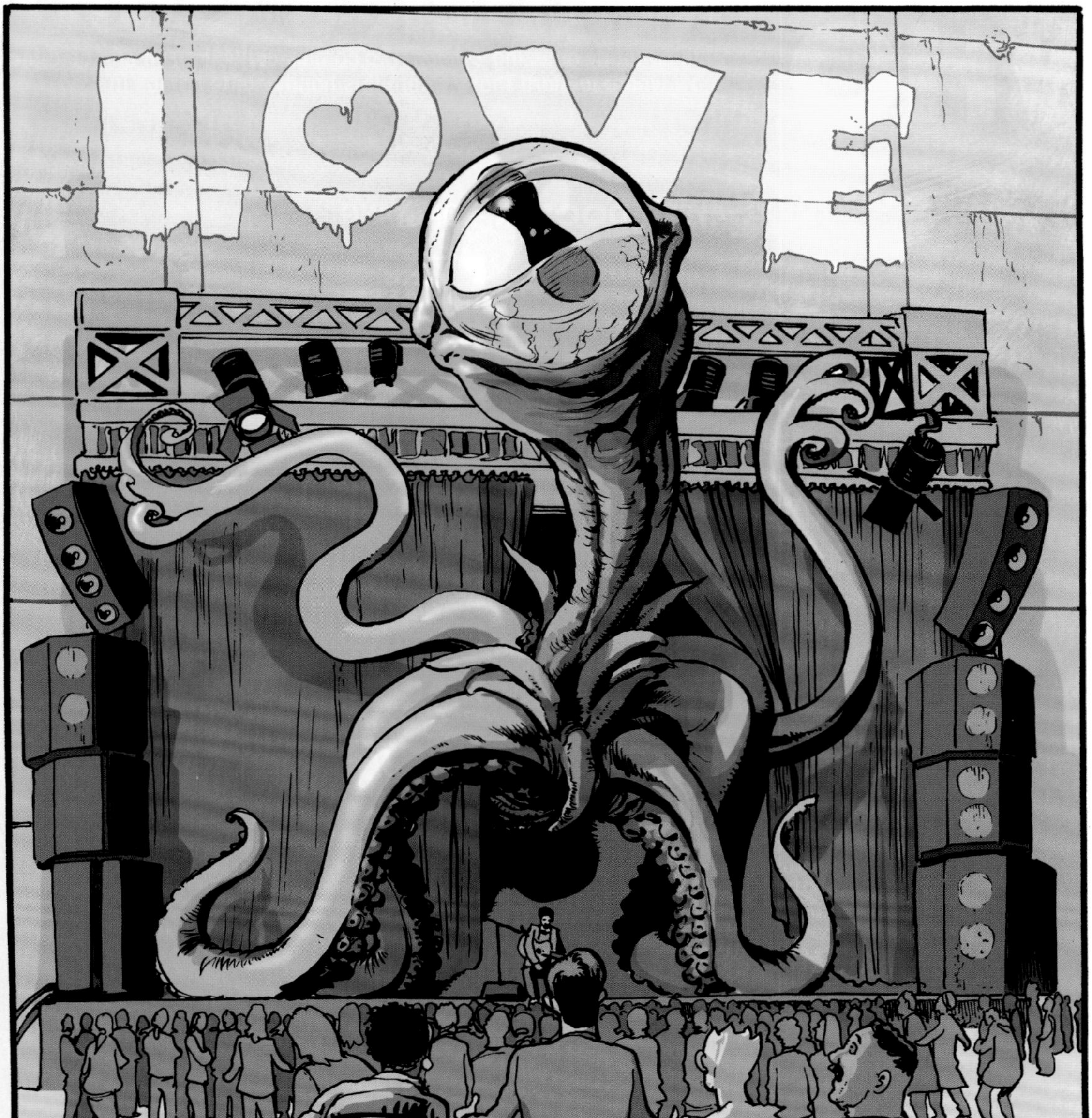
LOVE

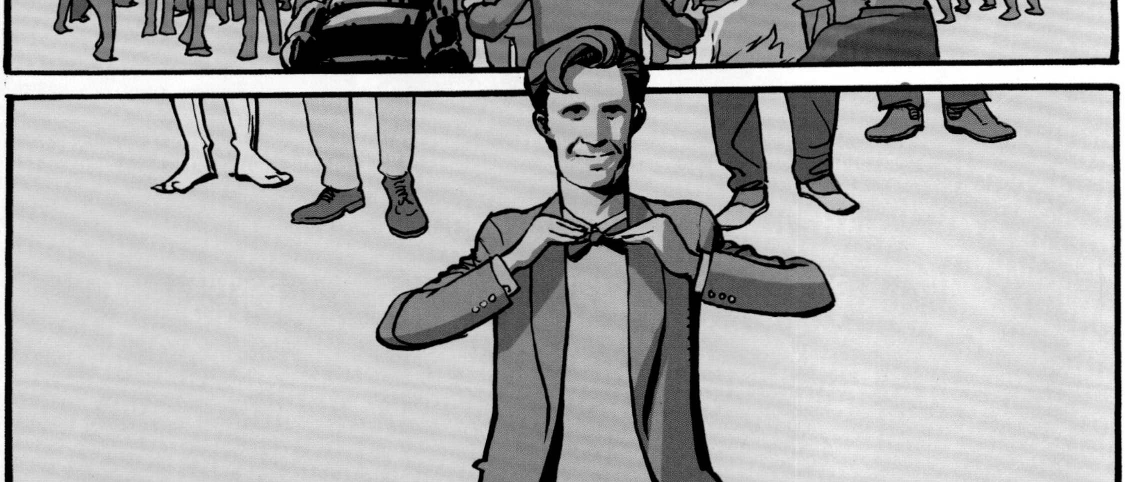

READER'S GUIDE

With so many amazing *Doctor Who* comics collections, it can be difficult know where to start! That's where this handy guide comes in.

THE TWELFTH DOCTOR – ONGOING

VOL. 1:
TERRORFORMER

VOL. 2:
FRACTURES

VOL. 3:
HYPERION

YEAR TWO BEGINS! VOL. 4:
SCHOOL OF DEATH

VOL. 5:
THE TWIST

THE ELEVENTH DOCTOR – ONGOING

VOL. 1:
AFTER LIFE

VOL. 2:
SERVE YOU

VOL. 3:
CONVERSION

YEAR TWO BEGINS! VOL. 4:
THE THEN AND THE NOW

VOL. 5:
THE ONE

THE TENTH DOCTOR – ONGOING

VOL. 1:
REVOLUTIONS OF TERROR

VOL. 2: THE WEEPING
ANGELS OF MONS

VOL. 3: THE
FOUNTAINS OF FOREVER

YEAR TWO BEGINS! VOL. 4:
THE ENDLESS SONG

VOL. 5:
ARENA OF FEAR

THE NINTH DOCTOR – ONGOING

VOL. 1: WEAPONS OF
PAST DESTRUCTION

VOL. 2:
DOCTORMANIA

VOL. 3:
OFFICIAL SECRETS

VOL. 4:
SIN EATERS

There are currently **four** ongoing *Doctor Who* series, each following a different Doctor.
Each ongoing series is **entirely self-contained**, so you can follow one, two, or all of your favorite Doctors, as you wish! The ongoings are arranged in season-like **Years**, collected into roughly three books per Year. Feel free to start at Volume 1 of any series, or jump straight to Volume 4, for an equally-accessible new season premiere!
Each book, and every comic, features a **catch-up and character guide** at the beginning, making it easy to jump on board – and each ongoing has a very different flavor, representative of that Doctor's era on screen.

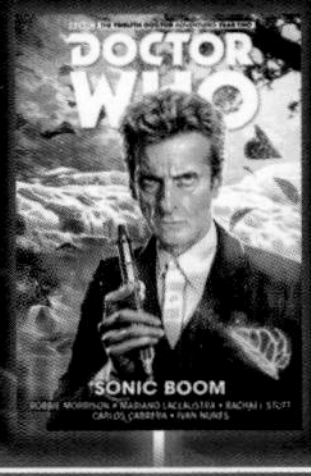

DOCTOR WHO
SONIC BOOM

VOL. 6:
SONIC BOOM

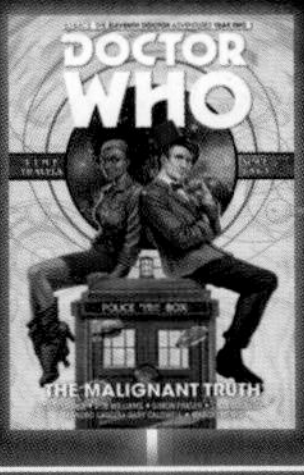

DOCTOR WHO
THE MALIGNANT TRUTH

VOL. 6:
THE MALIGNANT TRUTH

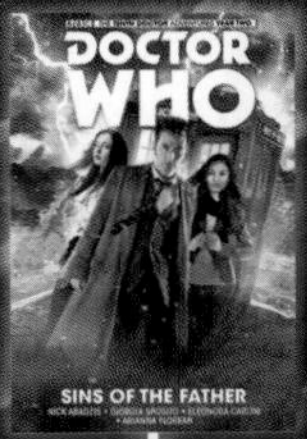

DOCTOR WHO
SINS OF THE FATHER

VOL. 6:
SINS OF THE FATHER

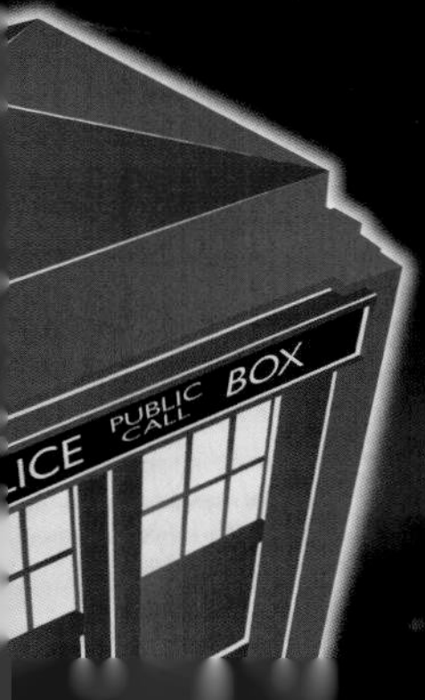

PUBLIC CALL BOX

THIRD DOCTOR

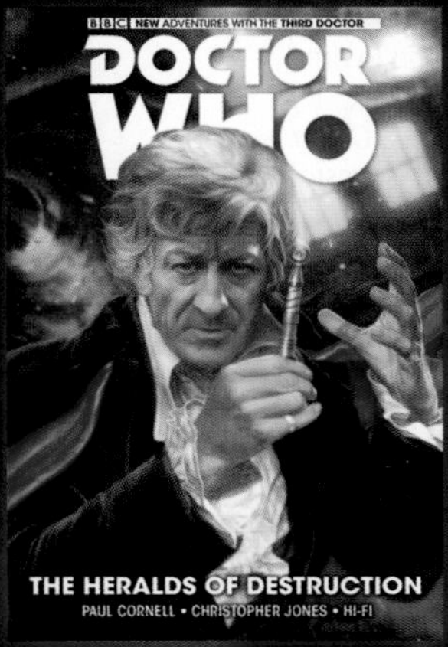

NEW ADVENTURES WITH THE THIRD DOCTOR
DOCTOR WHO
THE HERALDS OF DESTRUCTION
PAUL CORNELL • CHRISTOPHER JONES • HI-FI

As well as the four ongoing series, we have published three major **past Doctor miniseries**, for the Third, Fourth, and Eighth Doctors. These volumes are each a **complete** and **self-contained** story.

There are also two fantastic **crossover event** volumes, starring the Ninth, Tenth, Eleventh, and Twelfth Doctors – the first, *Four Doctors*, sees an impossible team-up, and the second, *Supremacy of the Cybermen*, sees the monstrous cyborgs rule victorious over the universe... unless the Doctors can stop them!

FOURTH DOCTOR

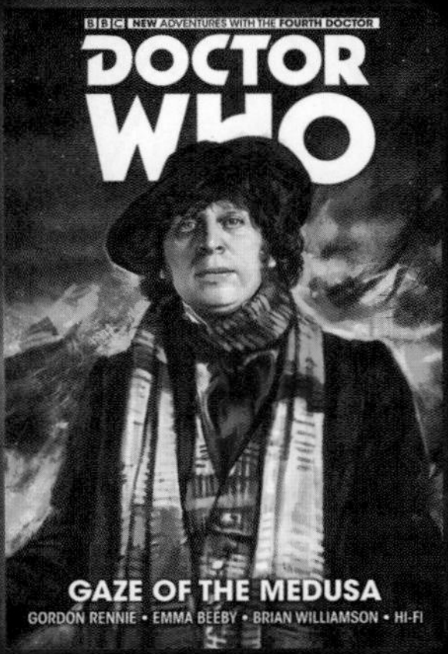

NEW ADVENTURES WITH THE FOURTH DOCTOR
DOCTOR WHO
GAZE OF THE MEDUSA
GORDON RENNIE • EMMA BEEBY • BRIAN WILLIAMSON • HI-FI

FOUR DOCTORS

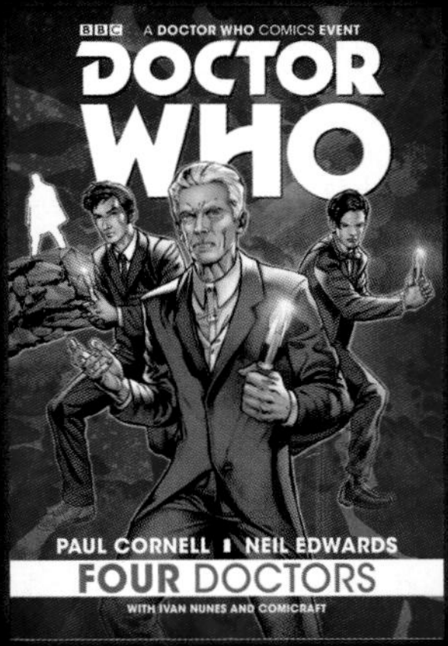

A DOCTOR WHO COMICS EVENT
DOCTOR WHO
PAUL CORNELL NEIL EDWARDS
FOUR DOCTORS
WITH IVAN NUNES AND COMICRAFT

EIGHTH DOCTOR

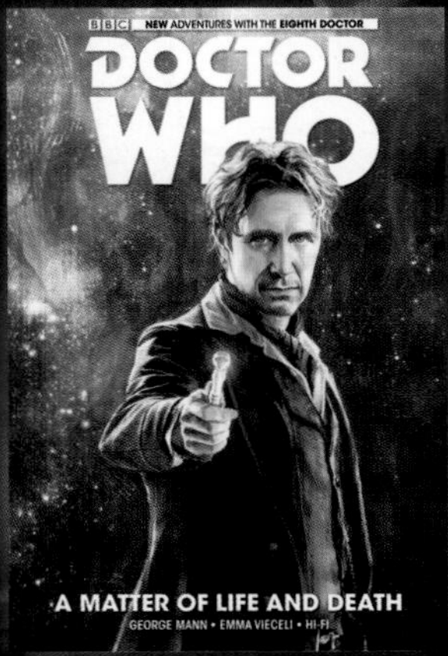

NEW ADVENTURES WITH THE EIGHTH DOCTOR
DOCTOR WHO
A MATTER OF LIFE AND DEATH
GEORGE MANN • EMMA VIECELI • HI-FI

SUPREMACY OF THE CYBERMEN

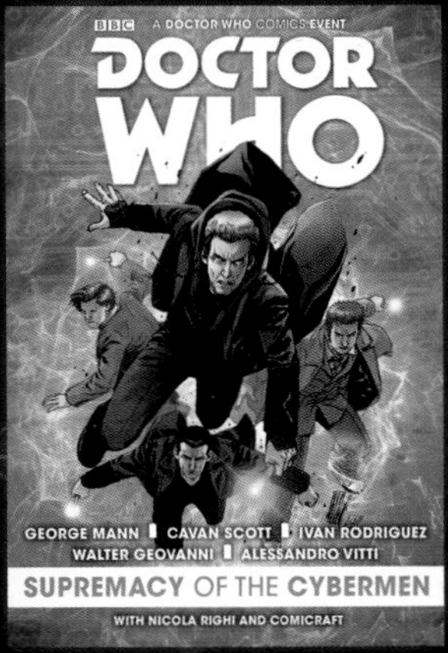

A DOCTOR WHO COMICS EVENT
DOCTOR WHO
GEORGE MANN CAVAN SCOTT IVAN RODRIGUEZ
WALTER GEOVANNI ALESSANDRO VITTI
SUPREMACY OF THE CYBERMEN
WITH NICOLA RIGHI AND COMICRAFT

VISIT **TITAN-COMIC.COM**

BIOGRAPHIES

Rob Williams began his comics career with *CLA$$WAR*, and now writes stunning work for *2000AD* (*Judge Dredd: Titan, Low Life, Trifecta, Ichabod Azrael*), DC (*Suicide Squad, Martian Manhunter*), Vertigo (*Unfollow, The Royals*), and Titan, which also publishes his creator-owned *Ordinary.* He lives in Bristol, UK.

Alex Paknadel is a talented writer who burst onto the comics scene with his creator-owned series, *Arcadia,* in 2015. He lives in Lancaster, UK.

I.N.J. Culbard is a British-based artist who has made waves with his independent work including *At The Mountains of Madness, The Princess of Mars,* and *The Picture of Dorian Gray*. He is also famous for his work on *Wild's End* and *Dark Ages.*

Simon Fraser is a world-traveling artist, born in Scotland, now based in New York City. Best known as the co-creator of *Nikolai Dante for 2000AD*, Fraser has drawn for *Judge Dredd, Grindhouse, Family, Hell House* and his own series, *Lilly MacKenzie*.

Leandro Casco is an up-and-coming artist from Brazil who has worked on *Doctor Who: The Long Con* and *Nikkei.*

Wellington Diaz is an illustrator and inker, who has worked on *The Man With No Name, Nova,* and *Superman: Grounded.*

Triona Farrell is a brilliant colorist who brings her unique style to all of the projects she has worked on to date, including *Weavers, Big Trouble in Little China, Joyride,* and *Assassin's Creed: Locus.*

Gary Caldwell has been coloring Simon Fraser's work for over 20 years, as Simon's right-hand man. Based in Scotland, he quietly knocks his pages out of the park every time.

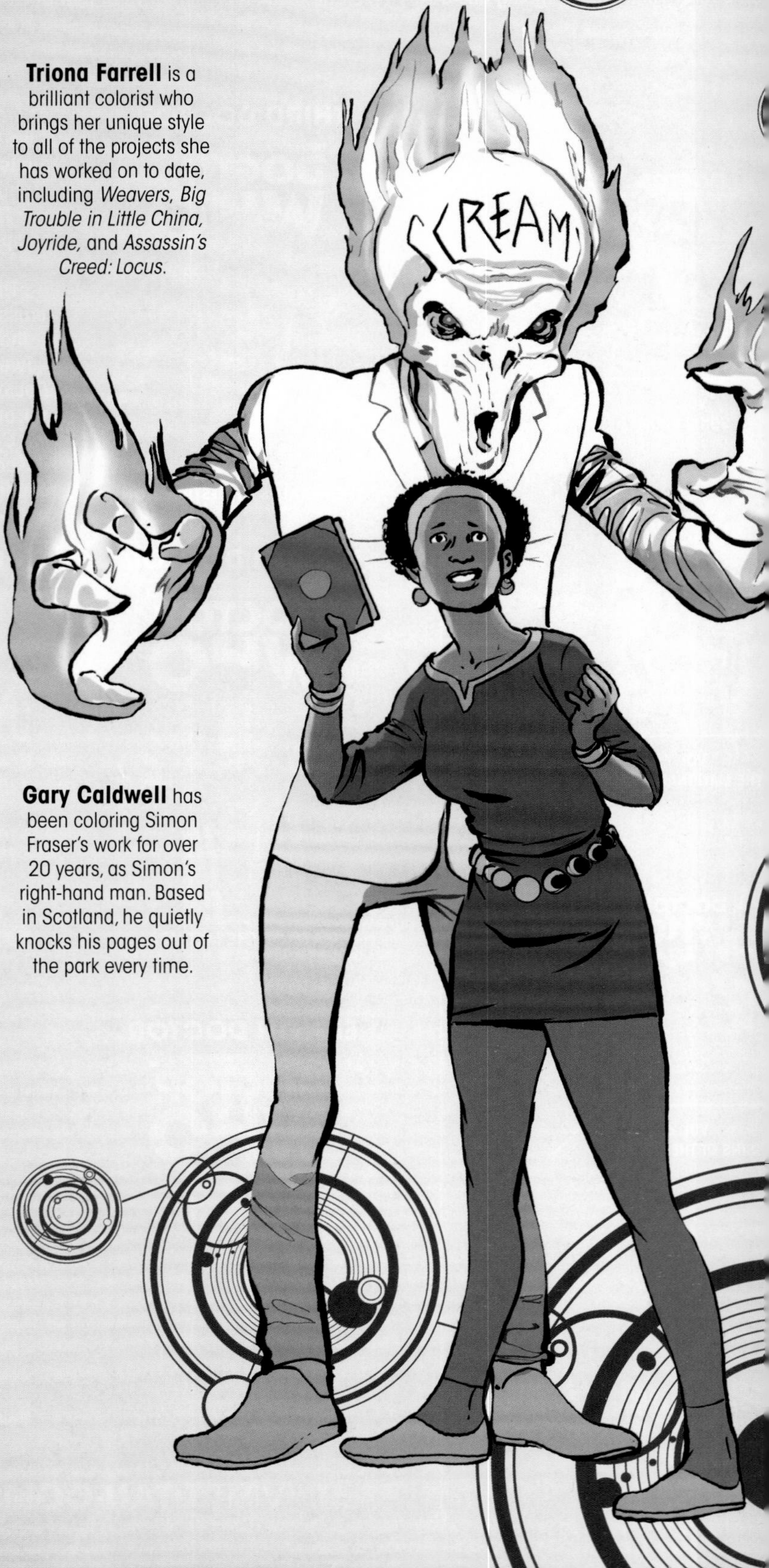
SCREAM